School-Age Child Care

F103

Available From
School-Age NOTES
P.O. Box 40205
Nashville, TN 37204
615-242-8464
FREE After School Resource Catalog

SCHOOL-AGE CHILD CARE,

An Action Manual for the 90s and Beyond

Second Edition

Michelle Seligson and Michael Allenson

Foreword by **Marian Wright Edelman**

THE SCHOOL-AGE CHILD CARE PROJECT
Center for Research on Women
Wellesley College

Auburn House
Westport, Connecticut • London

Library of Congress Cataloging-in-Publication Data

Seligson, Michelle.
    School-age child care : an action manual for the 90s and beyond /
Michelle Seligson and Michael Allenson.—2nd ed.; foreword by
Marian Wright Edelman.
        p. cm.
    Rev. ed. of: School-age child care / Ruth Kramer Baden . . . c1982.
    Includes bibliographical references and index.
    ISBN 0-86569-024-3.—ISBN 0-86569-025-1 (pbk.)
    1. School-age child care—United States—Handbooks, manuals, etc.
I. Allenson, Michael.   II. School-age child care.   III. Title.
HQ778.6.S45   1993
362.7'12'068—dc20   92-18359

British Library Cataloguing in Publication Data is available.

Library of Congress Catalog Card Number: 92-18359
ISBN: 0-86569-024-3
ISBN: 0-86569-025-1 (pb)

First published in 1993

Auburn House, 88 Post Road West, Westport, CT 06881
An imprint of Greenwood Publishing Group, Inc.

Printed in the United States of America

The paper used in this book complies with the
Permanent Paper Standard issued by the National
Information Standards Organization (Z39.48-1984).

10 9 8 7 6 5 4 3 2 1

This revised edition of *School-Age Child Care* was supported in part by a
grant from the Carnegie Corporation of New York. The statements,
findings, conclusions, and recommendations included herein do not
necessarily reflect the views of the Corporation.

This publication is designed to provide accurate and authoritative
information in regard to the subject matter covered. It is sold with the
understanding that neither the author nor the publisher is engaged in
rendering legal, accounting, or other professional service. If legal advice or
other expert assistance is required, the services of a competent professional
person should be sought.

*From a Declaration of Principles jointly adopted by a Committee of the
American Bar Association and a Committee of Publishers.*

CONTENTS

FOREWORD

Good child care is inextricably linked to the healthy development of children. It has also become basic to the economic health of large numbers of American families as more and more women have found it necessary to enter the work force, either because they are the sole support of their family or because economic changes mean their family needs two incomes to pay the bills. Millions of these women have school age children, children who spend significant amounts of time caring for themselves, both in the early mornings before school and in the late afternoons after school. Mounting evidence suggests that self-care among school age children has significant costs to the children, which take the form of increased fearfulness and loneliness, heightened vulnerability to peer pressure, and greater likelihood of substance abuse.

Michelle Seligson has devoted her career to ensuring that the best possible child care arrangements are available to school age children. Twenty years ago, Mickey was a pioneer. Working as a community child care organizer in Brookline, Massachusetts, she was shocked by the number of children in her community who were left home alone when schools closed at two o'clock. Always ready to act on what she felt children needed, Mickey helped parents organize one of the country's first city-wide school age child care programs.

Shortly after this model program got off the ground, it became clear to Mickey and her early associates that the school age child care crisis was national in scope. In response to the voices of desperate parents as well as the concerns of policy makers, school administrators, and child care providers, Mickey and Jim Levine founded the School Age Child Care Project in 1979.

Under Mickey's leadership, the SACCProject has grown into a national force dedicated to improving the quality of life of school age children, their parents, and their caregivers. While Mickey and her colleagues continue to speak out for an expansion of school age programs, they also understand the importance of providing technical assistance and support to ensure that these programs offer children a positive and constructive experience. They are committed to developing a skilled network of caregivers who understand the special needs of school age children.

In addition to providing the most comprehensive written materials in this field, the SACCProject also works quietly on a daily basis in countless communities to encourage the development of school age child care. It has, for example, joined forces with the National Association of Elementary School Principals to launch an extensive project designed to assist principals in working with their communities to develop high quality school age child care programs.

School-Age Child Care: An Action Manual for the 90s and Beyond is yet another feather in Mickey Seligson's cap. For all of us who work for a better future for America's children and their families, Mickey and her co-author, Michael Allenson, have written one more invaluable resource from the SACCProject.

—Marian Wright Edelman

PREFACE

"Have you considered revising the book? It's been ten years since the first one, and it probably could stand a little updating. How about it?"

That was our publisher John Harney on the phone. For several years, he'd been calling to ask me this question. For several years, I'd been successfully avoiding saying yes. In 1982, *School-Age Child Care: An Action Manual* was a first. Ruth Baden, Andi Genser, Jim Levine, and I gathered information from more than a hundred programs around the country. We documented organizing strategies, public awareness campaigns, model program designs, financing solutions, and policy changes. We discovered an array of initiatives, many of them from grass roots groups. We described parents' struggles to gain access to public schools as locations for their school-age child care (SACC) partnerships.

Up until then, SACC had received little public policy attention and little interest from the early childhood and education sector. The first Action Manual seemed to help change that. Many people bought it. Some of them even used it. And a few called to say they couldn't get along without it.

After ten years, there had been a phenomenal growth in the number of programs. All levels of government were getting involved. The business sector was contemplating investment in afterschool programs for employees' children. Mass market publications had started featuring "latchkey" stories. Foundations had begun to fund academic and social outcome studies. We had done our work. With so much already going on, my initial feeling about the revision was, "Do I really need this headache?"

In my role as SACCProject director, I traveled around the country, speaking and visiting with many providers and directors. Seeing program people still wondering what they were supposed to be doing with the children in their care. Feeling their frustration as children with deeper and more complex troubles kept on coming. Realizing that high caregiver turnover rates would only get higher if salaries stayed so abysmally low. Observing many programs that were *containing* children instead of *holding* them.

Mountains of books, papers, and videos about school-age child care had surfaced—well-intentioned, coming from that place in us that says we need to do something about a problem, that summons up our best efforts. Some were even visionary.

Then I knew that the first Action Manual had only gone so far. It hadn't gone far enough. That's when I said yes to John Harney.

I felt that in much of what I'd seen and heard, something was missing. The essence of what is possible in afterschool programs comes from facing some unpleasant truths about our society and then, in response, finding ways to make things different. To go in a different direction. Away from accepting inadequate space. Away from a norm that has children sitting at cafeteria tables all afternoon. Away from prescribed curricula and commercially packaged television products. Away from robbing children's free time to compensate for unmet educational goals.

That's where this new edition hopefully takes us. What John Harney asked for was a text revision. But what we did went far beyond. This book is a *re*-visioning of what is possible for school-age child care. Ideas that were hinted at in the first edition have been engaged, expanded, and enriched. Some earlier ideas and assumptions have been challenged. Some have been translated and updated in an attempt to guide *School-Age Child Care: An Action Manual*—and its readers—into the twenty-first century.

This new edition wouldn't work the way it does without coauthor Michael Allenson. A background in the entertainment industry doesn't exactly prepare someone to write a book about child care—unless, of course, that someone comes equipped with the intellectual ability to absorb vast amounts of information, the acumen to question assumptions, and an insatiable desire for moral and social integrity. Anyone who sees Michael around children—or, I should say, children around Michael—would immediately understand his passion about the ideas and concepts in this book. He respects children. He knows how to play. And he is deeply troubled by the ailing condition of American childhood.

He is also a writer. I hope that fact will be evident to you from the pages that follow. It became evident to me during the year and a half in which we ate, slept, and breathed school-age care. Perhaps profound change can come about only from authentic self-scrutiny, the kind that comes when someone with a fresh perspective, someone like Michael, says, "Hey—

look what you've got here. Look what it could be. How come you people don't use the authority you have as society's caregivers?"

This edition had a long and sometimes painful gestation. Michael's intense longing for the perfect way to turn a phrase, the exact image with which to illustrate a point, and his uncompromising adherence to principle were challenging to us both. At times we wondered if we would get through in one piece, but I believe the result speaks for itself. And if there's music in this book, it's Michael's orchestrations that you hear.

Together, we drew on many sources from beyond the child care field. We sought to inspire understanding through the richness of history, literature, philosophy, and contemporary culture. Many child care texts tend to sound like computer manuals, informed by data quickly codified by the field. In the humanities, life expresses itself in all its facets, and school-age child care is about life.

Of all the depths we plumbed, we found our deepest wellspring in *The Chalice and the Blade: Our History, Our Future* by Riane Eisler. Her book heralds a vision of society transformed by the concept of true partnership. It raises an analysis of historical patterns in societal and economic behavior, patterns distorted by greed and by a lack of reverence for human life. It isn't explicitly about school-age child care, but in our search to articulate the possible, we found that her vision blended beautifully into our revision. We gratefully acknowledge Eisler's gift to our work and our lives.

We have others to acknowledge here, people who have given our inquiries their focused attention, who have graciously supported our attempt to renew our outlooks. To thank them all would fill the pages of another book.

Sue Lawyer-Tarr, director of The Clubhouse in Tulsa, Oklahoma, shared her books, her thoughts, and her prayers with us. Lillian Katz read an early draft of a chapter, and in her crisp and considered review she pushed us to new definitions and expression. We telephoned some people late at night: Joan Lombardi, Diane Genco, Paul Sully, Roger Neugebauer, Jim Greenman, and Ellen Clippinger. They were kind enough to answer, both our phone calls and our questions, with their utmost insight and patience.

SACCProject colleagues at Wellesley read and critiqued our rough material while they bit their tongues waiting for us to hurry up and finish. Our thanks go to Ellen Gannett, Fern Marx, Lillian Coltin, Susan O'Connor, Lynn Hatch, and Dale Fink for sharing their research, their time, and their observations.

School Age NOTES' *Before and After School Programs: A Start-Up and Administration Manual* figures as one of our most prominent sources of illustrative material. Its recent publication relieves us from having to reprint many examples of lists and forms. Of course, we thank Rich Scofield and Mary McDonald Richards for making their volume generally available.

Ten years ago, the Carnegie Corporation of New York helped fund the research and publication of our first edition. A revisitation of this magnitude would have been far more challenging without present-day discretionary financial support from Carnegie and the encouragement of Program Officer Michael Levine.

There were also times when close personal friends helped us get through the rough spots. When our computer failed, Yang Xiaodong gave us his. He and Song Xiaoli made us dumplings when only dumplings would do. We thank them for sustaining us.

As we wrote in the preface to the first edition, the passion behind this very pragmatic book—behind all the nitty-gritty details and technical information—stems from a deep concern for the future. We still believe that the future belongs to the children. Because hundreds of thousands of children are forming their view of the future in school-age care programs, we hope this new edition frees program people to exercise their awesome responsibilities with some passion of their own.

Michelle Seligson
Newton, Massachusetts

Chapter 1

A STATEMENT OF MISSION

Can't get along without it. Big waste of money. A necessary evil. Powerful tool for social development. Sign of the times. A luxury for those who can afford it. The only chance these poor kids have.

Ask seven different people what they think about child care, and it's likely they'll come up with seven different answers. On a factual basis, it's simple. When parents take care of their own children, whatever the result, it's called parenting. When someone else does it, whatever the result, that's child care.

In 1840, German educator Friedrich Froebel coined the term *kindergarten*—literally, the children's garden—to describe group care and training of five- to six-year-olds. Most American parents probably lived through the common American version of the concept: blocks, fingerpaints, and naps. It's as firmly embedded in the national consciousness as is the Stars and Stripes.

Somewhere along the line, someone decided that five years old wasn't young enough to get started, so along came *preschool*. In preschool, children two, three, and four years of age get a leg up on kindergarten competition. Parents with demanding schedules, many of them mothers who can't afford not to work, also have the option of *infant care*. They entrust babies as young as eight weeks of age to group care settings.

As workplace demands and economic contractions become more stringent, all these types of care become more common. But for some reason as soon as a child reaches school age, many parents find themselves as outcasts from family support systems. All too often, that first school bell rings an end to available child care.

Few people's lives uniformly fit in between first and last school bells. Too many empty before- and afterschool hours remain in the day. School-agers' lives go on twenty-four hours a day. Consequently, many parents thrust doorkeys into their children's hands with instructions to come straight home, lock the door, and wait in isolation. For lack of reasonable alternatives, other children simply wander into the streets at 3 P.M. and look for somewhere to hang out. Parents and children alike must wonder why the family support service marketplace has suddenly abandoned them.

School-age child care (SACC) seeks to redress these concerns. Given their institutional histories, kindergarten and preschool classes seem almost like automatic cultural fixtures. Not SACC. It requires far more perception and perseverance to organize, fund, and operate a school-age care program.

Perhaps working parents sense that their children could enjoy something more productive or comfortable to do after school. Perhaps these parents want some assurance that their children won't be roaming the streets, risking all sorts of dangers. Perhaps a community-based agency needs a way to update its services. In any event, *a successful SACC program comes about as the result of a successful partnership.* How well the partnership works depends upon how well the partners answer the following questions:

1. MISSION STATEMENT—What is the purpose of SACC?
2. CHOOSING PARTNERS—Who joins, and in what capacity?
3. ADMINISTRATION—Where does the buck stop?
4. CURRICULUM—What is supposed to actually happen?
5. FINANCIAL MANAGEMENT—How do dollars affect things?
6. THE BUDGET—How do the pluses and minuses stack up?
7. RESOURCE DEVELOPMENT—Who besides parents might pay?
8. PROGRAM PEOPLE—Who makes a school-age program worth going to?
9. INTERNAL POLICIES AND PROCEDURES—Who handles what?
10. SCHEDULING—When will various events take place?
11. TRANSPORTATION—How do children get to and from the program?
12. LEGAL AFFAIRS—What does the law have to say?
13. ASSESSMENT—How well is all of this going?

This manual seeks to frame these general considerations for SACC program planning. However, the most important planning question does not receive its own chapter. Some well-meaning planners and administrators take their understandings about children for granted. With honorable intentions, they plunge into organizing and fund-raising, marketing and enrollment. Too late, they discover that they forgot to ask: What are the specific attributes of school-age children? How do they differ from preschoolers? From adolescents? That is, they forgot to ask: *Who is the school-age child?* Because it runs through every meaningful discussion about SACC, this question runs throughout the entire book.

Go back to your childhood—as far back as you can remember—and create an image of a happy memory and of the place where it occurred. Pay attention to the feel of things around you. What was happening to your body? What did you see? What could you touch and feel and taste? . . . The images that you come up with are the starting place for a good model of day care. It's the things that we experience as being good and positive in our childhood that we have the capacity to pass on to the children we care for. You will come up with images that have to do with outdoor places, with cozy places, with smells of good cooking, and with memories of being in physical contact with adults. I hope that your images have reminded you of how powerfully in touch children are with their environments.[1]

It's easy to observe children's similarities. They commonly seek pleasure and challenge. Their feelings of happiness, sadness, and boredom stem from the same human condition. They enjoy colorful stimuli and funny voices. With children, disappointments are usually soon forgotten and all things seem possible.

Yet even when children belong to the same age group, very specific characteristics distinguish one child from another. Children's developmental abilities can vary tremendously. Their physical capacities differ. They operate at different levels of emotional maturity. Their own parents, guardians, and home life give them separate and distinct handles on life.

For many children, the school day can mean silently paying attention, obediently following rules, and doing "work." Punishments may lurk in the wings for those who don't comply. Teachers' industrial employee patterns of coffee breaks and lunch hours afford children their own recess periods and lunch. However, what regulates these intermissions are school district/teacher's union contracts, not the natural ebb and flow of children's activity.

If budgets allow, children sometimes get other breaks from their curricular routines. Music, drama, and recess invariably top lists of children's favorite segments of the school day. Not coincidentally, these are also the times of the school day when real life gets its closest acknowledgment.

Like the day's-end siren that sends Fred Flintstone surfing down his rockasaurus's back, the final bell of the school day signals the school-agers' dash into their real lives. Riding bikes and writing secret notes. Playing house and playing ball. Going over to a friend's and a friend's coming over. Raking up leaves and diving into the pile. Making friends, gossiping, choosing sides, playing videos, getting dissed, getting even, running away, running back—lives potentially quite diverse when compared with the schoolday routine.

Although there is no typical school-age child, there are certain characteristics that seem to stand out for different ages. It is important to know what these differences are if we are to be responsible for planning and implementing programs that meet school-age children's day care needs.

It helps to know, for instance, why five-year-olds in general need more supervision and guidance than ten-year-olds. Five-year-olds stay nearer to home base; they have problems with sharing and losing; they wiggle when sitting and get into all kinds of body positions and screw up their faces when drawing or writing; they are active, busy and vigorous; they know the difference between right and wrong, are easily embarrassed yet can handle most routine situations; they use adult gestures, mannerisms, postures, affectations and intonations; and they act out what they know of the adult world and change roles rapidly to meet the demand.

Ten- and eleven-year-olds, on the other hand, are more sophisticated, but they are also more moody. They tease, test, talk back, are more rebellious, and yet are open to distraction. At one center, the children have a chant: "Don't blame me, don't blame me, I did it 'cause he told me so, so don't blame me." They sing it, dance to it, act it out and laugh when one child admits, "O.K. I did it." They are involved with team sports and competition, with cooking, billiards, puppet shows, records (jazz, rock and roll), joke books, projects, clubs, rituals, riddles and rhymes (like "Inka Bink, a bottle of ink, the cork fell out and wow you stink"). They keep journals, write plays, are interested in making money, and like to move beyond the home base to the community. They want to have the freedom to make choices about what to do and where to go. They are gaining in height and weight. Girls may be menstruating and may be concerned about their looks, especially their skin and hair. Peer relationships are all important. Usually, they are not neat about clothes or rooms.

Planners of day care programs must take these differences between age groups into consideration. I have seen many programs in which children who have been in a center for five or six years are still being fed the same daily schedule that long since has been outgrown—a pabulum, patty-cake program, boring and inviting trouble. However, an activity that is handled well by the staff can be appropriate for children of different ages.[2]

These are generally idealized, benign, and supportive views of children. However, there are other opinions and perceptions that may seem to some adults to be just as valid or even more so.

To keep their own lives manageable, some professionals whose work affects hundreds or thousands of children take a detached view. These professionals include school district administrators, city and state agency personnel, and community organization staffers. For them, taking a deep personal interest in each particular child their work affects is hardly possible. The more children there are, the less personal and, by necessity, the more stereotyped their views of children become.

Some adults take a jaundiced view of children. For them, a child may be no more than an irritant, to be remanded into other people's custody whenever and wherever possible. Or they may treat their children as direct extensions of themselves, possessions to be pressed and formed into replicas.

The difficult reconciliation of these and other adult views of children makes the job of planning SACC highly political. This manual aims to aid that political process. But to find what something *really* is, one cannot look to a book. One must look into a deeper place than that.

Thus we come to the first formal point of inquiry for SACC planning.

1. THE MISSION STATEMENT

A SACC program doesn't just fall out of the sky. Somebody chooses to bring it into reality. Somebody has a particular purpose in mind. Put down in writing, who that somebody is and what that purpose is becomes the program's mission statement.

Mission statements abound in world culture. Dominant ones always receive the implicit salute of capitalized letters. The Pledge of Allegiance is a mission statement. So is the Lord's Prayer. So is the Declaration of Independence. Their authors distilled their intents and purposes into unmistakable clarity. By carefully selecting their words, they also eliminated others. Of course, these mission statements have gone on to inform much of American culture.

Mission statements always look great on paper. When spoken aloud, they ring with authority. They emblazon in people's minds overriding concerns meant to inform all subsequent actions.

A SACC mission statement answers two basic questions. First, how do planners believe children can benefit from a program? Second, what exactly do planners want to give these children? No one reasonably expects an Eleanor Roosevelt or a King Solomon for a SACC planner, but people look for ideas and phraseology they can believe in.

Child care experts often speak of social, emotional, physical, and intellectual development. Seeking general approval, program planners and providers echo these terms in their mission statements. Although some try to make good on the developmental promise, too many others just whip out the bingo set and call it a day.

The inherent challenge of deciding how to help children productively fill their leisure time is too often swept under the rug by attempts to *negate the undesirable*. When he was asked what method he used to achieve a masterful sculpture, Michelangelo is said to have replied that, in effect, he saw the finished piece of work inside the raw marble and simply chiseled away everything that *wasn't* it. Similarly, the late Neil Bogart, who saw huge success in the 1970s as president of Casablanca Records, was once heard to offer the philosophical observation, "Life is a series of 'not this-es.' " With little else in common, both men saw in their respective missions an imperative to do away with certain objects and behaviors. Such a view may work well enough with respect to commercial sculpture and music production, but what about with respect to children's lives?

What is the objective of a program mission to keep children quiet in their chairs at all times? What kind of mission is it that confines fifty children all afternoon in an echoing cafetorium? Precisely how do these programs' planners believe children can benefit from these practices?

By naming "safety" as their primary mission, perhaps these planners are *negating the thrill of surprise*. By naming "supervision" as their goal, perhaps they are *negating children's choices*. In some cases, by choosing a mission that shadows a mediocre public school system, they are *negating their own responsibility* to help prepare children for a fast-changing world.

If it is to have any meaning at all, a mission statement will account for real conditions, not ideal ones. Platitudes and lip service belong in the circular file along with the junk mail. SACC is a frontline business in a nation where business is trench warfare, and SACC planners had better realize what's happening sooner than later.

It's a time of open racial tensions that are flaring and raging through the heart of society. It's a time of dissipation when hard-fought gains in civil rights and bourgeois values alike are being supremely reversed on a daily basis. Instead of freeing up the typical worker to pursue personal interests, the "convenience era" has turned the forty-hour work week into the sixty-hour work week—and has turned school-age care from a feminist-inspired vision of social esteem into an institutional means of child containment.

Mission statements written through rose-colored glasses by the side of the yellow brick road only compound the problem. It's not enough to think happy thoughts and hope it all turns out for the best. It's time to come to terms with the socioeconomic inequities hiding behind the bushes. What are called for are missions that address fear and hate; that open the door to racial heritage, global conditions, educational disparities, world religions—in short, every subject that directly affects the world our children will shortly inherit.

Professor Howard Gardner has formulated a theory to describe what he calls *multiple intelligences*. At this writing, research currently under way at Harvard and Tufts universities seeks to determine some statistical evidence to support or reject the theory. Gardner supposes that in addition to verbal and math skills, there are five other areas of human accomplishment that deserve equal attention and recognition (Figure 1.1).

It may prove difficult to measure someone's sculpting talent, musical prowess, or dancing ability. However, for millions of children, excellence in musical, artistic, and athletic expression currently provides the brightest

Figure 1.1

---

7 WAYS TO BE BRIGHT

LINGUISTIC
Language skills include a sensitivity to the subtle shades of the meanings of words

LOGICAL-MATHEMATICAL
Both critics and supporters acknowledge that IQ tests measure this ability well

MUSICAL
Like language, music is an expressive medium—and this talent flourishes in prodigies

SPATIAL
Sculptors and painters are able accurately to perceive, manipulate and re-create forms

BODILY-KINESTHETIC
At the core of this kind of intelligence are body control and skilled handling of objects

INTERPERSONAL
Skill in reading the moods and intentions of others is displayed by politicians, among others

INTRAPERSONAL
The key is understanding one's own feelings—and using that insight to guide behavior

Source: U.S. News and World Report, Nov. 23, 1987.

rays of hope for socially approved accomplishment. In hierarchical American society, the more of these multiple intelligences a child develops, the more chance a child stands of "trading up" to a valuable material existence.

Schools aren't getting the job done on verbal and math skills, so it falls to SACC programs. But a developmentally appropriate SACC program then has its hands full. Even with this mandate, putting together a program that revolves around all seven areas of human accomplishment takes time, resources, and a great deal of experience.

Therefore, begin a SACC program from a position of philosophical strength. Begin with a segment of service that can be done and done well; work through the rough spots with conviction; witness the program expand and grow from day to day. See it through new eyes every day. Seek to see it through the children's eyes.

2. CHOOSING PARTNERS

SACC programs come and go. Some, which are funded by one-time research grants, disappear upon completion of the research. Others manage to put down real roots in the community, becoming an honest bastion of family support. One criterion of a program's value is *service continuity,* which relies almost exclusively on who partners into that program.

Simply finding the right partner can be an education in patience. Like rushing into a doubtful marriage, going with the first potential partner that says "yes" may seem to solve a lot of problems, but experience indicates otherwise. It always makes sense to examine the differences between what people say they want and what they're really looking for.

As in marriage, people often choose SACC partners on the basis of the role they seem able to satisfy. It might be as an agency funder, a board member, an accountant, or a playground supervisor—any role that seems necessary to fill. But behind partners' roles lie their powers, so make no mistake about the connections between power, control, and program success.

While others are wooed, the most important program partners are often overlooked or pushed to the side. The children themselves generally have the least amount of political power and the most changeless administrative role. As a result, they often find themselves at adult organizers' mercies. Note this developmental difference between school-agers and toddlers: School-agers can reflect on their experience and verbally express preferences, often quite cogently. Their input, as well as that of their parents, informs the appropriate program.

3. ADMINISTRATION

The mission statement's first real test comes with the selection of an administrator. This person or group takes the responsibility for running the program. Whoever implements the mission by means of setting agendas, making policy, and deciding day-to-day issues is the *program administrator,* who is not to be confused with the *program provider.* Both roles are described in Chapter 2.

Generally speaking, the successful administrator is one who fulfills the mission statement. More specifically, the administrator operates at two levels, one internal and one external. The *external administrative arm* handles the overall operation. It deals with governmental entities, regulatory agencies, multiple site programs, and the like. The *internal administrative arm* dedicates itself to the daily nitty-gritty of children away from home. Because administration is just another way to describe control, a successful administrator displays an in-depth understanding of existing as well as potential centers of control. In practice, a school or YMCA board that holds titular responsibility may have little or nothing to do with the day-to-day details of a program; such an expectation would be unrealistic. Similarly, an inner-city fieldhouse staff probably would be out of its depth negotiating with White House funding administrators. Recognizing the political pecking order, and assigning administrative duties accordingly, makes for smoother operations in the long run.

Of all the possible managers, is there a "right" or "best" one? Again, what's best for one program may result in disaster for another. A careful, selective analysis of existing options includes some or all of the following:

- Parent groups
- Community agencies (Youth-Serving Agencies [YSAs], recreation departments)
- Centers of worship
- Public schools and school boards
- Private schools
- Community schools
- Corporations and businesses
- County and state agencies
- Volunteer and charitable organizations
- Entrepreneurs
- Urban or rural aid societies
- Family day care providers
- Special-interest groups (e.g., League of Women Voters)

Any one of these may appear suited to the tasks of administration. But, although each may seem to offer certain advantages—for example, handy location, good standing in the community, management by a friend—pay close attention to the administrator's primary agenda. It's not likely to let a SACC program disrupt that agenda.

Prior to start-up, whoever ultimately administers the program will want to:

—agree upon lines of responsibility, accountability, and projected costs; with legal counsel, put agreements in writing.

—solicit substantive input from children and parents on a continuing basis.

—pave the way for institutional cooperation with the program.

—interpret and adopt policies, codes, and regulations in accordance with current law and practice.

—determine and establish means of recordkeeping.

—make an unswerving commitment to accomplish the philosophical goals of the program.

Treatment of these points ought to be re-evaluated following start-up and reviewed at intervals during the course of operation.

4. CURRICULUM

Of all the questions about SACC programs, perhaps the most problematic is "What will the children do?" (In contrast, adult-centered planners ask, "What will we do with the children?" Notice the child-as-object sentence structure.) A number of SACC people answer the question the easy way: by default. They seem to think that limits of space, budget, and physical safety somehow dictate the scope of activity. Coloring today, coloring tomorrow . . . ?

Conversely, some planners interpret "curriculum" to mean formal classroom-style activities, but even the U.S. Congress wishes to protect children from overstructured afternoons. The Child Care and Development Block Grant Act of 1990 puts a notable restriction on grant recipients. It requires that SACC not be "intended to extend or replace the regular academic program" (Sec. 658Hb2B). The language of the Act clearly reflects input from knowledgeable child care advocates who lobbied in favor of informal environments for SACC programs.

Raw numbers also have a profound effect on curricula. Programs with too many children and too few adults tend either (1) to restrain children from any physical activity whatsoever, or (2) to impose overly regimented activities, such as running laps and the like. Of course, neither strategy is developmentally appropriate.

Each of the various planning factors has a direct bearing on the others. This principle of interrelatedness extends beyond the confines of the SACC program. It penetrates into and emanates from the homes, workplaces, and neighborhoods of participating families. An appropriate curriculum doesn't come out of one square brightly colored box, no matter whose name is on it.

Although overlap between strategies is common, the four most popular strategies can be summarized as follows:

• *Imitation.* As in the old game of "monkey see, monkey do," children love to imitate much of the behavior they witness. When they become adults, they continue to do so. Unfortunately, some child care planners and administrators use inappropriate models for their copycatting. Trapped between SACC and, for example, preschooler day care, a program falls into an expanded administrative shell that only imitates preschool arrangements. School-agers six years old and up will ask, "What is this baby stuff?"

• *Intervention.* On the heels of validated research and documentation, some programs purport to offer remedies for some perceived social ill. Their emphasis rests on nutrition, academic tutoring, training in moral codes, or keeping children out of the street. According to this strategy, simply stopping children from going hungry, putting needles in their arms, or getting pregnant is the measure of success.

• *Athletics.* These strategies acknowledge high energy levels and motor skill improvement among school-age children. Facilities and equipment are provided for either organized or informal exercise and active play.

• *Enrichment.* Some program leaders fully recognize Piaget's conclusion that children's imaginations become less static around age six. They strive to guide school-agers into areas of advanced interest. Often, these areas receive little or no attention during the traditional school day. Identifying and capitalizing on individual bents and interests, the program encourages children to explore what, to them, are new things and ideas. Of course, depending on the cultural norm, one child's enrichment may be another's basic skills.

These four strategies make up the curricular mix. Since inertia can take over and make any changes appear frightening or uncomfortable to adult participants, the mix may be difficult to alter once it has been established. And, to a certain extent, making a real change in any one element of the program means making changes in others as well. This usually makes any change a considerable undertaking. Since curriculum exerts such a powerful institutional presence, it's wise to combat inertia by keeping the mix as fluid and responsive as life itself.

5. FINANCIAL MANAGEMENT

There's an old joke about the SACC program that had to close because it couldn't afford to buy any more red ink. Outside of Washington, D.C., the idea of spending into a deficit doesn't thrill too many people, but that's the dependent nature of a SACC program. One of the most challenging aspects of program design is the never-ending battle of the balance sheet.

As with any type of business—profitable or otherwise—three components make up a SACC program's financial picture. The first of these is financial management. This involves procedures for managing cash and resources, as agreed between planner(s) and administrator(s). When a staff worker saves a purchase receipt for crayons, and when a state agency submits an annual report to Washington, the principles of financial management come into play. At each administrative level, accurate financial management depends on accuracy at all other levels.

6. THE BUDGET

This second component of finance requires more than a little imagination. While some anticipated expenses will appear as static figures, other costs can fluctuate dramatically. By and large, personnel represents the major program expense, often consuming between 70 and 85 percent of budget. While this may seem disproportionate, keep in mind that *to care for the children is the fundamental program service.* The material cost of a loaf of bread that retails for a dollar amounts to about twelve cents; the rest goes to the people who put that loaf in the shopper's hands. That is, the intangible service costs much more than the tangible goods. The same holds true for SACC.

Tangibles such as rent, utility fees, custodial services, and program supplies generally occur as stable costs. Aside from people's pay, fluctuating costs may include transportation and regulatory compliance. A workable budget reflects the impact of both stable and fluctuating costs.

7. RESOURCE DEVELOPMENT

To secure outside funding inevitably presents a stiff administrative challenge. Because parent fees traditionally provide the bulk of funding, child care costs for low-income families can account for as much as 20 percent of these families' annual incomes. Upscale programs may institute a flat fee system, with a fixed direct cost per enrolled child. More often, sliding fee scales allow parents to pay according to ability. Sometimes a program offers "scholarships" or supplemental credit on a case-by-case basis. If planners hope to receive federal or state funding, the sliding fee scale plan appears to be a good prerequisite.

The Child Care and Development Block Grant Act of 1990 authorized new federal funding for SACC programs. After funds are appropriated, they are channeled through the Department of Health and Human Services to individual state agencies, which in turn allocate the funds according to a combination of state and federal regulation. In some cases, the states—

and county and city governments—also earmark their own funds for child care providers. Notably, program providers can more easily secure government monies for start-up or service expansion than for ongoing operations.

Private funding sources—foundations, corporations, and others—also contribute to SACC program operations. A growing number of companies sponsor both preschool and school-age child care as a benefit or service for employees. Civic-minded companies invest in their local communities' well-being, and SACC presents itself as a means to do so.

When partners' cash management policies prohibit direct funding, they can still make in-kind donations. This might entail allocations of space, utilities, transport, equipment, or personal time. Conventional wisdom regarding underutilized school facilities has a direct bearing on the movement to centralize all child and family care inside the schools. Whether child care is synonymous with public social service and welfare remains, at this writing, another point of political debate. Not all schools and school districts offer significant potential for SACC program budgeters, but some do.

Bringing all three finance components into harmony takes the sensitivity of an orchestra conductor, the nerves of a trapeze artist, the strategic awareness of a football coach, and, sometimes, the tranquility of a Zen master. Because no single person can function in all of these roles simultaneously, the battle of the balance sheet requires a joint effort from the partnership. Anything else results in disharmony and dysfunction.

8. PROGRAM PEOPLE

What kind of people want to spend a quarter, a third, even a half of their waking hours in the company of children? Responses on this range from "People who love children" to "People who can't do anything else." Both are correct, but school-agers can usually tell the difference between those who talk the talk and those who walk the walk.

Setting up school-agers with disinterested minders makes the worst of all possible programs. During an average afterschool day, the practicalities that crop up call for training, knowledge, and experience, as well as an authentic concern for children. The main advantage to hiring whoever walks through the door is that they're usually willing to accept a low wage. Propping up a program's budget by offering minimum wages to unqualified warm bodies suggests a desperation that is unsuitable for the care of children.

People who seek a professional child care role *and* who enjoy caring for children don't come cheap. However, they appear more likely able to help plan and implement programs that meet a variety of partners' standards.

For this, they ask a living wage, a job environment in which their contributions are valued, and a little personal acknowledgment.

Somehow, the familiar image of the friendly neighborhood teenager (remember the pony-tailed bobby-soxer who watched toddlers for fifty cents an hour?) remains deeply entrenched in the collective memories of many Americans. Current professional standards entail a broader-based expertise supported in part by child development research, social ecology, pedagogical training, and a host of other specialized elements. The knowledge gap between 1950s babysitter and 1990s child care professional represents as great an advance as the technological difference between Sputnik and the Space Shuttle.

Finding, hiring, and keeping child care professionals poses planners another challenge. The rest of the business world has elevated the job of "personnel" to the science of "human resources." The business of SACC cannot linger in the ways of the past and sustain itself in the future. Modern human resource theory calls for an understanding of interrelatedness between SACC people's salaries, hours, staff-child ratios, personal backgrounds and tendencies, division of responsibility, capacities, physical environment, and job satisfaction.

To this end, as in any professional field, higher rates of pay may attract and retain more highly qualified staffers. Of course, capital outlay never guarantees desirable results, but consider the alternative. Institutional babysitting looms as the unavoidable consequence of a failure to recognize child care professionals as professionals. Accept less, expect less.

9. INTERNAL POLICIES AND PROCEDURES

• A suburban developer seeks an inducement for prospective home buyers.

• An inner-city housing project frames an alternative to gang and drug exposure.

• A public school with falling enrollment tries to attract middle-class white students.

Each of these real-life motivations led to the development of SACC programs. Each program wraps around a specific cultural imperative. Each program's planners gear each of their operating policies to reflect that imperative.

Whether it is highly selective or open to all, program admission policy communicates its planners' social outlook. When parents and children pick up on that outlook, it affects their participation. Exclusionary admissions that are aimed at weeding out potential partners can branch to other exclusionary policies. By the same token, a policy designed solely to gather up children according to entitlement can lead to overreaching.

Demographics are the biggest factors affecting admissions. Regarding children, these include:

Age
School grade
Gender
Number of brothers and sisters
Physical health

Regarding families, additional characteristics include:

Economic status
Cultural imperatives
Language immediacy
Employment status
Hours of employment
Custody status
Primary residence
School affiliation
Special needs
Religious affiliation

The wider the range of "acceptable" characteristics, the more complex the policy planning. Narrowing the margins of acceptability may simplify a planner's job, but making them too narrow erodes general support. Some planners conceive and implement a SACC program as a kind of private country club for children, replete with tenured access and award dinners. But most SACC planners consider their clients—and, in turn, their programs—in more down-to-earth terms.

Coming down to earth also means coming to grips with the actual numbers of latchkey children a program can realistically serve. Even badly overloaded programs maintain waiting lists. Child care R & Rs (resource and referral agencies) consistently report that demand for SACC services far outstrips the available supply. Given real-world limitations, no program can hope to satisfy a demand that exceeds capacity.

10. SCHEDULE

Some work/family advocates have suggested that before- and afterschool programs aren't enough. They suggest that the global economic war has had the same effect on parents' working lives as would a military war. They have observed more and more people working all hours of the day and night. This hard reality ought to have some bearing on a program's *external schedule.*

For the future, some advocates envision year-round, 24-hour-a-day, total-care programs. For the present, days and hours of operation usually still revolve around educational agendas, classroom sites, and school sessions. While year-round programs are what parents with job, job training, and higher education goals probably want most, such a schedule may not be immediately feasible. Still, a service-oriented view takes into account people's real-life schedules.

To justify funding or to tighten budgets, some program operators demand attendance just as a school does, holding up threats of fines and punishments for those who don't comply. But minimum daily attendance requirements can also hinder the program operation. With the advent of voucher and choice systems, parents may be able to opt out of these arbitrary impositions. Care-wise and cost-wise, it's better to have two children attending on a part-time basis than neither attending full-time.

Fixed hours of attendance can affect a program in the same way. On the plus side, knowing precisely who comes in when permits a bit more confidence in staff and curriculum planning. If transportation arrangements are necessary, organizing the comings and goings also becomes easier. But parents and guardians don't live their lives on paper, and anything unexpected can change parameters of personal obligation. Program planners who are more interested in people than rules create flex-hour programs.

The timing of various events during the course of each day constitutes the program's *internal schedule.* Leaving too much time for one thing and not enough for another usually results when planners structure time too rigidly. Cultural differences aside, creating an evenhanded flow to the day means being able to see time for what it is: a fluid thing, expanding and contracting around experiences, not just measured but *sensed.*

11. TRANSPORTATION

Like the story of Mohammed and the mountain, conventional wisdom says that if children are already at school, bring the programs to them. One at a time, several working parents in Washington state approached the same elementary school principal. Each wanted to know what to do about his or her children after school. The principal himself had noted that some children were hanging around school without supervision after classes let out for the day. He contacted the local YMCA youth director about the possibility of the Y administering a SACC program in his school. Since the children were already there, transportation didn't arise as an issue.

However, not all programs come into being as a means of supervising an at-hand group of children. Practicable programs may build on an area magnet approach in which planners situate and budget a program to reflect population density, residential geography, availability of public transportation, and the like. An established and respected neighborhood center, such as Chicago's Carole Robertson Center for Learning, can capitalize on its organic role, that of a place where people independently wish to go and will choose to do so.

A direct relationship appears between enrollment—which, in one way or another, translates to program viability—and transportation. While case-by-case accomodation needn't set planners another Herculean task, parents and guardians respond cooperatively when institutions recognize their valid imperatives. So, if transportation availability changes, how quickly a program's transportation policy responds to that change strongly determines program enrollment.

Transportation planning doesn't only entail busing, subways, and carpools. Even the logistics of walking from point A to point B may require close scrutiny. Confirming common street sense, a University of Chicago report explains that walking through a housing project presents a severe risk.

The Lower North Center is located in the middle of the Cabrini Green housing project. This puts the center squarely in the middle of many of the stresses and difficulties of life in a public housing project, but at the same time puts it close to many of the social and cultural resources of the near Northside. Cabrini Green is divided into different communities by strong gang boundaries, themselves defined by the type of building (red brick, white brick). Children often will not cross hostile gang territory to go to an after school program.[3]

It's hardly a unique circumstance. Transportation planning here goes hand-in-hand with life and death.

12. LEGAL AFFAIRS

Making the divisions of responsibility clear and certain stands out as an overriding concern in the first nine planning factors. "Chain of command" can be either a choke chain or a linkage of accountabilities. The latter, which allows for self-determining behavior, implies political or legal accountability. At each level of operation, legal concerns make themselves felt.

Many states and school districts photograph and fingerprint their potential employees, much as arresting police officers would. These I.D. elements pass through to the U.S. Department of Justice, which screens and reports the potential employee's federal criminal status. This procedure helps indemnify the state and the district in the event of some unexpected contingency. Although programs that seek state licensing renewals and government funding may have these and other protective mechanisms in place, not all planners and administrators are compelled to resort to such time-consuming and expensive measures. Still, from compliance with minimum health regulations to civil lawsuits, the legal ramifications of SACC program operation require close attention. One unforeseen legal complication can close down a program overnight.

Whether program funding and approval comes from the federal government, a church, a school board, a state agency, or private sources, very specific questions about legal accountability will have to be answered. Not infrequently, already existing groups collaborate to offer a SACC program. These organizations in particular find legal affairs a sensitive area of ongoing concern.

13. ASSESSMENT

Taken together, the planning factors listed here constitute the mechanistic whole of a SACC program. No partnership can proceed equitably with a program's start-up, improvement, or expansion unless it considers these factors together. Consequently, no partnership can determine whether it is achieving its objectives or fulfilling its mission unless its members periodically review and evaluate these factors together. The assessment process involves sharing observations and information about the program. When assessments motivate positive change and personal growth, then *and only then* does a SACC program blossom.

NOTES

1. Elizabeth Prescott, "Dimensions of Day Care Environments" (Keynote address, Day Care Environments Conference, Iowa State University, June 15, 1979).
2. Docia Zavitkovsky, "Children First: A Look at the Needs of School-Age Children," *School-Age Child Care, Programs and Issues* (Urbana, IL: ERIC/EECE, 1980), p. 8.
3. Robert Halpern, "The Role of After School Programs in the Lives of Inner-City Children" (Chapin Hall Center for Children, University of Chicago), p. 20.

FOR FURTHER REFERENCE

Alexander, Nancy. "School-Age Child Care: Concerns and Challenges." *Young Children,* November 1986, 42 (1): 310.
Bender, Judith, Barbara Schuyler-Haas Elder, and Charles Flatter. 1984. *Half a Childhood: Time for School Age Child Care.* Nashville: School Age NOTES.
Gardner, Howard. 1983. *Frames of Mind.* New York: Basic Books.
Scales, Peter. 1991. *A Portrait of Young Adolescents in the 1990s: Implications for Promoting Healthy Growth and Development.* Chapel Hill: Center for Early Adolescence, University of North Carolina.
The Unfinished Agenda: A New Vision for Child Development and Education. 1991. New York: Committee for Economic Development.

Chapter 2

CHOOSING PARTNERS

A plotted course of action requires a concerted effort from every participant in the SACC program partnership. Willingness to learn—as well as being prepared to fail in the process—distinguishes the long-lived SACC program from the short-lived folly. As in any other collaborative effort, the choice of partners and players stems from, suffers from, and succeeds by the choices that partners make along the road to discovery.

To acknowledge a partner means, in effect, to surrender a certain amount of direct personal and political power to that partner. Partnerships of all kinds generally form around what the partners perceive as desirable outcomes. On this score, a SACC program partnership comes about in no different way than any other organized mutual effort: a theatrical troupe, a professional sport team, or a quilting bee comes about as a matter of interpreting roles and outcomes.

GETTING THE BALL ROLLING: THE ACTION GROUP

Recognizing a situation that calls for new school-age care options might be as simple as looking out the window. Young children are hanging around in the street, waiting for something to happen; forlorn faces stare out through the same security grillwork every day; a frantic mother shrieks her child's name all over the street. It's easy to say, "Somebody oughta do something."

But who? Who'll bring unified effort to create new options, new programs? Who'll care enough to see a SACC program through from its conception to the first day the children arrive? Who'll keep an eye on the fits and starts of these new creations?

It may be a parent-teacher organization. An urban task force might take up the challenge, as might an interagency coalition council, an employees' union committee, or the League of Women Voters. It might even happen that a few concerned parents band together in common interest. Whoever moves the concept forward from good intention to living reality, that's an *action group.*

Action groups sometimes form spontaneously in response to a particular situation. They may work together to reach a single mutual goal and then disband, or they may continue on as a political presence, advocating public attention and support for child care issues. Other action groups take up SACC program advocacy as a natural outgrowth of their usual work. Either type may later undergo a transition into more formal program administrators. However, at the outset, action groups revolve around and, one hopes, further inspire the first prerequisite for appropriate SACC: collaborative partnership.

CANARI IN A COAL MINE

In days gone by, coal miners tested their working environment for breathability with a caged canary. If the canary died, the mine air was unfit to breathe. If it lived, the air was deemed acceptable and the work would continue. If the canary lived long enough, the miners used it again the next time concerns arose.

A Community Assessment of Need and Resource Instrument (CANARI) sounds much more complicated than it really is. In principle, a CANARI does the same thing for SACC that the caged canary did for coal miners. Those considering SACC start-up or expansion can use it to test the socio-economic atmosphere for potential program usage. It supplies local officials a meaningful profile of child-related public opinion. It offers parents a chance to help mold policies that directly affect them and their children. It also creates paperwork, but then, what doesn't?

Informal assessments have an air of the suggestion box about them. If they can't see any reasonable connection between their honest opinions and the implied authority structure, why should respondents, especially parents, express their concerns at all? With a caring focus on child care solutions, CANARIs help crystallize informal connections. Shared experience can't help but cement understandings between people with desires in common. A proper CANARI speaks directly to those desires and opens the door for fulfillment.

Information collected by a well-designed and minimally biased CANARI can make care planners' lives much easier. Whether or not the CANARI supports an immediate start-up, the data it provides can fuel efforts to enable other developmentally appropriate forms of child care. It provides the least refutable snapshot of immediate and imminent conditions affecting local child care. Keeping in mind that child care happens locally—not in well-meaning research centers or seats of government—the critical picture is the local one.

In the often-cited case of a recalcitrant school administrator, it's one thing to present self-supported opinions and feelings. These are easily and necessarily suborned by busy bureaucrats. However, it's quite another thing to document demand, including specific information that x number of children from y number of families remain unattended and unsupervised after school; that n families express willingness to pay z dollars a week for SACC; that those families indicate preferences about the SACC program site. Administrators tend to be more responsive to demonstrable claims.

To return for a moment to the coal miners, their canary gave them limited information. It couldn't tell them whether the mine supports were structurally sound or whether the coal dust would precipitate lung disease over a long period of exposure. The canary was a tool of the moment.

A CANARI survey suffers from similar limitations. By itself, a CANARI cannot directly determine:

- whether or not the expressed desires can be satisfied;
- whether or not those who express interest will act upon it;
- whether or not desired service is financially viable.

A CANARI can help to reduce the immediate risk of ill-conceived offerings and the greater risk of leaving perceived needs unrecognized. It can aid in re-prioritizing and re-organizing existing services, matching them more closely with the real requirements of the community. It can help blueprint site selection, design, and budget for a variety of child care options, including SACC.

Starting from scratch, the entire process that begins with a CANARI and results in a SACC program can take more than a year. In that time, any amount of survey information could be outdated or invalid by the time a program actually begins operation. So, as tempting as it may be, don't get stuck on the idea that CANARI data has to remain fixed and constant to be useful. Despite changes in circumstances, SACC start-up can be designed, offered, and funded much more easily with a CANARI. Without it, any attempt at organized child care is a leap into total darkness.

Getting the Bird Off the Ground

Any state, school, community organization, local agency, parent group, civic group, parish, county extension, or human resources department can fly a CANARI. Quite commonly, the survey gets done as a cooperative venture between two or more partners. Two examples bespeak this approach.

> *In sixty rural Wisconsin communities, a University of Wisconsin*
> *professor provides technical support, the local school serves as the*
> *data collection point, and a county extension home economist or*
> *4-H agent coordinates the effort.*

Dave Riley, child development specialist at the University of Wisconsin, describes the genesis of his state's child care movement as a somewhat self-defeating attempt to raise awareness:

In this initial effort, a standard "dissemination model" of education was used: university experts disseminated their knowledge about problems and solutions to local people. This method . . . can make some learners feel ignorant, and thus increase their dependence upon professional experts. Other learners, who have sufficient self-confidence, will sometimes defend their sense of personal control by resisting [such] efforts to instruct them about their problems. When we saw the lack of response to our initial educational efforts, our first response was to blame the learners. In some cases, no doubt, this was justified, as some members of the public seemed intent on denying the existence of local problems. But when we stopped blaming the learners and began taking their viewpoint seriously, it led to a new approach that has been surprisingly effective.

In our revised effort, we helped local groups conduct their own research. This method, quite different from the dissemination model, is more akin to conducting a demonstration or field test [in which] farmers are invited to see for themselves what seed grows best in their local soils. Farmers would place little faith in the results of seed tests conducted far away at the university. They know that their local soil is different, that the natural ecology varies from locale to locale. But so does the human ecology, we realized. One small town is often different from another, and they are certainly both different from the nearest major city. We should not be surprised, perhaps, that a local school principal is like a local farmer: both want to see evidence of what will work locally.[1]

Figure 2.1 shows the CANARI used by the University of Wisconsin–Extension to determine local needs.

Ironically, while much of the past research about SACC concerns itself with testing children for locus of control, the measurable shift in parental locus of control that mandated SACC programs harbor often goes unaddressed. Using this type of CANARI shifts decision making back where it belongs: into the neighborhood. Subsequent action then takes place in concert with the special attitudes, conditions, and comforts of the people who are affected.

Program viability depends heavily upon neighborhood involvement, which may be slower to start in some communities. After a time, SACC methods

Figure 2.1
UW-Extension Survey of School-Age Child Care Needs

Please answer each question as it best describes you and your family. There is no "right" answer. All information will be kept COMPLETELY CONFIDENTIAL.

I. CURRENT CHILD CARE

1. Thinking just of your school-aged children, what grades are they in school this year?

    Grades: _____ _____ _____ _____ _____ _____

    Please circle the grade of your youngest child who attends school. We will ask questions about this child.

    ---

2. What kind of after-school child care do you use for your youngest school-aged child? Please check all the types of care that you use in a normal week.

    Child stays:

    (1) _____ At home with a parent.
    (2) _____ At home with another adult. (Who?_____.)
    (3) _____ At home with older child. (How old is other child? _____.)
    (4) _____ At home alone or with younger brothers/sisters.
    (5) _____ At a relative's house.
    (6) _____ At a friend's house.
    (7) _____ At a parent's workplace. (What kind of work? _____.)
    (8) _____ In the home of a paid child care provider (a family day care home, or neighbor's or sitter's home).
    (9) _____ In a child care program (for example, at a day care center).
    (10) _____ At a meeting, lesson, class, team practice, recreations activity or something like that.
    (11) _____ Other (please describe):_____.)

3. What problems do you have with child care for your youngest school-aged child?   (check all that apply)

    (2) _____ Difficult to coordinate child care with my working hours (or school).
    (3) _____ Trying to arrange transportation for my child after school.
    (4) _____ The cost is too high, $_____ per week.
    (5) _____ I can't find child care that I like.
    (6) _____ I worry about my child while I'm working.
    (7) _____ Our problem is before-school care.
    (8) _____ My child misses out on activities or time with friends.
    (9) _____ Providing care when my child is sick.
    (10) _____ It's a problem if I need to change my work hours or work overtime.
    (11) _____ No problems experienced.
    (12) _____ Comments? _____.

Figure 2.1 (continued)

4. The lack of good child care keeps me (or my spouse) from working as many hours as we would like.

    ___ (1) No, false.
    ___ (2) Yes, true.

5. In the last year, how many days and/or part days have you been absent from work because your child was ill? (fill in the number for each)

    ___ (1) full days
    ___ (2) part days

6. If you (or an adult relative) could not be there after school, which of the following would your youngest school age child prefer? (check one)

    ___ (1) To go to a child care program or family day care home.
    ___ (2) To have an adult or teen "sitter" come into our home.
    ___ (3) To be cared for by an older brother or sister.
    ___ (4) To care for himself/herself alone after school.
    ___ (5) Other (please specify): _____.

7. Has your youngest school age child ever told you that he or she wanted to care for himself/herself, without adult supervision, after school?

    ___ (1) No
    ___ (2) Yes

8. How does your child (or how would your child) feel about being home alone for 2 hours after school this school year? (check one)

    ___ (1) My child would enjoy taking care of himself or herself.
    ___ (2) My child might worry a bit, but would probably feel O.K.
    ___ (3) My child would be unhappy or afraid.

II. CHILD CARE NEEDS

9. How often would you use supervised child care for your youngest school-aged child, if it was available? (check one)

    ___(0) Probably not at all.
    ___(1) Every school day.
    ___(2) Two to three times each week.
    ___(3) On an irregular basis.

10. If you used child care after school, what would be the latest time you would normally need such care? (check one)

    ___(0) No need.
    ___(1) 4:00 p.m.
    ___(2) 4:30 p.m.
    ___(3) 5:00 p.m.
    ___(4) 5:30 p.m.
    ___(5) 6:00 p.m. or later.

Figure 2.1 (continued)

---

11. What is the <u>earliest</u> time you would need <u>before</u>-school child care?

     ____(0) No need.
     ____(1) 6 a.m. or earlier.
     ____(2) 6:30 a.m.
     ____(3) 7:00 a.m.
     ____(4) 7:30 a.m.

Would you be willing to spend up to $2 per hour for. . .

---

12. An AFTER-school program?
     ____ (1) No.
     ____ (2) Yes.

COMMENTS on these costs?

_____
_____

13. A BEFORE-school program?
     ____ (1) No.
     ____ (2) Yes.

_____
_____

III. EDUCATIONAL NEEDS

Please answer --Yes or No-- whether each of the following questions is true or not.
My youngest school-aged child needs to know more about:

14. ____No ____Yes How to deal with strangers at the door or on the phone.
15. ____No ____Yes What to do if there is a fire in the house.
16. ____No ____Yes Preparing food safely when alone.
17. ____No ____Yes Applying first aid.
18. ____No ____Yes Dealing with boredom or loneliness when alone.
19. ____No ____Yes Dealing with fear when alone.

20. If you were to receive information on the topics listed above, how would your family like to receive it? Please check the <u>most preferred ways</u> below: (check one or more)

     ____ (1) A series of evening classes you would attend with your child(ren).
     ____ (2) A Saturday workshop you would attend with your child(ren).
     ____ (3) A series of classes for your child, taught at school.
     ____ (4) Written information, you could use with your child.
     ____ (5) Video tape program you could check out.
     ____ (6) Other (please explain): _____

21. While age is not the only consideration for parents when leaving a child alone, what age do you think most children can stay by themselves every day AFTER school? (circle the <u>age</u> below)

    4   5   6   7   8   9   10   11   12   13   14   15   16   17   18 <u>years old.</u>

Figure 2.1 (continued)

---

22. Living in our household during the week are: (check one)

 ___ (1) 1 parent.
 ___ (2) 1 parent and 1 or more other adults (grandparent, friend, etc.)
 ___ (3) 2 parents (or stepparents).
 ___ (4) 2 parents and 1 or more other adults.

23. How many adults in your household are currently employed at least 10 hours per week. (Check one).

 ___ (1) No adults
 ___ (2) One adult
 ___ (3) Two adults
 ___ (4) Three or more adults

24. We live: (check one)
 ___ (1) In town
 ___ (2) Out of town, non-farm
 ___ (3) Out of town, on a farm

THANK YOU! PLEASE HAVE YOUR CHILD RETURN THIS TO THE TEACHER

such as telephone reassurance lines and parent-child care workshops can engender initial trust between neighborhood members and SACC provider. This can engender the greater confidence necessary for full-service SACC program support.

In Boston, a parent group recruits assistance from the city's public and archdiocese schools to obtain formal survey data intended to bolster its contention about popular demand for more SACC programs.

Four-fifths of the U.S. population resides within thirty miles of ocean coastline, and the majority lives in or quite near major urban centers. Accordingly, none of these cities is stranger to the upheavals of drug trade, tax revolt, industrial downturns, and the concomitant economic fallout. Even though SACC-oriented action first began from feminist and social welfare agendas, many segments of urban society now have taken up the challenge to widen the range of SACC program availability.

Parents United for Child Care, an organization made up primarily of low and moderate income parents, identified as its top priority in 1989 the need for more Boston-area school-age programs. Although such programs have proliferated in Massachusetts for decades, a 1987 SACCProject study found that available supply could accommodate only 5 percent of the school-age population in Boston. This figure fell far short of discernible existing demand.

Thus, Parents United for Child Care partnered with the Wellesley SACCProject to design their own confidential CANARI—not to test the waters, but to solidify their political stance. Here, informal demand for improved breadth of SACC program services overrides the survey's investigatory function. The City of Boston seems farther along the road of discovery, so obtaining vital details for planning, funding, and staffing SACC programs makes better sense than running through the mechanical motions of an opinion poll. Figure 2.2 shows part of the survey used by Parents United for Child Care.

While reviewing the preceding CANARIs, keep in mind that they are not intended as templates. DO NOT COPY THEM. Instead, allow them to demonstrate what is possible. Creative interaction among planners, providers, and the people to be served is essential.

Depending on projected scope and the predisposition of the participants, a CANARI may be

• a printed questionnaire
• a telephone interview
• a door-to-door survey
• a congregational gathering

- a PTO meeting
- a voice mail or e-mail inquiry
- a combination of any two or more of these
- something else

There is no "right" way in which questions must or should be asked. An appropriate CANARI will match form to function. Sophisticated survey instruments won't necessarily ensure useful results. Neither will volume suffice, since the return rate of printed surveys can fall as low as 4 percent of the mailout, making generalizations or predictions based on the responses difficult or misleading.

The Wright brothers didn't get their first design off the ground. So, as Dave Riley described, be prepared to fail the first time out. On the other hand, there's no need to re-invent the wheel, either. The following general guidelines can aid the creative process.

- *Make the CANARI simple to answer.* Few, if any, people enjoy the prospect of filling out long complicated forms or of being grilled at length by an officious interviewer. Responses garnered by such methods are unlikely to reveal an accurate picture. Therefore, keep the main body of the survey simple. If printed forms are used, an optional "Comment" or "Opinion" section catches the more complex descriptive remarks. Similarly, in the case of personal or focus group surveys, leave respondents adequate time after the primary discussion to bring up personal concerns. Otherwise, the limited information that the CANARI collects may be statistically accurate but woefully inadequate.

- *Design questions that elicit relevant responses.* So that information gathered can be easily analyzed, compiled, and summarized, the most important CANARI feature is clarity. Questions and definitions must be easily understood. For example, the question "Do both parents work full-time?" might imply that only paid or full-time work qualifies parents to enroll their children. Data summaries would then unwittingly exclude those cases in which the child of a parent working part-time, attending school, or obligated in another way might benefit from SACC. More informative would be a question regarding specific hours of parental obligation outside the home.

Here's a good case in point. Planners in one Connecticut town send out a printed CANARI to parents. Responses seem to indicate potential enrollment of seventy children. The planners overlook affordability (they set high fees without inquiring about ability to pay) and frequency of need (most parents' obligations are only part-time, a few days a week). Their CANARI doesn't even ask the parents about these factors. Result: Planners barrel ahead with a program designed and budgeted to accommodate all seventy children, but only about a third of the children actually enroll.

- *Keep it short.* Ask the questions that must be answered, but keep the CANARI as brief as possible.

Figure 2.2
After School Survey

This survey asks about after school arrangements for your child. It is confidential—DO NOT PUT YOUR NAME ON IT. Thank you for taking the time to fill it out—you will help make after school care possible for children who need it.

How many of your children brought home a copy of this survey? [6]

If you got more than one, PLEASE FILL OUT ONLY ONE SURVEY—FOR THE YOUNGEST CHILD WHO BROUGHT A SURVEY HOME.

PART I. ALL PARENTS. Please answer these questions for only ONE child—the youngest child who brought a survey home.

1. **What grade is he or she in:** (check one)
   - ☐ Kindergarten (K-1) (7-1)
   - ☐ Kindergarten (K-2) (-2)
   - ☐ 1st Grade (-3)
   - ☐ 2nd Grade (-4)
   - ☐ 3rd Grade (-5)
   - ☐ 4th Grade (-6)
   - ☐ 5th Grade (-7)

2. *Answer if this child is in kindergarten:* **What type of kindergarten does this child attend?**
   - ☐ Half-day kindergarten (8-1)
   - ☐ Extended day kindergarten (full school day) (-2)

3. *Answer if this child is in kindergarten:* **Would you like to send this child to an extended day kindergarten?**
   - ☐ Yes (9-1)
   - ☐ No (-2)

4. **Which school does he or she go to?**
   - ☐ Bates (10-01)
   - ☐ Condon (-02)
   - ☐ Everett (-03)
   - ☐ Kilmer (-04)
   - ☐ Quincy (-05)
   - ☐ Blackstone (-06)
   - ☐ Dever (-07)
   - ☐ Hamilton (-08)
   - ☐ Parkman (-09)
   - ☐ Stone (-10)
   - ☐ Parochial school (name): _____ (-11)

5. **What neighborhood of the city do you live in?**
   - ☐ Allston-Brighton (11-01)
   - ☐ Back Bay/Beacon Hill (-02)
   - ☐ Charlestown (-03)
   - ☐ Chinatown (-04)
   - ☐ Dorchester (-05)
   - ☐ East Boston (-06)
   - ☐ Fenway-Kenmore (-07)
   - ☐ Hyde Park (-08)
   - ☐ Jamaica Plain (-09)
   - ☐ Mattapan (-10)
   - ☐ Mission Hill (-11)
   - ☐ North End (-12)
   - ☐ Roslindale (-13)
   - ☐ Roxbury (-14)
   - ☐ South Boston (-15)
   - ☐ South End (-16)
   - ☐ West Roxbury (-17)

6. **Are you: employed?** ☐ Yes (12-1) ☐ No (-2)
   in school or a training program? ☐ Yes (13-1) ☐ No (-2)

7. *Answer if you are not employed or not in school:* **If this child could go someplace after school that you liked and could afford, would you:** (check any that apply)
   - ☐ look for a job (14-1)
   - ☐ enter school or training (15-1)

8. *Answer if you are employed:* **If this child could go someplace after school that you liked and could afford, would you:** (check all that apply)
   - ☐ work more hours at your job (16-1)
   - ☐ change jobs (17-1)
   - ☐ work different hours or a different shift (18-1)
   - ☐ seek a promotion (19-1)

9. *All Parents.* **If this child could go someplace after school that you liked and could afford, how likely would you be to send them to:** (Check one answer in each row)

	Very Likely	Somewhat Likely	Not Likely	Already Use This
An after-school program at school	☐ (20-1)	☐ (-2)	☐ (-3)	☐ (-4)
An after-school program near school	☐ (21-1)	☐ (-2)	☐ (-3)	☐ (-4)
An after-school program near home	☐ (22-1)	☐ (-2)	☐ (-3)	☐ (-4)
A family's home near school	☐ (23-1)	☐ (-2)	☐ (-3)	☐ (-4)
A family's home near your your home	☐ (24-1)	☐ (-2)	☐ (-3)	☐ (-4)
Summer care	☐ (25-1)	☐ (-2)	☐ (-3)	☐ (-4)

10. **During the school year, how many days a week would you be likely to use such after school care?** [26]

11. **How many hours each day would you use such care?** [27] [28]

12. **What would you like in this program/home for this child?** (Check all that you would like.)
   - ☐ Help with homework (29-1)
   - ☐ Sports or exercise (30-1)
   - ☐ Outdoor play (31-1)
   - ☐ Field trips (32-1)
   - ☐ Arts, music, crafts (33-1)
   - ☐ Multi-cultural activities (34-1)
   - ☐ Bilingual providers (35-1)
   - ☐ Other_____ (36-1)

13. **In the past two years, have you looked for care for this child and been unable to find it?**
   - ☐ Yes (37-1)
   - ☐ No (-2)

• *Anticipate the human factor.*

—A program coordinator in Virginia explains, "We don't want to put undue pressure on principals in the schools . . . having people knocking on the door, saying, 'We demand this service!' "

—Concerned about the issue of confidentiality, a parent group decides not to request names, addresses, or phone numbers of CANARI respondents. Later, when programs open to low enrollment, the group can't follow up with those parents who had indicated they would definitely enroll their children.

—One afternoon, the League of Women Voters distributes an exploratory CANARI through a local public school system. That same afternoon, the League president receives a call from a parent, voice filled with desperation, asking, "When can I enroll my child?"

Before distributing printed CANARIs or scheduling any investigatory meetings, group leaders and program initiators would do well to freshen their familiarity with human behavioral response—not just of children, but of adults as well.

The coordinator in Virginia evinces a familiar concern. If such a demand for SACC exists that parents would indeed flock to administrators with cries for programs, won't such a hue and cry bring about action? Perhaps the coordinator's fear arose from a realization that public action for SACC becomes tantamount to class warfare, as public sector service demands often do. Historically, this antagonism toward SACC—and publicly facilitated child care in general—has tended to diminish as the economic climate worsens and the number of children at risk rises. For example, in the wartime U.S. economy of 1942–45, little or no opposition arose; the need was assumed and understood. Bringing popular pressure to bear on people charged with serving people hardly seems an unwanted outcome. Even if the only result of the initial CANARI is a call for change, the process has begun.

On another note, false impressions and failure to identify partners can seriously set back SACC action. Parents and other concerned parties won't easily shrug off misrepresentation or the raising of false hopes. The CANARI is the SACC program's calling card; treat it accordingly.

• *Never fear the power of publicity.* An invaluable method for stemming neighbors' opposition to a party is to invite the neighbors themselves. Just the act of offering an invitation often soothes ill feelings. Occasionally, it makes for an even better party.

Purposefully excluding or avoiding contact with someone whose interests might be affected by a SACC program can severely undermine the CANARI effort. Don't inadvertently alienate people who have hands to lend, resources to supply, and appropriate experience. Take steps to make the CANARI public knowledge.

Local papers and in-house publications often print information of immediate concern, especially if the press release is delivered by hand. In a large metropolitan or countywide effort, utilize electronic media coverage. Most radio and television stations offer not-for-profit organizations opportunities to air a no-cost public service announcement (PSA). Pursue every outlet to generate broader awareness and interest in your CANARI.

So that interested individuals can obtain further information, always include a contact name and phone/e-mail number in memos, press releases, and PSAs. In some areas, publicity can still generate some dissent, and the dissenters may focus their efforts on the given contact. In a democracy, this is the price of change. If any opposition arises, try to be informative and to open a dialogue, but don't be discouraged by cranks.

Turning the CANARI into a Homing Pigeon

Getting a questionnaire out is one thing. Getting it back is another. Not too many people enjoy the idea of filling in long forms. And parents working long, swing, or night shifts aren't likely to be waiting by the phone for an afternoon interview. In some communities, *any* type of interrogation gives cause for suspicion and avoidance.

Promising nothing for the effort of returning yet another form to another form collector usually ends as badly as promising too much. One neophyte observed in dismay, "We only received nineteen out of six hundred fliers back, even though we knew more people needed and wanted the program." This shotgun approach also fuels environmental concerns about solid paper waste, since most of the fliers fly right into the neighborhood's big curbside circular files . . . if not onto the curbside itself.

Getting reliable information from the CANARI depends on creating a reliable way to get the information. Good intentions alone won't attract a significant response. Like anything else that depends on family participation, a successfully conducted CANARI encourages parents and rewards children.

When thinking of ways to bring the CANARI back, consider the following points:

• *A specific and coherent plan for obtaining CANARI information must reflect an intelligent grasp of respondents' cultural values.* In some communities, even the choice of language might inadvertently blunt response. For one Florida county's printed CANARI, planners wisely anticipated local ethnic composition by writing in Spanish and Vietnamese as well as English. No doubt these planners obtained a higher response percentage and, one hopes, a better profile of parents' self-perception than if they had written in English only.

• *A penny saved keeps forms unreturned.* Instead of worrying about what looks like an unnecessary expense, many successful enterprises can testify to the benefit of using self-addressed, postage-paid envelopes. Both for-profit and nonprofit groups use such envelopes to facilitate ease of re-

sponse and so increase the rate of return. Keep in mind the possible headaches and debacles for a SACC provider who goes ahead with limited or inaccurate information. Even deeper financial difficulties may be avoided with a small up-front expense like this.

• *Get the children involved.* After all, any action that ultimately stems from CANARI information will affect their lives. In many cases, distribution of a printed CANARI can take the form of a public, private, or religious school take-home. Naturally, there arises the possibility of encouraging parent cooperation by pegging returned forms to "happy-face," "special treat," or some other reward system normally employed at the school. Also, increasing the form's visual impact by making it colorful and entertaining also makes it less likely to be lost on the way home or misplaced unseen on a kitchen counter.

• *Personalize.* Magazine subscription sellers flood mailboxes with millions of "You have already won!" announcements, each prominently bearing the addressee's name in huge block letters. Even the most basic personal computer programs make it possible to do the same with form correspondence. Make no mistake: The CANARI is a *request.* How likely is anyone to respond to "Dear Mr., Ms., or Mrs. Child's Parent"? The same consideration holds true for in-person meetings. For the timid as well as the vocal, the care of their children is a highly personal issue. Treat it as such.

POWER, POWER, WHO'S GOT THE POWER?

The U.S. Constitution vests governmental power in the nation's citizenry via the electoral process. Economic power emanates from a checkbook. An entrenched bureaucracy absorbs and re-directs all other energies with even greater power.

Navigating these deep waters may appear to be a mind-numbing and daunting prospect, especially inappropriate to the meager scale of a private, exclusive child care program. However, whether promoting a limited closed-end offering or a district-wide public effort, SACC advocates repeatedly discover themselves engaged with "the powers that be." The results of this particular engagement do more to determine who plays which roles than any other type of interaction between partners.

Every community has its old guard, its moneyed interests, its political power brokers. True, these are important partners in SACC. The trouble is, power is often miscalculated as residing solely with recognized institutions. But power takes many forms. Successful community-based action stems from the authority of natural community leaders. The big question here is: Who's going to run the program?

To distinguish between various forms of political power is to distinguish various *elements of authority.*

PRESUMED

This is authority taken upon oneself without permission. Presumed authority denies the value of any external input. It often leads to arrogance and intransigence, which makes it a most difficult obstacle to cooperative action.

ADMINISTRATIVE

Bureaucracies carry administrative authority to license, regulate, allow, or restrict access, as well as to transmit information in whatever way they choose. Here is the filter through which executive directives are transformed into either action or stagnation.

VESTED

Vested authority likens to moral authority in the sense that every sane individual of majority age owns the responsibility for his or her own actions. One increases vested authority through relative achievement and success in one's environment. A parent or guardian also has a vested authority for the actions and treatment of a child.

EXECUTIVE

Whether empowered by appointment, organic ascendancy, or election, an individual or committee with executive status assumes a prescribed authority that shapes events. Executive decisions can enable or disable with sweeping impact.

WAGE

Having the ability to provide or withhold money, those who cut the checks certainly have their say. In any economic model, the deeper the pockets, the wider the wage authority.

ASCRIPTIVE

Ascriptive authority arises not as a result of individual achievement but by virtue of some predetermined demographic characteristic. For many years, its influence has been the focus of human and civil rights advocates. Age, race, gender, religious affiliation, and national origin, to name just a few, may be used by those trying to justify this type of authority.

YIELDED

In some specific instances, a situation may exist in which no one is willing or able to exercise any other kind of authority. This surrender creates a kind of decision-making vacuum. In these cases, anyone who steps forward and offers a course of action probably wants that yielded authority. Although other elements of authority may be clearly in evidence, it is not uncommon for someone wresting presumed authority to promote it as having been yielded.

Because combinations of these elements pave the way for a successful program partnership, the acronym PAVEWAY signifies the seven main types of authority to be considered:

Presumed

Administrative

Vested

Executive

Wage

Ascriptive

Yielded

The degrees to which each authority influences a SACC program can be seen as that program's fingerprints; they identify that program as a particular entity, separate and unique from any other program.

A LOOK AT THE PLAYERS

Each member of the SACC partnership plays one or more roles, each role consisting of different tasks and responsibilities. Shared and shifted responsibilities account for most of the flux in everyday life. The same holds true in SACC programs in that, once initiated, roles quickly become a part of program life.

One role roster consists of positions specifically called for by the definition of school-age child care programs, including the following:

CAREGIVER—also called staff, personnel, worker, teacher, employee, helper, assistant (and, unfortunately, other terms of lower regard); the actual person who interacts with and takes care of children;

ON-SITE DIRECTOR—the individual charged with direct supervision of program site activity, as well as that individual's surrogates;

SACC PROGRAM PLANNER—as discussed in Chapter 1, the person who identifies and codifies program factors;

SACC PROGRAM ADMINISTRATOR—as discussed in Chapter 1, the person who performs executive duties as set out by the planner;

SACC PROGRAM PROVIDER—an intermediate function that bridges planner to administrator; an organizational and financial conduit that is approximate to middle management in private corporate structures; the person who authorizes satellite sites of multi-site programs.

Another roster lists the mechanistic roles of which any successful partnership ordinarily must avail itself, including the following:

LANDLORD—holds the land or structural rights to the program base location and building;

MAINTENANCE CONTRACTOR—provides cleaning, repair, and upkeep services;

ACCOUNTANT/TAX CONSULTANT—maintains and analyzes financial records;

LEGAL ADVISER—reconciles program partnership and practices with standards and regulations in current force;

TRANSPORTATION MANAGER—correlates and solves minutiae of client-related arrivals and departures.

Still another roster contains roles of incidental or variable importance to a SACC program. Whether a particular program enjoins these partners depends on its size and scope. This list includes the following:

OUTSIDE FUNDER—provides cash and credit flow that supplements operational income;

PUBLICIST—raises general awareness of a particular program as a desirable option to potential partners;

SOCIAL SERVICE COORDINATOR—establishes case-by-case agendas linking SACC to the chain of family care program services;

POLICY ANALYST—acts as a consultant to planners and administrators; amasses, digests, and extrudes appropriate directives for program start-up and implementation;

RESOURCE AND REFERRAL AGENT—sometimes called a resource broker, identifies human and financial resources currently available to a given program;

NUTRITION SPECIALIST—carries out mandated procedures for food procurement and distribution, generally to multi-site programs.

On the receiving end comes the roster of direct, indirect, and implied beneficiaries of a SACC program, including the following:

CHILDREN AND PARENTS—those who participate as service recipients;

IMMEDIATE COMMUNITY MEMBER—an individual, such as a neighbor, relative, or local merchant, whose residential or commercial status sometimes leads to direct interaction with children and parents;

EXTENDED COMMUNITY MEMBER—an individual or entity whose residential, commercial, or occupational activity depends, to some extent, upon children and parents.

Even a brief look at these role rosters shows that perhaps thousands, perhaps tens of thousands of people may be either directly or indirectly affected by a given SACC program's operation. Because of these potentially far-reaching societal implications, no SACC program may be undertaken casually or lightly. In fact, if there is only one observation about SACC that remains unchanged since publication of this manual's first edition, it is this: *The key to eventual success is the formation of a broad-based coalition.*

BRINGING PARTNERS ON BOARD

Given the variety of partner roles and PAVEWAY elements, program initiators can begin to appreciate the importance of consultation. The more isolated the program, the less chance a need may arise for negotiations and concessions. On the other hand, a group of only twelve individuals with diverse perceptions can come to be known as a hung jury, unable to agree about even a single proposition. No matter how unpleasant or difficult it seems, protocol and personalities must be heeded to the extent that all partners may cooperate in support of each other.

Some potential partners may be more attracted by a program's superficial qualities, others more reassured by its quantifiable results, still others convinced by its indirect long-term effect on the very children it serves. One way or another, if a concern is conceivable, someone will express it. It is better that this input comes from consultation within a partnership that embraces diversity, rather than from disgruntled and disenfranchised outsiders.

The foremost mandate to planners and providers is the mandate for inclusion. To make good on that mandate, they must adopt certain precepts about vox populi, the voice of the people. They must organize themselves in ways that encourage exchanges of ideas and feelings. In almost all cases, they must follow certain organizational guidelines that spur such exchanges between all concerned parties. They can accomplish this in a number of ways, but perhaps the most common is the formal directorship, also known as *the board.*

A board formally and often legally represents the program. It ratifies program missions and internal policies. It establishes and oversees hiring procedures, budget affairs, and funding mechanisms. It determines the program's relationships with other agencies and partners. It concerns itself with regulatory compliance and liability matters. Equally important, a proper board serves as a forum for the regular exchange of information affecting the program.

Traditionally, a chairperson sits as leader of board meetings and activities. Two co-chairs can share the role and its duties, each assuming complementary responsibilities. Chairpeople may assign themselves their role, or they may be elected to sit for a predetermined amount of time.

More modern boards replace the fixed chair with the position of *facilitator,* a regularly rotating assignment that falls to each board member in turn. Rather than laboring under a top-down hierarchy, members of these boards strive for a more creative and trustworthy balance of power. The facilitator concept can more suitably inspire the essence of partnership that is so crucial to successful SACC.

A board normally accomplishes its business through a system of standing and ad hoc committees. *Standing committees* handle regular business.

Ad hoc committees come together only for unusual situations, one special issue at a time. Committees function like mini-boards, then bring their results to the entire board.

Parent Boards

Official members come from among the people whose children attend. Usually, boards consisting solely of parents can be found administering parent-run programs (see Chapter 3). Occasionally, *parent advisory boards* form to make parents' varied concerns clearer to multi-agency and multi-site programs. The following excerpt from the Madison, Wisconsin, *After School Day Care Handbook* illustrates this.

The structure within the association shall be a representative democracy, with parents at each center electing representatives to the governing board. It is the right of every element of the association (staff, parents, children) to expect support from every other element, to appeal decisions involving them directly, to sit on the board as a representative or concerned party, to carry through in the objectives of the association for creative, enthusiastic daily care, to express opinions for that potential.

The Board of Parent Representatives: Responsibilities/Duties

Policy	Determination of all policies re: the administration and program goals Has the responsibility to request information to determine those policies Sets all policies for future of organization as well as present operations
Hiring	Responsible for all hiring/firing of staff (usually in consultation with curriculum coordinator and director) Responsible for all hiring/firing of administration staff Responsible for committee personnel (volunteers)
Appeals	Hears appeals regarding all decisions, policies, differences with other elements within association Hears grievances of all decisions, including its own
Finances	Responsibility to work with director on budgets, fee setting, fundraising, proposals (including appearances before potential donors if necessary), and ascertaining cash flow appropriateness on a monthly basis
Publicity	Aid Central Staff
Committees	Functions of the board are handled by various committees of the board: Standards & Guidelines (Policies), Personnel (Hiring), Financial (Finances), Publicity (Publicity)

Authority   The Board shall have the ultimate authority and responsibility for all actions of the ASDCA and all decisions of the board are final

Officers   Shall be elected according to the bylaws and each officer shall chair one committee[2]

Boards with a Capital "B"

These are directorships of politically powerful entities: school districts, major corporations, banking institutions, county governments, health maintenance organizations, and so on. Many people sit on boards, far fewer on Boards. And when little boards come up against big Boards, guess which one has to try harder.

Very few Boards actively seek an inclusive consensus. Some are simply isolated from their constituents' real-life concerns, either by geography or work schedules. Following the path of least resistance usually means never knowing just how out of touch they really are. For them, revelations may be slow in coming but never impossible.

CLOSE-UP: The Nashville and Middle Tennessee YMCA

CEO Clark Baker and vice-president for operations Robert Ecklund were feeling pretty good about their child care programs. The Y was serving 1,868 children daily at 56 sites in five counties. Income from the program amounted to nearly $2 million a year.

But Baker and Ecklund had never visited a site.

Said Ecklund, "We were doing an excellent job of monitoring the ratios and setting goals, but we had lost sight of the external environment—new trends in child-centered and child-directed activities, state political and education communities, and other providers."

Y staff members in Nashville discovered that people were talking about them, and it wasn't good. Parents, school personnel, and others weren't satisfied with the way the Y's child care programs were being run, but they also weren't sharing their criticisms with the Y staff.

"We think nothing of adding a Stairmaster to a wellness center," Ecklund said at one point, "but when have we invested $3,000 in a site for child-centered/child-directed activity centers?" He thought leaders of large Ys were good at things like fitness testing and Indian Guides. But, he wondered, "How many Urban Group CEOs or COOs have directly worked in child care?"

Baker and Ecklund determined they needed to make some radical changes. They called in local resource people in the child care field to tell them how they thought the Y was doing in school-age care. They called a special meeting of all executives and program staff people to talk about what they had heard and where the Y needed to go. These people were very open about the problems they saw.

The two developed a new public policy statement, which was unanimously accepted by other Ys throughout the state. The Y's child care program cabinet created an aggressive work chart and gave its full support to program changes. On board came two new program managers, one assigned to internal issues, the other to external issues and site evaluation. Baker became active on a task force of the state's Department of Human Services, and several other staff members joined forces with the National School-Age Child Care Alliance.

By fall 1991, the YMCA was committed to invest $115,000 in SACC supplies and equipment.

The Y may be the largest SACC provider in the nation, but "we are not the best, although we may be well intentioned," observed Ecklund.

Source: Ken Vogt, Program Services Division, YMCA of the USA.

Trying to work with big Boards from outside the Boardroom can be very confusing. To assuage parental concerns, big Boards sometimes carve out one or two token seats for parent representatives. All too often, parent representatives end up being cowed or co-opted by the other, more powerful Board members. To forestall this paralysis, reserve as much administrative authority as possible for the parent board or the program director (PD).

Intelligent Life beyond Boards

Popular though they are, formal boards won't necessarily fit the situation or the tastes of all program people. Planners and directors may only be looking for some political and moral support, not a new layer of bureaucracy. Others who already work for corporate boards or departmentalized agencies, and who don't know the SACC field well, just want technical assistance from working SACC professionals. They won't feel the need to initiate citywide CANARIs or to plan community-wide action.

Numerous coalitions and professional networks can offer the benefit of their experience and the support of shared purpose . . . without large-scale political obligations. SACC associations are generally anxious to expand their training and assessment imperatives throughout the family service field. Generally speaking, they're more than happy to include new partners in their drive for better SACC programs.

Interdependence-minded program people can initiate this type of partnership through:

• Local SACC coalitions
• Child care resource and referral agencies

- Municipal human services departments
- Early childhood professional associations
- Community colleges
- Universities
  —child development divisions
  —elementary education departments
- 4-H extension services
- Urban mayors' coordination offices

Bolstered by these formal or informal connections, program providers can move along to the next tier of SACC program action: defining the administration.

NOTES

1. Dave Riley, "Grass Roots Research on Latchkey Children Leads to Local Action" (Paper presented at Extension National Invitational Conference on School-Age Child Care, St. Louis, Missouri, May 1990), pp. 3–4.

2. Kay Hendon et al., *The After School Day Care Handbook: How to Start an After School Program for School-Age Children* (Madison, WI: Community Coordinated Child Care/4-C in Dane County, Inc., 1977), p. 12.

FOR FURTHER REFERENCE

Day Care Association of Montgomery County, Inc. 1989. *Partnerships: Solving the School-Age Child Care Crisis* [videotape]. Bellefonte, PA: Central Region SACC Project.

Doyle, Michael, and David Straus. 1976. *How to Make Meetings Work.* New York: Berkeley Publishing Group.

Eisler, Riane, and David Loye. 1990. *The Partnership Way.* San Francisco: HarperCollins Publishers.

Eller, Carole, et al. 1985. *The Hours We Can't Be Home: Developing a School-Age Child Care Program.* Hartford: Collaboration for Connecticut's Children.

Friedman, Jane, et al. 1984. *Managing the Media Maze.* Oakland, CA: Child Care Employee Project.

League of Women Voters Education Fund. 1991. *Expanding School-Age Child Care: A Community Action Guide* (pub. #923). Washington, DC: League of Women Voters.

Toffler, Alvin, and Heidi Toffler. 1990. *Powershift: Knowledge, Wealth, and Violence at the Edge of the 21st Century.* New York: Bantam Books.

Chapter 3

ADMINISTRATION

Any successful service business, including SACC, operates within an organizational framework. It delivers services in clearly structured, accountable, and dependable ways. Whatever group, agency, or company manages the business, success demands a flexible and responsive framework.

Each community or company poses unique problems to SACC providers. Each also possesses unique intrinsic resources. A rational assessment of problems and resources will suggest a particular approach to administrative organization. The models and profiles contained in this chapter represent only a sample of options used in current practice. Elements of any or all of these should aid planners and administrators in tailoring their own frameworks.

Administrators take one of three main approaches: (1) *societal institutions* play the dominant role, (2) *community-based approaches,* in which concerned parents and others with shared personal interests organize the program, and (3) *collaborative approaches,* a blend of community and institutional leadership.

In any administrative approach, the primary objectives of the SACC administrator remain constant. Understanding these objectives is prerequisite to any further discussion of options.

Establish clear policies that facilitate school-age child care

No Time to Waste: An Action Agenda for School-Age Child Care, makes the following recommendations specifically to school boards. However, the same goals concern any SACC administrator.

Schools are better able to operate quality SACC programs or play supportive roles as partners when their governing boards have established clear, well-thought-through policies on school-age child care. The lack of clear policies, on the other hand, can seriously retard the initiation of needed programs, preclude consideration of alternative models of school-age care, jeopardize access for low-income and special needs populations, and at times, produce public friction and private frustration among and between various parties. Policies should, *at a minimum,* address the following: the relationship of SACC to the organization's mission and/or legislative authority; the goals, scope, and purpose of the program; the level of responsibility of the organization and other parties involved; the governance of the program (e.g., by a parent board); eligibility for enrollment/access for low-income families and populations with special needs.

Sometimes, a school or a community organization plays only a supporting role. Even so, it should agree to clear policies about: (1) use of and access to space it provides; (2) extent of accountability and limits of responsibility to the program; (3) liability in case of accident or injury to child or staff; and (4) its role in regard to program licensing.

Transportation to off-school SACC sites is a key issue. Local school boards need to respond with proactive transport policies.[1]

Utilize the CANARI and changing community conditions to determine appropriate sites

As in any marketing effort, careful analysis of the client base reveals the location and disposition of *opinion leaders,* those whose interests must be satisfied if others are to be attracted and served by a program. While over-flowing demand and political pressure will affect site selection, CANARI data will help substantiate it (see Chapter 2).

Administrators must also look beyond their own immediate impressions and try to forestall adverse response to a program. Some sites will attract, others will repel. Successfully gauging community reaction to SACC's physical location means staying in touch with the various groups within the community.

Openly solicit parent and community involvement

A policy advisory group, comprised of opinion leaders, can solidify the SACC program's community image. Limiting input solely to parents whose children are currently enrolled violates the CANARI clause regarding untoward exclusion. Give anyone with an interested opinion—including children—an opportunity to express it.

Coordinate program planning with government officials

From town council to U.S. Congress, sheafs and reams of child care officialese constantly issue forth. One SACC program might find itself operating under more regulations than a tree has leaves. Another might have to answer to nothing but conscience. Administrators must stay on top of an ever-changing legal landscape, determining whether a program must observe regulations and which ones apply.

Recognize specialized skill requirements when hiring program people

No SACC program can go forward successfully without clear distinctions between traditional schoolroom procedure and child care skills. Just as teachers are trained in the rigors of cognitive pedagogy, caregivers must exhibit an applied talent for informal child guidance. If caregivers are held to no higher standard than that they be warm bodies who show up on time, the resulting "program" makes a mockery of child care rationales.

SOCIETAL INSTITUTIONS

Public Schools as Sole Administering Agency

Schools and school boards represent a fast-growing segment of SACC providers. Drug abuse, malnutrition, child neglect, declining enrollment, and a host of other ills have drawn many schools into the role of social interventionist. Although cognitive development remains their foremost priority, more and more school administrators have come to see that they can't do the right thing without having a broader picture of children.

The typical public school takes its authority from a combination of sources. An elected school board maintains executive authority. A school district wields administrative authority through a controlled bureaucracy. The board, in turn, charges principals with vested authority for their particular school's functions. With this impressive array of authority sources, schools naturally lend themselves to the role of SACC provider.

Schools and their assignees conform SACC program administration to their own existing hierarchies. This makes a program only as accountable and dependable as the existing system allows. School boards make decisions that affect program budget, salaries, hours of operation, placement/expansion/reduction of sites, and so on. With in-kind resources and even some school budget funds going to finance a SACC program, one school board member observes, "If I'm administering the dollars, I want to administer the program."

School-age care programs may shadow a crumbling school's standards, but what's the point? It cannot hope to remediate them. What a program *can* hope to do is provide an informal laboratory for the development of more modern standards. If staid school administrators feel a draft, there's a reason. Appropriate SACC isn't about maintaining status quo. It's about making things better.

Arguments against Public Schools as Sole Administering Agencies

Institutional psychology. By their very institutional nature, schools share common characteristics. School authorities tend to be defensive of their turf. They exhibit concerns about any kind of change that threatens the status quo. New programs are cause for fear and suspicion. Risk-taking exposes school authorities to criticism and/or censure. In an atmosphere of dwindling discretionary resources and fallen scholastic achievement, school insiders lean toward sustaining their bureaucracy and away from anything that might be deemed extracurricular. The survival of the existing institutional framework takes precedence over any other consideration.

Conflict of mission. In 1990, voters in Fremont, California, considered a ballot initiative meant to raise taxes for, among other things, school-based child care. They resoundingly defeated the proposal. It remains uncertain whether general resistance to tax-financed child care or a specific dislike for school-based child care caused voters to reject the initiative. In either event, taxpayers' feelings about public schools can red-flag this administrative option.

Relatedly, private sector complaints about unfair competition and subversion of free enterprise may arise, as they did when Hawaii's governor introduced legislation that placed the state's solitary school district in sole charge of statewide school-based SACC programs. Citing precedents of public schools' broad powers, courts have generally held against such complainants. But how much ill will should a SACC program cost?

Lack of dedicated facilities. Depending upon the philosophical aims of program planners, school space usage ranges from incidental to integral. School-administered programs tend to unfold exclusively within the confines of school space. Program activities rely on availability of classrooms, cafeterias, and playgrounds.

An essential SACC ingredient, the impression of constancy, can get lost in the shuffle. If formal classes or other school activities take precedence, the SACC program staff may be hustling its young charges in and out of storerooms, broom closets, and basements, trying to stay one step ahead of the next contingency. The resulting sense of transience cannot possibly be conducive to meaningful program conduct.

Is the school willing or able to house a program during summer months, school holidays, and alternative hours of greatest demand? Operating a SACC program while all other school functions have shut down doesn't exactly make things easy. If school policy doesn't allow child care at these times, parents' inconvenience and children's reduced options implicitly contribute to the "latchkey" practices SACC was intended to combat.

Developmental disharmony. School-run SACC programs must guard against resembling nothing so much as more school. The Child Care and

Development Block Grant of 1990 explicitly states that SACC programs receiving federal assistance shall "not be intended to extend or replace the regular academic program" (Sec. 658H62B).

The practical difference between a kindergarten schoolteacher and a caregiver of five-year-olds often rests solely on formal training. Giving them both the same group of children in the same basic environment may yield little in the way of visible differences. On paper, for reasons having to do with liability or budget, schools may separate the extended day from the school day. Schools may call the latter portion school-age care, but throwing a threadbare carpet on a cold cafeteria floor and naming it "The Cozy Corner" doesn't make it so.

In general, a child's traditional classroom experience entails order, compliance, trained responses, and memorization. It puts pressure on a child's attention span, rewarding the docile and punishing the disruptive. To discharge their instructional duties, many classroom teachers first assume the role of disciplinarian.

Especially at schools attended by large numbers of at-risk children, school educators may fear what they see. They may even harbor contempt toward children and parents. These educators may believe they must constantly tell their young charges what to do—or else.

Child care advocates believe SACC programs ought to contribute to critical thinking skills. But many schools operate on a mechanistic agenda to impart pre-digested data. Prosocial behaviors depend on people's skill at figuring things out for themselves, not just following the leader.

Appropriate school-age care seeks to complement the classroom experience by creating the opportunity for independent personal growth. Thus, such things as enforced seating assignments, mandatory tutoring, and adult-dictated activity agendas have no business dominating a SACC program.

Arguments in Favor of Schools as Sole Administering Agencies

Expedience. From tabletops to toilets, schools contain a wide array of facilities scaled to the size of a typical school-ager. Playground equipment, books, activity materials, and storage space that might otherwise go underutilized can be brought into play, allowing budget directors to cut capital outlay. Concerns regarding transportation planning can be reduced or allayed. To the extent that parents trust the school, parental involvement or oversight can remain relatively level.

School-administered multi-site programs can provide both continuity and diversity for children who relocate within large districts. Since a mechanism already exists for school funds disbursement, purchasing, and food procurement and preparation, a school district can administer SACC programs in conformity with equivalent school rules and regulations. A broadly represented constituency can further a program's claim to appropriateness and, in due course, respectability.

Comprehensive child development. Head Start founder Dr. Edward Zigler has long propounded his opinion that a concerted system of prenatal care, nutrition, parent education, community outreach, preschool care, school-age care, and traditional schooling, centralized within a single administrative framework, would streamline family service delivery. The primary advantage of centralizing services through the school, he contends, is that the school is already there.

Whether or not schools become the equivalents of family support service "shopping malls," the potential advantage of closeness between classroom instructors and school-age child caregivers can still be appreciated. Caregivers and instructors who work at the same location with the same children can quite easily exchange pertinent information regarding those children.

With regard to children at risk, fundamental human needs such as basic health care and nutrition underlie children's ability to learn and develop. Coordinated practices of schools, SACC programs, and other human service agencies form the basis for collaborative administrative models. See the section on collaborative approaches later in this chapter.

Complementarity with school board agendas. School-run SACC programs can sometimes serve intentions other than those of "pure" child care.

In 1982, the Denver, Colorado, Board of Education transformed an old school located in a low-income, high-crime downtown neighborhood into the Gilpin Extended Day School. Prior to the change, Gilpin's Anglo (white native English-speaking) enrollment stood at 3 percent. The new school's policy required children residing outside the neighborhood to qualify for the school-run SACC program by enrolling as regular school students. The policy also required parents of all extended-day enrollees to pay program-related fees. In a short time, Gilpin's Anglo enrollment rose from 3 percent to 14 percent.

If the board was indeed motivated to alter the racial composition of Gilpin's student body, the SACC program certainly did the trick.

Youth-Serving Agency (YSA) as Sole Administering Agency

At the turn of the last century, the proliferation of community organizations, designed to address situational social dilemmas, very neatly coincided with the advent of mass European immigration to the industrial United States cities. Faced with the prospect of absorbing and acculturating millions upon millions of impoverished families into an American workplace, churches, charities, and even some city planners created these havens of hope. All sought to ameliorate the havoc and recklessness stemming from these immigrants' inexperience with their newly adopted society.

In the absence of child labor laws, two million children were put to work until they dropped from illness, injury, or death. Outside the workplace, they frequented the city streets in search of an honest nickel or, failing that, a dishonest dollar. Too often for the dominant society's taste, animal survival took precedence over the transcendent value of human decency. Around the country, agents of social reform consolidated resources, forming various associations, centers, and clubs, which they hoped would attract children and serve the dominant social order.

Although a larger population has cut the percentage they represent, two million children in the United States are still working under illegal and unsafe conditions. Suburban schoolgrounds witness the dealings of youthful extortionists and drug peddlers. Inner-city gangs ride roughshod over entire localities, replicating their own brand of social order through nationwide criminal networks. The last three generations of social reform seem to have been no match for human tendentiousness.

Despite this, YSAs pursue their historical missions to bring health to children's body, spirit, and mind. For providing James Naismith a venue in 1891 to invent basketball, the Young Men's Christian Association established itself as a nineteenth-century innovator. Other nationally known groups such as Boys' and Girls' Clubs, Inc., and Camp Fire Inc. also owe much of their relatively high profile to their relative longevity.

Overall, YSAs can be counted on for their "brand name" recognizability and the traditional administrative aims on which their charters rest.

Arguments against YSAs as Sole Administering Agency

Complacency. Agency designees must have the knowledge, time, and willingness to perform the specialized tasks associated with a SACC program. Absent these, a program can easily be "tacked on" to the agency's larger service mission and summarily handed down the chain of command. School-age child care is decidedly not just a new name for an afternoon recreation class. Some YSAs have a problem identifying the difference.

The "service to all" backlash. A YSA with an open-arms tradition may be mishandled by parents who see it as a perennial fixture in the community. They could expect that agency to absorb late payment or nonpayment of client fees. In that event, even a program budgeted to break even cannot sustain itself. When asked why he was forced to close some programs, one YMCA director explained, "We simply didn't pursue people who didn't pay."

Transportation. After caregivers' salary and benefits, transportation can account for a greater share of SACC program costs than any other factor. Travel between home, school, and the agency's facility must be made cost-effective and logistically feasible and must be controlled for liability. In the case of after-school care alone, the agency must functionally arrange for the equivalent of five field trips a week. In cases of before- and after-school care programs, that's ten a week. And if the children don't travel together, or if they walk between school and the agency facility, or if a school bus picks up before school but won't drop off after . . . Clearly, transportation planning brings up a great many "ifs."

Arguments in Favor of YSAs as Sole Administering Agency

Expedience. Being an incorporated, tax-exempt agency with a pre-existing administrative structure simplifies start-up procedures. Already staffed by accountants, social workers, food service workers, recreation or arts specialists, and drivers, an agency can more easily assign duties. A reputable YSA that currently receives financial support from community, state, or federal sources will usually get comparable cooperation from new funders. Year-round agency operation contributes to the possibility of fuller service schedules.

Variety of experience. In an agency's hands, a SACC program may more easily widen the potential for off-schoolground activity. Extending a child's supervised day into alternative spaces, and not just into extra hours of restricted movement, eases the problem of children's emotional and social responses to prolonged confinement. This also applies to the cost of transportation, which need not necessarily equate with the idea of lost program time; the very essence of physical transitions between program base and other locations can impart to children feelings of relief and expectancy. And feelings count for a lot in SACC.

Community School as Sole Administering Agency

Many states, cities, and towns favor the concept of the community school as a valuable resource to both children and adults. At the national level, legislation encapsulating this philosophy exists in the form of the Community Schools and Comprehensive Education Act of 1978. Several states have enacted their own legislation to promote the concept.

Where they haven't already done so, local authorities can apply the formal designation "community school" to almost any tax-supported school. Some communities must lobby the municipal government to sponsor such a designation; others deal directly with the school system. With regard to SACC, active citizen participation with community school councils and planning groups carries the potential to maximize facility and tax-dollar value.

A community school can tie in with its sponsoring school system's administration, receiving some financial and in-kind support for its operations. Or, like many SACC programs, its administrative functions may exist wholly apart from the school's, making it a stand-alone, self-supporting organization that contracts with the school for space and maintenance services. In either case, funding for SACC programs administered by com-

munity schools primarily derives from parent fees and contracts with social service agencies.

CLOSE-UP: The Adventure Club, Robbinsdale, Minnesota

For over a decade, the Robbinsdale Community Education Department
has funded its own SACC program, The Adventure Club. A program director at each Adventure Club site supervises day-to-day operation, and
a single coordinator oversees the total program. The Adventure Club is
administered by the Education Department and all club staff are Education Department employees, although there is a separate salary scale and
employee bargaining unit.

From an inauspicious start, with only six children at one inhospitable
site, The Adventure Club has grown to encompass hundreds of children,
multiple locations, and a myriad of services and activities on a year-round
basis. In large measure, it owes this success to integral linkage with other
community organizations. The city Parks and Recreation Department co-
operates with no-cost team sport, drama, and gymnastics offerings. During summer months, it teams with the local Y to diversify options for enrichment courses and recreational diversion. At some sites, the Club offers
before-school breakfasts subsidized by the USDA federal school lunch
program. With an ever more diverse program and energetic public relations efforts, the Club continues to attract the families it needs and who
need it.

Arguments against Community Schools as Sole Administering Agency

Untoward economic dependency. When a community education department runs into financial trouble, its SACC program can run rather rapidly
into the budget-cutter's axe . . . unless the SACC program can justify
itself as a core component of the community school's viability. By virtue
of star attraction status, a SACC program may prove more operationally
valuable than some other incidental offerings. Otherwise, come the end of
the fiscal year, its complexities may doom it.

Peripheral treatment. Community schools won't necessarily take well to
child care. They primarily bank on adult education, remedial studies, and/
or nightly room rentals to local entrepreneurs. An affiliation with a community school may lend a program some credibility. But if the community
education department's primary goals conflict with an "unwanted" SACC
program, any leftover credibility could end up being more trouble than it's
worth.

Indistinct policy and practice. The same deficiencies that lead to peripheral treatment of the program can also cause the program to suffer from a
lack of clear administrative direction. Even in the event the community

education department supports SACC program efforts, an inability to demonstrate leadership or a failure to assimilate the distinctive requirements of a formal SACC program can hamper the overall effort.

Arguments in Favor of Community Schools as Sole Administering Agencies

Built-in approval. One community school director comments, "When you're part of the system, it's always easier to get things done." Depending on the definition of "things," programs run by community education departments can conceivably build on existing administrative relationships. Such programs can more easily obtain access to school buildings, playgrounds, and equipment than many other potential administrators.

Possible dollar cost incentives. In Portland, Oregon, the school board's facility usage policy permits community education programs the use of rent-free space. Says a Portland school administrator, "It's cleaner in terms of relationships and communication to have SACC under the community school umbrella." By its very nature, a community education department retains the legitimacy of regular school administration, but without the usual rigidity.

On top of this, when state legislators increase community school funding, it's not unheard of for SACC programs to get a piece of the pie.

Cross-curricular coordination. To a logical extent, pre-existing community education activities can absorb children. This somewhat relieves the PD and caregivers from daily planning overload or curricular tedium for children. Much of community education centers on the humanities, like music appreciation and practical arts; this gives the children an excellent opportunity for elective breadth and personal expression, which may be otherwise lacking in the school day or at home.

Local Government Agency as Sole Administering Agency

In the 1980s, the laissez-faire climate of the federal government of necessity began to stimulate more state and local participation in child care. SACC was no exception. By the end of the 1980s, at least fourteen states had enacted special legislation (some with money attached) earmarking SACC program development. A few cities administered their own SACC programs to eligible clients.

In the 1990s, federal government funds earmarked for child care are made available to the states for direct services. Funds are also used indirectly for training and technical assistance (see Chapter 7 for financial resources discussion). However, more city and county governments appear to be providing SACC directly to eligible families. Others have mounted coordination and training projects, and these efforts primarily focus on conducting needs assessments, convening citizen groups to aid program development, and facilitating program improvement. Mayors' offices and human services departments typically provide leadership in a style that is best described as a municipal "brokering" of SACC.

Some city recreation departments have expanded hours and days of drop-in activity offerings, thereby aspiring to the role of government SACC providers. Programs administered so use a combination of fee mechanisms: tax-supported facilities and staff, parent fees, and funding for low-income clients derived from state/federal sources.

Arguments against Government Agencies as Administrators

High vulnerability. When budgets get cut, government-run child care programs tend to be among the first "luxuries" to go.

Taxpayer opposition. Many people are opposed to publicly funded child care, health care, and other human services. Many of them fund government through taxes. They vote, too. Governments dominated by these people don't make excellent SACC providers.

Bureaucratic weight. Appropriate SACC offers children an alternative to strictly institutional settings. This purpose could get lost in the government process.

Arguments in Favor of Government Agencies as Administrators

Centralization. In addition to property management and maintenance, governments can make available a variety of other citywide services. Co-ordination of specialized personnel, transportation, and funding are—theoretically—a government's forte. Incidentally, this is why cities often limit their involvement to coordination and task forces. (See city and county funding section in Chapter 7.)

Fund-matching. When public monies become available, it's not uncommon for local government agencies to know about it before anyone else does. City and county agency funding proposals can show something funders really like: a capacity for *fund-matching.* Funding amounts often relate to how many dollars a recipient can raise without the funding. Governments can hold up in-kind resources as collateral, which makes them attractive recipients.

Day Care Center as Sole Administering Agency

In certain communities, polarized attitudes about "creeping child care" are responsible for people drawing a line in the sandbox. School unions can freeze out a potential school-sited program with scheduling barriers. Town councils may view school-agers as being ready for regimented recreation and no longer deserving of softer care programs. Just bringing the authorities into an era that includes appropriate developmental practices can be a full-time advocacy job.

However, a preschool day care center generally has built-in community approval. As a recognized institution, it may seem the likeliest candidate for SACC administrator. Preschool "graduates" could conceivably move on to a second tier of service. With sufficient space to run a SACC-style component at the same location, the day care center might initiate a program more easily than anyone else.

While the SACC component develops, the preschool administration furnishes it a chance to establish its own identity, its own intrinsic value to the community. Then, like a seedling that outgrows its starter pot, the SACC program may be transplanted to a larger facility or another administrator. Or the day care center may continue as the provider. Either way, the center has created an opportunity for program care that is better suited to these growing children.

Arguments against Day Care Centers as Sole Administering Agency

Transportation difficulties. Unless the center operates close to elementary schools, getting children to and from the center can cause logistical problems. Having children traveling unnecessarily long distances defeats the purpose. See Chapter 11 for a discussion of alternatives.

Compulsory age-mixing. Wonder-years children can spatially co-exist with first-graders for only so long, especially in small enclosed spaces. Developmentally speaking, ten-year-olds have gotten on to personal and sexual interests that just don't jibe with most preschoolers. Being stuck in with "a bunch of babies" won't sit well with older children—and won't do the younger ones any good either.

Early childhood orientation. Day care center directors and caregivers may possess great skill and knowledge from their preschool experiences. Still, school-agers are not preschoolers. Designing a set of dynamic daily experiences for school-agers, hiring program people with a grounding in middle childhood education, even setting aside the appropriate environment and materials might fall beyond the center's administrative capacities. Maybe well beyond.

Short shrift. The youngest children in a care program always tend to get the most attention. With preschoolers and school-agers side by side, the SACC component may lose out. This can hold especially true when the center co-mingles funding from both components, because expenses for preschool care rise disproportionately.

Arguments in Favor of Day Care Centers as Sole Administering Agency

Socialization buffer. Five- and six-year-olds just entering traditional schools sometimes have rather weighty hurdles ahead of them: lots of unfamiliar faces, strange adults telling them what to do, doorknobs too big to turn.

The SACC component offers children continuity in a drastically changed social order. With the freedom and comfort of the program's "extended family" to depend on, the shock of transition eases.

Dedicated space. Day care centers can much more easily resolve the pressing floor-space concerns that trouble school-site SACC providers. A 1991 Southern Illinois University report states that 69 percent of Illinois day care centers that offer a SACC component provide separate space for school-agers. Conversely, 60 percent of SACC programs in the state's public schools and 54 percent in its non-public schools are compelled to share space with others.[2] To be fair, it must be noted that the schools serve an average of three times as many children as do day care centers, but capacity alone rarely translates to appropriate care.

Consolidated care. To better serve parents, a two-tier care service permits a situation in which more than one child can get care at the same location from the same provider. This can be a major convenience for working parents at afternoon pick-up time. It also reinforces lines of parental input and builds on existing partnership.

Open more often. Schools generally close on many more days than day care centers do. When schools are closed, so often are school-run and school-sited programs. Day care centers aren't as hampered by school district schedules, custodial unions' overtime demands, and other such impediments to working-day care requirements.

Private or Parochial School as Sole Administering Agency

Since 1978, many private schools with no religious affiliation have become bastions for children of white middle-class parents. Due to the tax revolts that began with California's Proposition 13, control of education dollars—and therefore wage authority—has shifted out of the public sector's property tax base and into the property owners' hands. This permits them to re-direct monies to privately managed schools.

With the freedoms of church-state separation, authority at parochial schools tends to be far more ascriptive than in public schools and, consequently, less a topic of external negotiation.

In both instances, SACC program administration issues are somewhat distinct from those faced at public school sites. The National Association of Independent Schools (NAIS, 75 Federal Street, Boston, MA; 617-451-2444) offers information and networking.

COMMUNITY-BASED APPROACHES

Citing a variety of sources, sociologist Alan Wolfe attempted in 1989 to describe then-current child care perceptions and arrangements in the following manner:

In working-class families, where "the emphasis is on help, cooperation, and solidarity with a wide range of kin," there is greater reliance on relatives to watch children than among professional and managerial workers. In black communities in particular, grandparents are still a much-relied-upon source of support for child care. Among middle-class families, by contrast, which put "strong emphasis upon the self-sufficiency and solidarity of the nuclear family against all other kinship ties and groupings," child care needs tend to be contracted out in the market. As [Kathleen] Gerson discovered in her research, "reluctant mothers" did not "seek help from relatives or friends unless it was voluntarily offered." Afraid of the obligations that such ties would entail, "paid child-care arrangements were overwhelmingly favored by the group." The career mobility needed for success in the corporate world makes impractical any kind of child care except hired help.[3]

Wolfe's treatment of economic and race-based social compartments leads to some very specific questions about the definition of *community*. Once upon a time, a community was solely a product of residential proximity; only neighbors could form a community. Today, a host of associations, based far more on demographic characteristics than home address, have usurped the designation. Terms like *medical community* and *financial community* refer to people joined by professional affiliation, no matter where they live. Phrases like *the nation's Hispanic communities* attribute functional unity between millions of disparate speakers of Spanish.

Thousands of members of these so-called communities may have little or no knowledge of each other's personal existence—yet, thanks to cultural, educational, or occupational sympathies, their interests and influence are deemed to be unified under the heading of community. Alternatively, a *community-based organization* (CBO) may charter membership in national umbrella organizations that facilitate interaction and communication with other CBOs, thereby bringing together otherwise disparate groups.

Still, the most frequently made connection continues to be one in which *community* relates to or is dependent upon family. By this standard, a correlation arises between family values and community values; where the family units have disintegrated or migrated, so then has the residential community.

Community-based approaches to SACC programs assume the existence—and desirability—of family-oriented residential neighborhoods. However, they need not cater solely to the previously mentioned reluctant mothers in middle-class settings, where sense of community has also given way to the market economy.[4] The SACC concept can permeate and adapt itself to any setting where, in the encroaching shadows of the urban complex, community values still linger.

Parents Run the Program

When several mothers and fathers, not affiliated with any other organization, observe their very own circumstances and agree to join together as a formal group, they may elect not only to plan but also to administer a SACC program. Frequently, the common connections of their residential proximity or of their children's school location bring these parents together. Sharing the vested interest and responsibilities of their children's care, parents with a unified will to improve overall conditions within their community can spur the thoughtful creation of highly appropriate programs.

At this writing, media coverage and research about American societal trends increasingly point out that, due to the marketplace demands of inflation, taxation, and international industrial competition, many parents have been left short of time, energy, and interest for community-building. In some long-established poverty zones where parental absenteeism and fatalism flourish, a social service agency already may have served, for quite some time, as the primary binding community force. But neither of these points diminishes the potential value of parental solidarity in the face of threats to their children's development and growth.

It is significant that in the social movement against white male ethnocentricity, women's rights activists and minority groups have long utilized child care issues as a rallying point from which to exert political influence. The fact that even affluent and middle-class families now feel compelled to adopt organizational measures to stem downturns in their ability to minister to their children only underscores that significance.

A parent-run SACC program makes the most sense for parents who realize they are also affected by policy decisions that affect their children and who themselves wish to make such decisions, democratically and representatively. For a parent-run program, half-measures just won't do.

Parents who run their own programs have observed several outcomes. They have noted that their perspectives and values permeate program policy and design, that they obtain political clout in the community, and that running a SACC program generates parental skill-building and esteem. For these reasons alone, *a parent-run SACC program might have an even more productive impact in those communities where it might seem least likely to succeed.*

About starting up, one organizer of a parent-run program remarked:

If you look back at some of the forms that we first used, you'll find that they were totally inadequate. If you look at our bookkeeping system, you'd laugh compared to what we have now. It was a sheet of paper with a list of children and with a sliding fee scale, and no way to check to see how many days they were there. The same thing happened with staff salaries. We just didn't think it through. We just sort of went in, and as problems came up, we tried to solve them.

In the decade since this remark was made, a cottage industry has sprung out of the experiences and hard lessons learned by just such organizers.

Publications such as this very manual contain the distillations of experimentation, trial-and-error, and just plain good luck on the part of modern SACC practitioners and advocates. For parents who can muster the strength and gumption, a parent-run SACC program offers all the benefits with much less bureaucratic difficulty.

The same thing that can scare people away from running their own program is also what makes it such a wonderful life and learning experience: *A SACC program is a business.* Being unaccustomed to formal supervisory positions or overloaded by job-related duties, some folks just see the hassle, the demands on time, the added pressure of SACC obligation. However, in all likelihood, parents who hone their organizational skills with a SACC program can easily transfer those skills to other community groups . . . and even into the workplace.

A Community-Based Organization (CBO) Runs the Program

Defining the difference between some community agencies and a CBO hearkens back to the PAVEWAY of authority (see Chapter 2).

Certain local offices or groups derive their authority hierarchically from a massive national or worldwide administrative bureaucracy. These offices and groups may be said to be *agents* of the larger body, acting upon the local environment under instructions from outside. The people giving those instructions may live thousands of miles away.

While it may share missions, cultural themes, and information through umbrella or radiating connections, a true CBO aspires to legitimacy through the authority vested in it by residential community members. A CBO answers to its constituents. It acts upon the local environment in the interests of local residents.

CBOs tend to exercise their powers not as outside agents but as neighborhood filters. They work as instruments through which community members assert and express themselves. Some serve as channels between philanthropic interests and the local community. A successful CBO develops interactive relationships between community members as well as with appropriate others outside the community.

CBO-run SACC programs reflect the specific perceptions and conditions that occur within the residential community.

CLOSE-UP: Guadalupe Center, Kansas City, Missouri

Since 1974, Guadalupe Center, a grass roots CBO on the city's west side, has weathered a divisive break with the Catholic diocese, a disheartening cutback of federal social program funding, and speculative land-grabbing that shaved its community population from 20,000 to 7,500.

By shifting into an aggressive gear, Guadalupe Center now obtains nearly half its funding from foundations, corporate sponsors, and the United Way, which funds specific programs. One of those programs, Academia del Pueblo, caters to school-age clients. A model curriculum offered by the National Council de La Raza, Academia del Pueblo brings together at-risk Hispanic children after school for experiences designed to create an esprit de corps, as well as to develop critical thinking and higher order mental processes.

For the program, Guadalupe Center staff built an environment containing cooperative learning stations, around which they sought to encourage community-building techniques. A typical two-hour program session might entail discussion and planning of new housing for the community. To combat provincialism, the program also encourages idea and information exchange with children at eight other Academia del Pueblo sites across the country. Parent involvement and participation receive requisite attention, and Guadalupe Center staff meet with children's regular school administrators and teachers.

Planners and administrators of parent-run and CBO-run programs might like to keep these additional points in mind:

• *Seek solid cooperation.* Intimidation won't wash. Hidden agendas and ulterior motives can doom the program. From the outset, set a welcoming and agreeable tone for all that is to be accomplished. Stem frustrations and disillusionment by establishing realistic expectations and goals. In the course of meetings, of which there will be many, employ methods of discourse that engender a comfortable and meaningful exchange of divergent views. This may or may not mean following Robert's *Rules of Order,* but in any case, allow an atmosphere of mutual respect.

• *Anticipate "drop-outs."* Human nature being what it is, some people will eagerly agree to something that they subsequently find themselves, for whatever reason, "unable" to do. Degrees of commitment can shift and vary, so division and distribution of various responsibilities must be attended accordingly. Avoid practices wherein seemingly unpleasant tasks are foisted on people who are unwilling to say no in public. One way to accomplish this is by giving each parent a *task partner,* one parent who will assist, train, back up, or, if necessary, replace another parent.

• *Put it in writing.* The last thing anyone hoping for results wants to hear is that fateful line, "Well, *I* didn't know." Create tangible records of meetings and agreements: a Parent Board Handbook, a Policy Statement, a Decision-Making Model, a Meeting Schedule, and whatever else comes to pass. Because some parents may think the program is run by school or church or private enterprise, make certain all handouts clearly identify the program as parent-run; include names and phone numbers of parent board members. If someone then says, "I didn't know," it won't be for the program's lack of trying.

It's also highly important to keep safe copies of all documents, so that any parent can gain access at any time.

• *Politicize.* This doesn't mean that the program has to endorse the Democrats or the Republicans. By its very nature, a SACC program makes a political statement to government, school boards, and the community at large; it seeks to engender a change in the status quo—and that, in and of itself, is political. Build on the inherent political nature of the program. Find opportunities to affirm it. Interact with other authority representatives: school principals, school board members and candidates, city service representatives, fundraisers, and the like.

• *Strive for self-sufficiency.* Even though a parent-run SACC program depends on its partners and its physical environment, its health and longevity call for independence from the whims or fancies of a particular person. Embrace what charisma, strength, and energy each partner brings to the program, but refrain from localizing or yielding program direction to one source. Too much is at stake to allow one partner's reticence or paralysis to bring everything to a grinding halt.

A Congregation Runs the Program

Black community churches care for thousands of at-risk children. Some receive substantial funding, but most manage on minimal budgets. Their SACC programs echo churches' historical role in the Underground Railroad during and immediately after the period of formal enslavement. At that time, a church was the only place where a child could receive organized secular and religious education.[5]

The powers of shared faith and religious conviction widely continue to exert binding force within a given residential community. Otherwise unaffiliated parents often relate through the commonality of their local church, temple, meeting house, or other place of worship. In their roles as spiritual leaders, local congregations conduct various outreach activities, one of which may take the form of an afterschool class.

CLOSE-UP: Project SPIRIT Afterschool Programs, nationwide

The economics of race affect all children. Black American children are affected more adversely than any other group: Two in every five black American families are poor, double the number for all American families. Faced with the fallout from rampant unemployment, unforeseen pregnancies, the drug economy, and gang culture, the Congress of National Black Churches (CNBC) decided to act.

A multi-denominational organization, the Congress offers afterschool training for 6–12 year old children at 15 affiliate churches in Oakland, Atlanta, Indianapolis, and the city of Washington. The program is one component of CNBC's Project SPIRIT, launched in 1986 with a grant from Carnegie Corporation.

While they vary slightly according to local requirements, the 15 programs share a core design weighted heavily with homework. Retired or active public teachers and other professionals supervise. A minister or layperson in each city coordinates to make sure the children undergo tutoring from approved workbooks and curricular materials.

But at the heart of Project SPIRIT lies the development of black cultural and ethnic pride. After three hours of homework and tutorials, a portion of the afternoon is devoted to improving self-conceptions and practical living skills through games, skits, songs, and role-playing. As Dr. Harriette McAdoo, the programs' principal evaluator, points out: "Western societies have consistently ranked light skin more favorably than dark, an evaluation often internalized by minorities, which Project SPIRIT attempts to overcome."

During the programs' first full year, parent evaluations yielded highly positive responses. More than 70 percent of parents reported their children had improved self-esteem and school performance. Parents also concurred that churches had reached beyond their own congregations, including parents and children from throughout their communities.

Source: Carnegie Quarterly (New York), Fall 1988.

Totally autonomous classes and programs for school-age children constitute only one segment of available congregational offerings. As this Close-Up illustrates, religious schools and houses of worship often contract with SACC providers from outside their own immediate administrative circle. This shifts the administrative focus to one of collaboration.

COLLABORATIVE APPROACHES

By far the most common administrative solution consists of a collaboration between two or more of the previously described entities. One reason is that after salaries and benefits, SACC program budgets' biggest line item usually turns out to be space rental—that is, of course, unless a school or congregation makes an in-kind contribution. Also, because so many children's lives revolve around school attendance, schools make the most natural candidates for some types of mutual arrangements. Here is where *school* often becomes the operative word in school-age child care.

SACC programs that result from collaborative approaches aren't necessarily better or worse than—or equal to—programs that are solely administered by a school, parent group, agency, CBO, or some other entity. In theory, extensive collaboration equates with a program's ability to acquire—to get more space, money, equipment, time, and so forth. In practice, however, what planners envision as a mutually beneficial partnership can easily dissolve into a political turf war in which the real losers are the children.

Collaborating with Schools

When formal entities wish to collaborate with schools, three primary administrative issues arise: schoolground usage/rental; program impact on day-to-day school operation; and legal responsibility and personal liability. Depending on a principal's personal style, the composition of the school board, and the strength of the collaborating entity, resolution of these issues can range anywhere from dictatorial conformity to relative indifference. Usually, though, outside groups and schools negotiate to achieve program goals within mutually agreeable limits.

Schoolground Usage/Rental

If they are approached by an outside entity wishing to run a SACC program, the first question school officials probably ask themselves is, "How much is this going to cost the school?" This makes sense, since from an outside group's point of view, the most desirable scenario consists of unchallenged limitless usage of schoolgrounds, with janitorial services, utilities, and all liability costs carried by the school. In fact, for reasons too complex to explore here, even the barest maintenance costs lie beyond the reach of many schools' budgets.

Frankly speaking, a majority of outside groups could not even begin to run a program unless a collaborator meets overhead expenses. This holds true particularly for programs that seek to care for children at risk, from low-income families, residing in blight and poverty. Yet this observation hardly mitigates the financial condition of many public schools, which are unable to properly staff and operate even traditional classrooms.

The fundamental purpose of public schools and the land they occupy comes to the SACC negotiating table in the form of cost. How many hours a day do school facilities remain open? Do reasonable agreements exist with maintenance workers' unions? If a program runs until 6 P.M., is the school looking at substantial overtime charges? What about heating? What about lights? Is there anyone supervising playground access after school? Simply, is the cost of making the school suitable for SACC too high?

Leasing school space remains a relatively new concept, and some school systems still have no consistent formula for calculating rent. In one school system, each participating principal establishes a different rate of payment—even though all of the schools' SACC programs are run by the same outside agency. In another community, no group wishing to use school space paid a rental fee—except the SACC programs. In the latter case, the school board eventually adopted a more egalitarian policy; they decided to charge rent to *all* groups capable of payment. Naturally, SACC programs are deemed capable. For descriptions of space rental options, see Chapter 6.

In terms of space usage, even programs with the ability to pay often find their lease terms highly restrictive. In the same way that a movie theater ticket constitutes a lease to do nothing but quietly occupy a seat for two hours, so school SACC leases often permit children to occupy classrooms and chairs but not to influence, decorate, or re-arrange the space in which they will find themselves programmatically "cared for." The secondary-use aspect of lease terms can and does inhibit creative tendencies, suppressing SACC's primary thrust of developmentally appropriate activity. Space usage terms deserve at least as much consideration as bottom-line cost.

Program Impact on Day-to-Day School Operation

The program comes in at 2:35 after the teacher is through, and the next day there are seven pencils out of place, and they didn't put two chairs up, and the teacher's down screaming at the principal, "They're ruining my classroom!" Or, let's be realistic. Sometimes bulletin boards are knocked down, somebody wrote on a desk, and somebody took something from somebody's desk. These are things that go on, no matter how closely supervised kids are.

This program director's remarks nicely illustrate "The Goldilocks Syndrome," also known as "Who's Been Jumping Around in *My* Classroom?" Classic territorial conflicts arise when SACC programs occupy traditional classrooms. Without *dedicated space,* the program inevitably draws this kind of fire. Being made to walk on eggshells through somebody else's domain cannot possibly lead to either warm feelings or mutual respect.

Whether or not the lease agreement calls for direct cash payment, it most definitely must allow the program to operate *freely* in whatever spaces are designated. The time for authoritative adult-centered regimentation must end with the final school bell, and a new time for self-exploration, self-expression, and child-centered behavior must begin. Obviously, this is not to imply that children are to be let loose to ride roughshod across countertops or to swing from light fixtures. However, the repressive extreme filled with negative reinforcements like "Don't touch that," "Don't sit there," "Don't talk," "Sit still," and "Do what I tell you," seems a better model for prison life than for SACC.

But classroom teachers are well within their rights when they stand up for the sanctity of their everyday environment. There is no reason why a teacher's regular students ought not to be entitled to a sense of security and stability when they return each morning.

Resolving these differences often results in SACC programs getting assigned to cavernous multi-purpose rooms and gymnasiums, inhospitable cafeterias, or close-quartered storage rooms and broom closets. Of course, confinement of program operation to the self-same classrooms in which children attend regular classes every day seems little more appropriate. Here again, the mandate for dedicated SACC program facilities becomes the focal point of programs' impact.

Ironically, conflict of purpose arises when a SACC program exceeds its mission to empower children. One observer noted:

We had a situation where some of the workers in the program let the children do so much—gave them so much freedom—that then teachers reported problems with these children in the classroom. You see, if you can misbehave in school from 4 to 6, then what's the difference between 10 and 12, when you're in class? And, if you're in the halls, and literally swinging from the chandeliers after school, then it tends to carry over, because it's the same physical environment.

Where a program is badly understaffed, where the staff-child ratio seems right but the caregivers are underqualified or poorly trained, where indifference characterizes program direction, such a program no longer qualifies as school-age child care.[6]

On another front, before- and afterschool SACC programs located at or near schools often combine transportation and food service arrangements. One might imagine that such arrangements would easily dovetail, but sometimes the reconciliation can be problematic. For example, suppose a before-school program group wishes to take advantage of the school's federally funded nutrition program. Can all children qualify for the nutrition program? Does the program make separate morning-meal plans for those who don't? Will the principal exercise any discretion in the matter? Might there arise a subsequent complication if even one child is included or excluded improperly? If the program operates off schoolgrounds and starts before the school opens, who transports the children—parents, SACC program, or school?

Legal Responsibility and Personal Liability

As one school superintendent explained, schools "expect the [outside] agency to have itself well protected and not to put us at any risk. We don't want to assume any additional liability because of the program."

For the most part, programs not run solely by the school itself are subject to this prevailing position. See Chapter 12 for a general review of legal issues.

Tips on Collaboration

The following suggested guidelines can help to ensure a more seemly collaboration with public schools.

• *Make a public announcement.* The After School Day Care Association in Madison, Wisconsin, prepared and widely distributed a newsletter entitled, "Our Doors Are Open: The Impact of an After-School Program on the School Building and Personnel." By addressing major issues head on, SACC programs clear the way for present cooperation and future goodwill. Announcing policy and practice changes won't hurt, either.

• *Meet, meet, meet!* At the start of the program year, bring together everyone who might encounter the program: teachers, maintenance workers, secretaries, resource specialists, even physical education instructors. Open a forum for discussion, review terms of the lease, or just introduce everybody to each other. Then, at regular intervals, continue the dialogues begun at the kick-off meeting with follow-up meetings and conversations. Get feedback, get input, involve others in the decision-making process. In the wake of open communication, intractability and indifference will both take a licking.

• *Understand "The Principal Principle."* In any event, the school principal must answer to his or her employers, the school system management. This fiduciary obligation cannot be broached, nor should it be. As the school's chief operating officer, the principal must approve the program director, may want to approve other program staff, and must be free and welcome to offer suggestions and opinions at any appropriate time.

Observable differences in managerial style between men and women principals, as well as between well-to-do neighborhood and impoverished neighborhood principals, must inform negotiations. A multi-site program's director in Southern California notes that "male principals are more regimented and discipline-oriented. And principals in impoverished areas allow more behavioral freedom, because expectations of program content are low, as are expectations of children's performance." If and when the principal tries to start dictating program policy, the collaboration has unraveled and it's time either to remove the principal (good luck . . . !) or to move the program.

• *Share mutual advantages.* Readers of this manual certainly must be familiar with the common admonition to young siblings fighting over a limited supply of cookies or toys: "Share it with your sister!" For some incomprehensible reason, many adults from whose lips these words issue set a diametrically opposed example when they themselves are engaged in compulsive possessive and territorial behavior. For those who claim, "It's different for grown-ups," this manual joins the children who ask, "Why?"

The childish idea that "what's mine is mine, and you can't have it" needn't be acted out by adults. At one time, the Hephzibah Children's Association (HCA) in Oak Park, Illinois, found it had been assigned more foster grandparents than its program could handle. Given that some HCA program site schools needed assistants for their traditional kindergarten classes, HCA shared these volunteerist riches with the schools. The same can easily be done with less valuable resources such as books, craft materials, and audiovisual equipment. Needless to say, this type of shared interest in child-centered goals can heavily contribute to mutual respect and goodwill between outside entity and school. For a relationship to work both ways, often it must first work one way before it works the other.

• *Examine the liaison option.* Some school systems authorize a liaison officer who can work as an intermediary, ombudsman, and roving diplomat with collaborating programs. Although it might be unrealistic to imagine a completely impartial liaison, it can help to have someone who possesses consistent knowledge of the history and status of current agreements between the collaborators. Schools might wish to nominate a school administrator; outside entities might seek a member of a PTO, an advocacy group, or a service organization involved in initial program planning.

THE DUTIES OF SACC ADMINISTRATION

As different as they are, all of the aforementioned groups and organizations that decide to pursue SACC administration will face the same basic set of duties. Most are carried out interactively and simultaneously. Some are conditional, applying only to new organizations or unaffiliated administrators.

Representing planners' interests, the program director often takes direct responsibility for the agenda, but an overview can help all partners understand ongoing concerns. Figure 3.1 sets out the primary duties that running even the simplest program entails.

NOTES

1. Michelle Seligson and Dale B. Fink, *No Time to Waste: An Action Agenda for School-Age Child Care.* SACC Project, Center for Research on Women, (Wellesley College, Wellesley, MA, 1989), p. 72.

2. Susan W. Nall and Carol S. Klass, "School-Age Child Care in Illinois" (Edwardsville: Southern Illinois University, March 1991), p. 21.

3. Alan Wolfe, *Whose Keeper?: Social Science and Moral Obligation* (Los Angeles: University of California Press, 1989), p. 56.

4. Ibid., pp.60–69.

5. Harriet McAdoo and Vanella Crawford, "The Black Church and Family Support Programs," *Prevention and Human Services,* vol. 9, no. 1.

6. Some child development "experts" and SACC critics charge that children must, at all times, be inculcated with restrictions, boundaries to prevent the children from getting out of hand. Some like to blame all social ills on permissiveness and believe it to be their duty to rectify the situation by enforcing strict behavioral codes of conduct. Rather than applying their efforts to orient children to the effects of choice and decision making, they work to reduce the children's effect on the environment into adult-dictated directives. Of course, this attitude has no proper place in developmentally appropriate school-age child care and gets no sympathy in this manual.

Figure 3.1

•DETERMINE VIABILITY OF SERVICE (COMPLETION TIME: 3 TO 6 MONTHS)

Identify potential areas and populations
Meet with members of community
Develop and conduct CANARI
Assimilate and interpret CANARI results
Follow up with survey respondents

•CREATE THE LEGAL ENTITY (COMPLETION TIME: 1 TO 8 MONTHS)

Form a board of directors
Elect officers
Choose legal name for organization [note: Children may still choose an
operating name later.]
Complete incorporation process
   adopt non-discrimination statement
   finalize by-laws
   formulate mission statement
File for tax-exempt status [IRS 501 (c) (3)]
Apply for taxpayer ID number

•RESEARCH APPLICABLE REGULATIONS (COMPLETION TIMES VARY)

Investigate licensing procedures, with regard to:
   health and safety
   zoning
   building codes
   fire codes
Appraise qualifications and ratios for Caregivers [Note: Prior to full
compliance, it may be possible to obtain a provisional license]

•SELECT APPROPRIATE SITE AND SPACES (ONGOING FOR MULTISITES)

Using CANARI feedback, survey potential locations
Negotiate potential terms of agreement
Apply for city zoning variance (up to 6 months)
Apply for specialized area usage permits
Confirm and sign written terms of agreement or lease [Note: complete
these duties prior to advertising or public announcement of service.]

•DEVELOP TRANSPORTATION POLICY (ONGOING)

Confer with school transportation officials
Negotiate for cooperative service
Explore alternatives to school transport

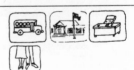

•CONFIRM OR SECURE INSURANCE (FINALIZE BEFORE OPEN)

Liability
Medical/dental
FICA
Workers' compensation
Fire and theft
Vehicle

PREPARE INITIAL BUDGET (COMPLETION TIMES VARY)

Determine tangible start-up costs
Research and factor in Caregiver training and development
Design parent fee structure
Assess availability of non-parent funding

Figure 3.1 (continued)

•INITIATE FINANCIAL RESOURCE DEVELOPMENT

Reconcile CANARI data and initial budget
Develop written funding proposals
Submit applications to targeted non-parent sources
Secure start-up funding (6 months before open

•HIRE PROGRAM DIRECTOR (PER FUNDING, 2 TO 6 MONTHS BEFORE OPEN)

Observe Affirmative Action guidelines
Create job description
Design an initial employment agreement
Initiate search
Interview and select
Negotiate and sign employment agreement

•PREPARE OPERATING BUDGET (ONGOING; ANNUAL IMPLEMENTATION)

Review anticipated costs and cash flow
Secure public funds contract or voucher agreement
Apply for Child Care Food Program reimbursements
Analyze developing macroeconomic trends
Synthesize projected three-yearbudget figures

•DEVELOP ADMISSION POLICIES AND PROCEDURES (ONGOING)

Establish qualifiers regarding:
    numbers and ages of children to be served
    group sizes relative to available space
    Caregiver-child ratios
    special and at-risk children
Determine enrollment procedures
Create and implement waiting list policy

•DEVELOP IN-SERVICE CAREGIVER TRAINING PLAN (ONGOING)

Devise opportunities for Caregiving team to:
    learn new skills
    engage in self-evaluation
    visit other programs
    participate in support groups
Engage and consult with SACC professionals

•PREPARE HANDBOOKS FOR CAREGIVING TEAM AND PARENTS
(COMPLETION TIME: 3 MONTHS BEFORE OPEN)

Evaluate workability of all internal program policies
Determine wording of policies and procedures
Commit wording to paper for review by board
Negotiate and, if appropriate, revise policies and wordings
Print and ready for distribution
Conduct periodic re-evaluations

•IMPLEMENT MARKETING, RECRUITMENT, AND ENROLLMENT (INITIATE 3 MONTHS BEFORE OPEN)

Select primary areas and populations for recruitment
Develop public relations approaches and materials
Print and distribute notices and press releases
Advertise /"Show-and-Sell" the program
Solicit pre-open enrollments

Figure 3.1 (continued)

•HIRE CAREGIVERS AND OTHER TEAM MEMBERS (ONGOING)

Observe Affirmative Action guidelines
Create job descriptions and basic agreements
Advertise positions (begin 1 to 2 months before open)
Interview and select applicants (begin 3 weeks before open)
Distribute Caregiver handbooks and sign agreements
Conduct background checks

•PREPARE AND EQUIP INDOOR/OUTDOOR AREAS (ONGOING)

Conduct regular inventories of all items and space usage
Secure and set up storage spaces
Acquire food, equipment, supplies, and other materials

•EXPAND THE PARTNERSHIP BASE (ONGOING)

Encourage participation of Friends of the Program:
   contact personal acquaintances
   seek out neighborhood volunteer support
Interact with community-based organizations and agencies
Approach high schools, colleges and job training programs
Assess relative contributions of skills and time offered

•FACILITATE CAREGIVER PROFESSIONAL DEVELOPMENT (ONGOING)

Sensitize Caregivers and Friends to SACC planning elements
Invite critical thinking and partnered policy planning
Design interactive, process-oriented training sessions
Identify and address gaps in awareness about:
   roles and responsibilities
   first aid/CPR
   cultural imperatives
   time, space and curriculum
Engage and consult with other SACC professionals
Stay abreast of professional development trends

•STEP UP MARKETING AND RECRUITMENT (AS CALLED FOR)

Compare pre-open enrollments with desired levels
Consult local R & R for information about competition
Target additional avenues of publicity and advertising

•OUTREACH TO PARENTS (ONGOING)

Distribute and conform receipt of parent handbooks
Edit and distribute periodic newsletter
Solicit parent input
Outfit program areas to be welcoming to parents
Make special arrangements and accomodations
Facilitate parent awareness of Caregiver observations

•DEVELOP LINKS WITH SCHOOL CLASSROOM PERSONNEL (ONGOING)

Obtain parents approval to query school personnel
Seek exchange of information with classroom teachers
Consult periodically with principals

•OVERSEE SERVICE AND OPERATION RESPONSIVENESS (ONGOING)

Prepare quarterly budget reports for board and I.R.S.
Perform overall program assessments (at a minimum, annually)
Keep the program from "falling into a rut"
Devote time to child advocacy and community-building groups

FOR FURTHER REFERENCE

Lefstein, Leah, and Joan Lipsitz. 1986. *3:00 to 6:00* P.M.: *Programs for Young Adolescents*. Chapel Hill: Center for Early Adolescence, University of North Carolina.

Neugebauer, Roger, ed. *The Best of Exchange* (reprint series). Redmond, WA: Exchange Press.

Scofield, Rich, ed. 1989. *School Age Care Administration*. Nashville: School Age NOTES.

Sisson, Linda. 1990. *Kids Club: A School Age Program Guide for Directors*. Nashville: School Age NOTES.

Chapter 4

CURRICULUM

Every good local journalist knows that reader involvement depends far more on answering questions of *who* and *what* than of *when*—recently, most likely—and *where*—somewhere in town. Designations of time frame and location can be repeated endlessly without generating interest or knowledge. It's the people, events, and changes in circumstance that make the story.

The same thing goes for a SACC curriculum, whenever and wherever a program operates. Ideally, the curriculum provides ample opportunity for exploring children's ideas, ambitions, sensibilities, and personal feelings; *informal learning* of new manual and interpersonal skills occurs much more naturally given such a curriculum. Rather than setting up an institutional container for interchangeable parts (read "children"), informed planners and administrators *personalize* a program's time and space to fit the unique personalities and interests of the children.

For brevity's sake, this manual's discussion of appropriate curriculum centers on before- and afterschool programs. In practice, much of it will apply to full-day programs as well. Aside from time and space, an appropriate curriculum is bounded only by imagination.

As a final point of introduction to the subject, the very word *curriculum* is itself inappropriate to this discussion. The idea of imposing "a fixed series of studies," as Webster's *New World Dictionary* puts it, runs 180 degrees opposite to the idea of SACC. This manual often substitutes the terms *experiences* or *activities* instead. However, popular usage has imposed the "C" word, so it is used here solely for the purpose of general comprehension.

MOLDING THE PROGRAM TO THE CHILDREN

From the start, all programs must recognize and acknowledge their children's interests and desires. As one program person puts it:

Unfortunately, our tendency is to say, "I'm having a school-age program, so I'll need balls, headphones, puzzles, etc." instead of listening to the kids and letting them help you figure out what you want for the program.

Truly capable program people can find out just by asking, listening, and observing. They support children's natural healthy interests by shaping the program around them. They thereby encourage children to take the initiative, to exercise responsibility, and to view the desires and values of others as exciting diversities rather than as obstacles.

• *The Younger Children: Ages 5 and 6.* Typically, new school-agers come up against an overwhelming mass of teachers, administrators, and other children. To acclimate comfortably to this major change in social circumstance, it's especially important that these children take part in new experiences in smaller groups, or even pairs. Additionally, kindergartners may or may not require a scheduled rest. A period of immobility enforced across the board for all children generally reflects either a teacher's desire for a break or a blanket application of casebook practice; neither motivation reflects knowledge about specific children.

• *Opening Up: Ages 7, 8, and 9.* Before school, it's anyone's guess whether these children will want a quiet breakfast, time to catch up on homework, or a boisterous verbal explosion. After school, it's much more likely that they'll opt for running around instead of having to sit down. In fact, until some of the pent-up excess energy gets blown off, a structured indoor activity could come across as some kind of punishment! Also, this is the age at which many children begin to engage in longer-term activities that directly correlate to adult behavior. For example, baseball card collecting and scripted playacting can convert at adulthood into wealth accumulation and social conventions. Clearly, the focuses designed into the program's longer-term activities can have a direct bearing on future vocations and avocations.

• *The Wonder Years: Ages 10 and Beyond.* Even before the opposite sex begins to exert a draw, pre-pubescent children's major interests lie in peer association and peer approval. What "everybody else" is doing takes precedence over just about anything else. Also at this time, some boys and most girls begin to experience a conscious awareness of their imminent physiological changes. In that they generally mature more rapidly than same-aged boys, girls quickly outgrow an unresponsive SACC program that continues to treat them like "babies."

With each different child comes a slightly different set of desires and values. Children of five, six, and seven years of age may long for comfy cushions, while older children's overflowing energies may require a gymnasium. Even so, it sometimes takes only one dissed young man to gum up the whole works. In his excellent book *Caring Spaces, Learning Places: Children's Environments That Work,* Jim Greenman relates his very first experience with children's response to an adult-centered child care environment:

I waited for my 18 four year olds to come in off the bus, putting the finishing touches on my classroom: tables with assorted activities, block corner, dress-up area, and bookshelf with colorful books. In they came, some shy, most excited. Then in came Carlos, two feet tall, with a foot-high Afro, and a look and bearing about him that proclaimed: here was a man among men.

The other children clearly looked up to him (figuratively speaking). Carlos coolly surveyed the room where he was to spend eight hours a day, five days a week, for the next twelve weeks. A sinister uneasiness hung in the air. I began to get nervous, because it was clear that the children were waiting for Carlos' judgement on my efforts. It soon came. "This place is dooky," pronounced Carlos. (Carlos always pronounced; he never spoke.) Soon all the children began chanting, "This place is dooky," and I saw my summer rapidly deteriorating. . . . It took me over ten years to learn all the implications of the lesson Carlos taught me. Carlos recognized at a glance that the church basement was a crummy place to spend a summer.[1]

The point here isn't that all church basements are crummy places. But Greenman's was, and everyone knew it. Children's input feeds into both short-term and long-term planning. This takes spontaneous as well as regularly scheduled planning sessions between caregivers and the PD. Continuous interactive communication between children, parents, caregivers, and the PD doesn't stand on ceremony or wait for a more convenient time. Rote conditions for such meetings will tend to generate rote responses, so keep the communication channels well oiled and fluid.

• *Program People.* Caregivers must be clearly apprised of their responsibilities as *program facilitators,* taking in and interpreting critical information between children and other program personnel. If caregivers are to commit themselves wholeheartedly to making the program work for the children, then their perceptions of curriculum—what works and what doesn't—must be supported, encouraged, and valued. Without caregivers' commitment to maximizing program effectiveness, all the planners' fine words and theories go straight out the window.

Given these points, all caregivers deserve inclusion in the activity planning process. For those more experienced—and possibly more jaded—a planning session jump starts the exploration of new ideas and activities.

For those less experienced, it's a chance to verbalize concerns, bounce observations around, and learn a little more about the way the partnership can work. For PDs, it's an ideal supervisory method of making sure that everyone gets the same information at the same time, of bringing up difficult situations in which all caregivers have a hand, and of mitigating fears and conflict in an open way.

• *Parents.* Some parents will want to participate in curriculum planning, although many may have nothing to say until they have something to complain about. Some parents, insecure or uncertain about dealing with organizations, may have little more to contribute than warnings to their children to "do what the teacher tells you." Other parents will call in every day with specific demands and expectations, right down to who pours the apple juice.

Making the program child-responsive may mean causing some parental dissent. Rather than shying away from the inevitable, PDs and caregivers can plan more confidently when they acknowledge argument as an element of growth and development. The minute any partner in the program begins to cower, the entire program's balance lies at stake.

No program worth its salt sets as silly an objective as to keep everybody quiet and happy all the time. Of course, inciting unnecessary conflicts can be avoided by making a practice of respectful outreach. (See the parental partnership section in Chapter 9 for more discussion about such policies.)

TENETS OF PARTNERSHIP PLANNING

When approaching discussions about program tone and tenor, successful SACC program planners will:

• *Capitalize on children's particular interests*—what they want to engage in, to safely learn more about, or to explore on their own.

• *Balance unstructured child-initiated pursuits into the total program plan*—providing adult-directed activity only as windows of opportunity, to facilitate children's ability to make healthy decisions for themselves. Leave exercises in obedience and conformity where they belong: in the punishment sector of the traditional classroom.

• *Encourage and recognize caregivers' personal commitments*—not as a luxury, but as an integral program component. And on interview, if a person exhibits no sign of interest other than a wan and defensive, "Yeah, I like kids," keep interviewing. No SACC program runs well without people who actually care.

• *Bring children to the world by bringing the world into the program*—making SACC as much a community member as the park, the corner store, or even the junk yard. With or without caregivers' conscious effort, each part of the world within—and beyond—the program's homebase community takes on some kind of identity, maybe positive, maybe negative. As a result of associating with particular partners, that identity rubs off on the program and its children. By definition, a fresh program beats a bogus one any time.

• *Set and communicate reasonable limits clearly, consistently, and with some respect*—otherwise, when testing those limits, children can play the both-ends-against-the-middle game, in which one caregiver says yes and another says no. The result of this: possibly pandemonium, but probably just total chaos. DON'T take the "easy way out" by setting up an adult dictatorship.

• *Allow for spontaneity, flexibility, and serendipity within those reasonable limits*—almost as if life in a SACC program could be the real lives of actual people. When first snow falls, children might rather run outside and build a snowman than sit inside at a bench making papier mâché robots. *Let them out*. A fight between two boys over who gets the carrot for his snowman's nose may precipitate anger, fear, and disappointment. *Work through it*. One seemingly unhappy child may wish to stay inside but won't say why. *Give that child a little extra attention*. After all, whose program is this, anyway?

PLANNING FOR THE THREE E'S

Picture a traditional fifth-grade classroom teacher whose idea of conducting class is to pass out third-grade textbooks, remand the children to silence and stillness on threat of expulsion, stand by the door and visually police the class for disobedience—and then do nothing more. Far from exaggeration, this basic approach still finds wide acceptance in many schools across the country. Whether it is due to socioeconomic forces or just plain ignorance, crowd control techniques matter more than instilling a desire to learn. That is, child management takes precedence over child development.

Such shrugs of the shoulders carry over into many so-called child care programs. Head-counting and happenstance are the orders of the day. Unskilled, untrained warm bodies, hired off the street, ramble into multipurpose rooms filled with corralled children and switch on a television to earn their minimum wages. The doors are locked and guarded. The air grows stale. Cartoon voices echo off the cold tile floor. And *this* they call school-age child care.

In both of the described instances, meaningful mission has been abandoned and administration has gone to sleep. No wonder the curriculum comes down the way it does. If the adults, ostensibly role models, have no apparently humanitarian goals, why should children?

As educators traditionally extol the virtues of the three R's, so SACC is elementally comprised of the three E's: *Experience, Events,* and *Environment.* Although traditional inculcation of the three R's tends to be mechanistic, successfully embracing the three E's calls for less mechanization and more mediation.

Events are what happen when children interact with their environment. Both internal and external experience result from and, at the same time, catalyze that interaction. Environment acts upon and is acted upon by the course of events, which is driven by the experience. No one of these elements can lay claim to greater importance than another: They are inextricably interdependent. If the three Es are not acknowledged, if planners and caregivers fail to recognize their equal importance, then SACC *isn't* what happens.

Planning a SACC curriculum does not mean writing down a list of things to do and times to do them. Making that list is the last stage of planning, not the first. Planning means thinking about, examining, understanding, and realizing what any event, experience, or environment means to children. For example:

All children will not learn the same thing from the same experience; planning should take this into consideration, particularly for group time.[2]

Herein lies the danger of so-called replicable curricula. To answer the ever-present question of "What do we do?" some people attempt a stock formulaic response. They seem guided by a mistaken impression—namely, that all children can be typed and categorized by demographic data, then inserted into predetermined events.

While it is true that social conformity and social acceptance often go hand in hand, molding a SACC program to a "proven" quantitative formula or to a gaily colored and slickly packaged set of instructions cannot possibly be appropriate. Before jumping onto any bandwagons, carefully consider the immediate nature of the three E's as they apply to a specific group in a specific location.

Any reader who still remains unconvinced about the importance of planning will do well to examine the following excerpt from the Madison After School Day Care Association's curriculum guide.

Children will generally find ways of occupying themselves, even if no plans are made. Why, then, should you bother to plan at all?

1. Planning insures variety for the children. Children will often only choose to do things that are familiar to them. Scheduling new choices opens up possibilities for them.

2. Planning specific activities cuts down on the number of petty conflicts between children. It has long been observed that children can "play" by themselves only so long before things begin to deteriorate. While children need scheduled "free time," they shouldn't have three hours of it.

3. Planning provides a means of assessing the success of the program, passing

useful information on to other staff, and recording for future reference what was done at the center.

4. Planning sets forth specific responsibilities for staff, aides, and volunteers.

5. Planning provides an outline which determines what supplies and materials will be needed on a given day.

6. Planning provides substitutes with information, in the event that a staff member is absent.

7. Planning makes it possible to inform the school administration and staff of upcoming activities. It is important that the After School staff are seen as professionals, and that program plans are available for school staff and administration to see if they so desire.

8. Parents must be informed of program activities, particularly when children will be outside the school building. Plans should be available at the center for scrutiny by any interested parent. In some cases, it is valuable to post a condensed version of the day's activities so that the children and parents can easily see it.

9. The A.S.D.C.A. Board of Directors and the administrative staff must be aware of the center's activities. The quality of advance planning is one aspect of staff evaluation.[3]

THE ESSENCE OF EXPERIENCE

Planning experience means translating the mission statement into discrete experiences for children. It does *not* mean circumventing, repressing, or otherwise squashing children's desires and interests. Some programs serve children with learning problems, atypical behaviors, insufficient diets, and severe home instability. In these programs, temptation often runs high to try to overcome children's other experiences. But intervention and remediation cannot substitute for *care,* the operative factor of SACC.

Picture a small sickly yellowing potted plant, badly in need of care. In order to revive this plant, would a wise horticulturist:

1. flood the roots, dump on fertilizer, shove in plant food stakes, tie each leaf and stem to rigid supports, surround it with stereophonic Vivaldi, and fry the mess with sunlamps?

2. throw the plant in a corner where it can be watched, pile a few gardening books next to it, and leave it there until it either dies or visibly shapes up?

3. find out about the plant, learn to understand its unique characteristics, and, realizing that there are no guarantees, incrementally institute an appropriate, well-planned recovery program?

Of course, children are much more complex than potted plants, yet it remains surprisingly popular among some child care programs to choose methods (1) and (2) for curriculum implementation. Too many PDs barrel ahead with little or no understanding of the children in their programs—their particular natures, their ages, phases of development, cultural imperatives, and the like. They blanket children with top-heavy curricular cure-alls, almost as if they believe themselves to be putting out grease fires. No wonder children in these programs find themselves suffocating from the experience.

During ongoing activity planning, the specific goals of each particular child deserve consideration. Quite a few PDs set goals without involving children in the decision-making process. Strange as it may seem, when a new curricular format or activity option comes up, successful PDs present it in such a way as to encourage children's active participation, and not as a means of stricture and intimidation. Autocratically enforced curricula, although usually replicable, do little to engender warmth or enthusiasm.

The point is this: *An affirmative experience equates with positive learning.* Each child's independent *idea of success* can be tapped, supported, and actively reinforced. This cooperative approach makes SACC tougher for adults unaccustomed to the idea of respect for children, but those who practice it can personally attest to its advantages.

HOW EVENTS FUEL EXPERIENCE

Some children bring with them many of their own ideas; they carry definite interests and objectives for exploration and creativity. Some children suffer from abuse and bring with them a deeply disturbing insecurity. Others who suffer from emotional neglect whirl, flail, and shout in a blatant bid for attention. Some struggle with physical, emotional, ethnic, or speech differences that clearly set them apart from others of their age or educational level. More than a few children exhibit all of these characteristics and more.

In the words of noted child development expert Lillian Katz, "The real challenge . . . is to develop activities that children will find satisfying over a long period of time rather than momentarily exciting—the kinds of activities that invite genuine and appropriate problem-solving, mastery of the difficult and concentration or absorption, and [some] that even may be a little routine."[4] Given the nigh-limitless range of potential experience, SACC program-generated events can reflect as much or as little imagination as PDs and caregivers possess.

Events That Facilitate Appropriate Child Development

The following descriptions constitute only a small sampling of events that take place during SACC time. Most require little or no initial capital outlay. All are adaptable to specific goal orientations.

• *Independent projects.* Many children actually have healthy, productive ideas about the kinds of things they'd like to do. They don't really need to be told what to do all the time, do they? Just encouraged to pursue their own interests. A child fascinated by the heavenly bodies might like to make a star chart.

Some children get the idea they'd like to do something on their own, but they're just not quite sure what it is. They don't really need to be told what to do all the time, do they? Just guided along to a few comfortable choices. A child intent on wastefully mixing up cooking supplies might be re-directed to a chemistry set, with a caregiver supervising the experiments.

Some younger children feel more comfortable when an adult gets something started or put together for them, then stands back and lets them take over. Even *they* don't need to be told what to do all the time. Just given a little boost. A six-year-old child who has shown an interest in puppets may be helped to build a lap-sized finger-puppet stage.

Independent projects can run the gamut of children's imaginations, sparked sometimes by an adult-initiated activity that grabs a child's longer-term interest, sometimes by something completely outside the SACC realm. In any event, projects chosen by children themselves hold out much greater promise for building and reinforcing self-esteem; they give a child a chance to see and feel the physical world as a friend.

• *Group projects.* Appropriate group projects also spring from children's expressed interests. Program people need only to lay the groundwork and contribute expertise. When developing such projects, afford each child leeway for interests that fall outside the parameters of group activity. Forcing children's participation benefits no one.

Caregivers and the director can unify group projects with the overall program. Even such "one-shot" ideas as making Halloween masks or modeling clay vases may still flow naturally from children's desire and experience. By getting to know each child personally, caregivers help determine whether the requisite skills, interest, and cultural orientation lie within the group. Then the director can make a more informed determination.

Outside a program, school-age children run through streets and subways with spray-paint cans, leaving their mark on any surface they find. In SACC, using those same spray-paint cans, children might be encouraged to design and paint a stylized exterior wall mural, beautifying the neighborhood and cutting reputations for young artists in the bargain.

• *Interest centers.* These organized sectors combine the initiative of independent projects with the broader goal orientation of a group project. Left to their own devices in an unstructured environment, children will actually develop their own interest centers—in closets, basements, tool sheds, alleys, and doorways. The properly equipped interest center qualitatively enhances children's natural inclinations.

In a sense, all PDs attempt to construct interest centers. Unfortunately, they sometimes do this simply by instructing children to perform certain activities "in this corner only" or "at this table only." A more developed program reflects a conscious understanding of the way interest centers invite, rather than prescribe, children's involvement.

For example, a scientific exploration center might include an array of seashells, dried leaves, and fallen insects, along with several magnifying glasses, perhaps a microscope, and laminated written fact sheets to stimulate examinations of these items. Naturally, whichever items children don't swallow can be studied at any time. Discussion of the Modular Motion Principle later in this chapter takes up the subject of interest center layout.

• *Excursions.* Known for many years as "field trips," these originated from the nineteenth-century agrarian society's practice wherein children might be led out of their one-room schoolhouse and into an actual nearby field for nature studies. In an urbanized twenty-first-century child's life, a field trip can mean a two-hour round-trip bus ride on clogged traffic arteries, sandwiched around a visit to a temperature-regulated indoor museum. The old familiar term only occasionally applies as it once did.

With a little advance work, any program can plan an excursion, ranging from something relatively simple—a seven-block walk from program homebase to the library and back—to a complex three-day weekend camping trip. Some practical prerequisites for excursions:

1. Get fully briefed about cost, regulations, and special details by pertinent people at the destination.
2. If not kept on file, obtain written waivers (permission slips) from parents.
3. Confirm any formal travel arrangements.
4. Confirm dates, travel times, and any parent-provided supplies with each child's parent or guardian.
5. Where possible, to avoid unpleasant surprises, scout destinations in advance of the actual excursion.
6. Prepare children with advance discussions about all phases of the excursion, and familiarize children with general facets of the destination.

For complex excursions, additional points pertain:

7. Solicit parents and guardians who may wish to accompany the group.
8. Hold a final pre-excursion conference with all participants, so that everyone shares the same information at the same time.
9. Clarify and communicate procedures for anyone who accidentally gets separated from the group.

• *Community resource enjoyment.* Envision the SACC program homebase as a child's "hub" in the community "wheel." To beat the heat in Birmingham, Alabama, the Homewood Summer Day Program schedules daily transportation to its district's high school swimming pool. "Extended

Day has opened the community door tremendously," says program director Sandra Vella.

• *Focused-interest groups*. Whether they revolve around video production, weaving, playing chess, hiking, or birdwatching, focused-interest groups make wonderful attractors for children. They aid children in making manageable, longer-term commitments, and they create a concentrated opportunity for skill and attention-span development. Such groups also provide children a critical avenue to self-esteem: a means by which to excel at something they enjoy.

Children in these groups can benefit most from an adult facilitator who possesses a degree of expertise in the specific interest area. Although choosing a group's adult facilitator from among paid program caregivers can offer some convenience, there's no sense making arbitrary assignments that compel an adult into somebody else's idea of fun. Perhaps a parent or Friend of the Program would be more than happy to share their interests in ecology or woodworking with like-minded children.

Also, going outside the program to choose facilitators gives children a chance to plug in to different generations, divergent cultures, and social diversity. Many SACC programs report excellent results from bringing together the children with caring volunteer seniors. Urban programs' proximity to cultural centers puts them within reasonable reach of many professional artisans and craftspeople, some of whom undoubtedly stand willing to share a few hours a week. Only adult apathy limits the possible dimensions of exploration.

Events That Undermine Appropriate Child Development

Many operating programs rely heavily—too heavily, in fact—on what are known as *fallback curricula,* comprised of events that require little or no direct creative participation on the part of children or caregivers. Fallback curricula find greatest favor where the emphasis lies in head counting or behavior control. Programs dominated by a fallback curriculum unwittingly exacerbate the very problems SACC programs seek to resolve, namely, the absences of creative freedom and productivity in children's lives.

The Video Babysitter

Acres of forests have been felled in service of literature that opposes indiscriminate television usage. Many more forests have died to provide millions of viewers with entreaties to plunk down, switch on, and zone out. Never mind the national networks' plaints of declining viewership. On average, according to one estimate, children gorge their impressionable brains on thirty hours of television every week.

For a moment, forget judgments about good and bad, about right and wrong. Even neurological researchers confess to relatively little understanding of most specific brain functions. To what extent and in how many ways television affects physiological and societal conditions may be a topic of debate for many years. Still, certain general conclusions have gained wide acceptance among well-informed observers. The simple scientific facts are as follows: The body affects society, the brain affects the body, and television affects the brain.

From direct experience, most readers will have observed behavioral effects of television exposure, effects that collectively constitute "couch potato syndrome." There seems little need to reiterate the symptoms of glassy-eyed vacancy, slackened jaw, desensitization, and anxiety or violence associated with deprivation. Such uniform symptoms in human beings can only result from a drug-like disturbance to normal brain activity.

Because a television appears to be a benign machine, resistance to the idea of television as anything else seems understandable. Only very recently, some traditional curriculum experts have devised the notion that comprehensive literacy aims must include not only written and spoken language, but also the language of electronic media. Television literacy concerns have begun to seep into pedagogical training courses, if only at a snail's pace.

The children in a SACC program can't wait; they are developing *now*. In a developmentally appropriate program, directors and caregivers do not surrender to the convenient effortlessness of televised drugs, not even "once a week for a special treat, and to take the extra burden off the program workers on early release day," as one sadly misinformed PD in Virginia puts it. Pawning off children to television represents a dangerous fatalism toward child care in general. Only TV-related events geared toward developing children's capacity to apprehend the language of television, events that lead children to a deeper understanding of the ways in which television affects them, make any sense for SACC. Any other use stands as a blatant failure of imagination.

Games of Death and Destruction

Too many children's games revolve around shooting, killing, smashing, crushing, and wiping out imaginary enemies. The age-old male-centered glorification of violent bloody conflict echoes today in the myriad toy guns, toy soldiers, animated ninjas, and transforming robots that proliferate as "consumable goods." Adoration of male role models whose popularity stems from an ability to injure, maim, or mutilate permeates mainstream American society. In the streets of urban war zones, gangs square off against each other with automatic assault weaponry. Some people take a shotgun blast in the face because they choose the wrong places to park their cars. And it all begins with a childhood game of "Bang, bang, you're dead!"

In that they are highly imitative, and in that they often channel their energies and enthusiasm into unfamiliar paths, school-age children learn interactively. One lesson begets another, and another, and then another. Using SACC time to foster hostility, prejudice, or intolerance toward imaginary enemies only perpetuates the vicious cycles in which death merchants prosper and babies die in the streets.

Developmentally appropriate SACC programs seek to overcome the lessons of death and destruction with comparable explorations of growth and acceptance. Games that encourage gratification through dominance or submission, through conquest or surrender, through fantasized obliteration of a vilified other, cannot be viewed as "just a game" . . . because next time, that game is life.

Gender-Specific Activities

In 1990, for the first time ever, an eleven-year-old girl fielded first base in the Little League World Series play-offs. That same World Series witnessed one team's pitcher unable to bear up stoically as the opposing team pounded his fast balls; sniffling and dejected, he broke down in tears.

Attributing masculinity to athletic competition or categorizing emotional sensitivity as feminine follows from a long historical thread of gender-based prejudice. Efforts to overcome these prejudices have been confounded by superficial policy whitewashes, which only serve to reinforce gender myths.

Take the incredible case of Zachary Toungate, an eight-year-old student at Mina Elementary School in Texas. For daring to sport a thin stylish ponytail, Zach found himself removed from his classroom, isolated from his friends at school, and even denied the opportunity to show his face at lunchtime. Proclaiming incontestable authority, the school board condemned Zach for violating the school dress code, which apparently remains well rooted in the World War II era. The incredible part is that this took place in 1991.

The Mina School dress code, like so many other antiquated institutional relics of days gone by, functions under the guise of health and safety regulation. In actuality, this code—not to mention its similarly conceived counterparts across the country—exemplifies the arbitrary authoritarianism that has fueled centuries of gender bias.

In their quest to maintain control, order, and conformity, potential SACC planners can quickly become civil authoritarians. Rather than blindly allowing this to happen, they might do well to examine the ways in which boys are plied with shovels and toy dump trucks while girls are shrouded in oven mitts and aprons. A child's cultural assimilation needn't be synonymous with preconceived and fixed notions of appropriate adult gender roles.

ENVIRONMENT: THE BRIDGE BETWEEN EVENT
AND EXPERIENCE

Planning, designing, and dedicating space for SACC involves recognizing and accepting the things that make children people. Some children, just as some adults, prefer to spend a lot of time indoors: making things, cooking, talking, playing quiet games. Some prefer more access to physical challenges, constructive and cathartic ways of expending youthful energies. Enough of most children's lives consists of rigor, compulsion, obedience, and resignation. Instead of these low-level motivators, why can't an environment supposedly designated for children's care consist of structure, encouragement, and cooperation?

Children often seek solace and satisfaction to the same extent that one might expect of any adult. They often seek out their own turf where they can "have the opportunity for the legitimate exercise of power, the ability to control territory, and opportunities for risk and daring."[5] An appropriate environment's structure encourages this.

As any adult might, children may seek "opportunities to be gentle, to play without intrusion."[6] This doesn't automatically imply a naughty game of "Doctor." A SACC program may be the only chance of respite or privacy for at-risk children, the only opportunity to quietly expand the limits of their imagination, away from peer pressures and harsher realities outside. This calls for an environment that gives children a sense of belonging—a comfortable environment, one in which they can relax and be themselves.

Young people's worlds can grow beyond the walls erected by short-sighted reactionaries, and their ambitions can swell beyond the rhetoric of smooth-talking homeboys. A SACC program environment can contain all the necessary raw materials for bringing options into perspective, for bridging the gap between desire and reality. Then, it's just a matter of creating those options and building those bridges.

The Place Is the Space

There's a direct link between indoor layout and how indoor interaction takes place. Architects design churches so that congregations face the pulpit. Librarians design shelving arrangements so that readers can navigate easily between the stacks. Inside even the most changeless brick building, changing the placement of furniture and objects helps or hinders the way people want to behave.

Consider the ways in which indoor design can help or hinder the goals of a school-age care program. For children to have a chance for low-pressure quiet activity, an environment must speak to that, even invite it. For children to pursue some independent project, for children who wish to join in some group activity, or for any reasonable option generated by children or caregivers, the same holds true.

At the same time, consider the chance of accomplishing these goals with thirty children and two caregivers squeezed inside a mobile trailer in a parking lot. In a multi-purpose room, capacity 200, with echoing ceilings and cold tile floors. In the school cafeteria, trapped between rows of tables and benches.

One obvious compromise usually leads to many invisible ones. That's why sacrificing school-age care goals on the altar of space limitation usually makes for an uncomfortable program. On the other hand, designing indoor space to serve the goals of a SACC program takes more effort and imagination, but it makes for a much more rewarding environment.

Room capacity plays a significant part in environment planning, but understanding room capacity takes something more than a quick eyeballing. A room may be licensed to accommodate forty children in a formal face-front seating arrangement. In the same room, appropriately furnished and equipped for SACC, trying to pack in forty children could be a recipe for bedlam!

Time and effort enter the calculations, too. Converting a space into an appropriate environment takes more than a lick and a promise. Shelves, countertops, and storage space may have to be built. Furniture will need to be moved or at least re-arranged. Like making any place livable, creating the SACC environment might take some heavier construction work, maybe some painting and plastering, signboard work, carpet laying, or some electrical and plumbing work.

And then there's *money*. In an echo of the 1960s child care movement slogan, "Spend tax dollars on the people, and let the Pentagon hold the bake sale," funding strategies and tactics frequently dominate discussions of SACC program start-up or expansion. How much money is there now? How much might there be later? How can the program afford all this?

Once again, to resolve these issues, savvy SACC planners, administrators, and directors turn to the power of partnership. Children's sense of pride and ownership in an environment they help to create, parents' and caregivers' strength of will to improve their own conditions—these desires create avenues of opportunity for the partnership-minded SACC staffer. When children and adults join together in the decision-making process, the resulting venture can bear sweet fruit.

The Line-of-Sight Principle

Indoor and outdoor, a healthy program's physical space provides possibilities for play, for solitude, for informal association, for physical mobility, for intellectual challenge. In fact, it provides these possibilities all at the same time. Yet some lawsuit-wary planners and PDs feel obliged to produce something less in order to satisfy a single logistical principle. It's the principle behind the most common directive in regard to the care of children: "Keep an eye on 'em."

To prevent untoward bullying, sexual activity, kidnapping, choking, broken bones, drug and alcohol usage, or just plain old running away, the line-of-sight principle always comes into play. So that they may be watched, children find themselves figuratively—sometimes literally—corralled within physical space that has been blocked, restricted, and boundaried for maximum visibility. Concurrently, no clubhouse construction projects or games of hide-and-seek are allowed, since they interfere with this principle of constant surveillance.

A favorite topic of futurists and speculative fiction writers has long been the issue of maintaining safety at the expense of humanity. One of the finest works of this type is Jack Williamson's 1949 classic, *The Humanoids*. It chronicles an imaginary world of tomorrow in which all humankind submits itself to the seemingly benign care of kindly humanoid servants, robots who are incapable of error and who can never allow a human to come to harm. In the final analysis, these conditions lead to total mind control and enslavement of the human race. For more than a generation since its publication, *The Humanoids* continued to be assigned reading at M.I.T., a literary warning to computer students of what may result from too narrow a focus on a single programming principle.

The issue of safety receives equally practical questioning from one SACC program staffer:

One of the things that is really sticky in day care is this question of safety, and one of my concerns is that it's very easy to start prohibiting everything. The day you have two children on a swing and one of them falls off and skins his knee, then the next day there's very apt to be a rule. No more two people on a swing. Yet two people on a swing is a neat thing to do, and the important thing is that you experiment doing it safely. When you are taking care of other people's children, you have a responsibility that is a little bit different from being mother. This is a sticky wicket that you have to keep re-evaluating, because you can't keep limiting children's experience because somebody might have an accident.[7]

It makes a good deal of sense to forestall injuries by keeping any environment free of broken glass, toxic waste, open pits, and other obvious hazards to health and safety. Less obvious threats, such as uncovered radiators, slippery stairs, or open parking areas, can also pose imminent danger. Rusting and jagged metallic surfaces or splintering wood surfaces require immediate replacement or repair. However, all of these points might apply to a hospital, a machine shop, or even a home. They should come as no surprise to anyone.

The environment might also be enhanced by security measures which prevent sudden intrusions by dangerous antagonists. Many schools use chain-link fence and barbed wire for this purpose. Some programs post guards. Some systems entail coded computer-operated access. Some just lock the door and stay inside. Although none of these may seem particularly desirable, the antagonistic intruder may seem less so.

Aside from these obvious points, what *appropriate* degree of watchfulness might directors and caregivers exercise? Rote adherence to the line-of-sight principle shapes many a PD's liability concerns; if an untoward incident occurs, it might give the director someone to blame. How many excellent caregivers have been dismissed from a program because they made the mistake of taking a close personal interest in something one child was doing, but then failed to notice another child fall off a swing? One can hardly imagine a parent forced to give up custody of a son who skins a knee in the driveway, yet this is often the underlying philosophy of staff relations in SACC programs: Watch all assigned children at all times or risk dismissal.

Relatedly, the line-of-sight principle inspires poor curriculum planning. In one program in the South, a lone caregiver was trapped in a small windowless classroom with twenty-two first-graders. The caregiver's assignment for the afternoon had been to keep the children seated at their tables, hand them some paper plates and shiny foil, and instruct them to produce "flying saucers." On the planning board, the event and the environment must have looked quite manageable, since line of sight would never be threatened.

In practice, the assignment didn't work out. Some children didn't want to wrap paper plates in foil. Some wanted to run around. Some wanted to talk with their friends, and the room was filled with a driving chatter. The despairing caregiver seemed hard-pressed to focus his line of sight on any one of the children. Unable to command attention or control of the impatient talkative group, he plaintively moaned, "I can't take this anymore."

None of the preceding remarks should be construed to imply that line of sight plays no critical role in SACC environments. Some children probably should be watched every minute. (For that matter, so should some adults.) However, the general idea here is to offer the calming knowledge that a caring other stands within reach. Children's emotional security is a core rationale for developmentally appropriate school-age care, so don't betray that rationale from the start. As Figure 4.1 describes, what underlies appropriate line-of-sight practices is understanding the importance of *the children's point of view.*

The Manufacture-for-Use Principle

Children project continuity into a physical space. They generalize their sense of its condition. Most children won't register a significant awareness of adult action or intention to alter the condition. For example, after a

Figure 4.1

Vermont Licensing Head Listens to Fourth & Fifth Graders, Changes School-Age Regulations

by Dale B. Fink

We often talk about capitalizing on children's interests and ideas in planning activities for school-age child care. A small group of children in Vermont went one step further this winter and became involved in statewide policy development.

Not that they planned it that way. They were just mad about the regulations, which said "Each child shall be supervised at all times by staff." To them, this was unfair. It meant they constantly had to have a adult watching over them. Why couldn't they be in an adjacent room, for instance, doing their homework or working on a project? They weren't babies: they had much more freedom during the school day, not to mention when they were at home.

Shelly Henson, the site coordinator for one of the 11 SACC sites of the Greater Burlington YMCA, explained to them how the regulatory process worked and where they could direct their suggestions if they had any. The children wrote a letter, saying forthrightly, in slanted, hand printed, lettering: "We don't like your rules. We protest. We think were (sic) old enough to be trusted." It was signed by Robyn, Tyler, Benjy, Christopher, Willy, Kerrie, Matthew and Ryan, "the 4th, and 5th graders of the Charlotte YMCA." Henson sent it along with an accompanying letter of her own, describing the discussion she had held with them,

to the state director of Child Day Care Licensing.

Thanks to that correspondence, Vermont is now the first state in the country to spell out in its regulations a separate standard of appropriate supervision for older children attending SACC - giving children above the third grade more freedom and independence. Coleman Baker, Director of licensing, seeing the children's letter as a good opportunity to explain to the youngsters that the rules were designed for their safety and protection, arranged a personal visit to the Charlotte YMCA site.

However, over the course of the discussion, they convinced him to reconsider the state policy. Within a few weeks, Baker issued a new one: *Fourth graders (and up) may be in a room without adult supervision.*

"We don't like your rules. We protest. We think were (sic) old enough to be trusted."

Vermont's new definition of supervision stipulates that fourth, fifth and sixth grade children do not always have to be in the same room with an adult caregiver. However, staff must know the whereabouts of each child and what activities they are engaged in; no child may be alone, except for toileting; children must be in approved, licensed space; staff must be within earshot of the children; and staff must monitor the children every fifteen minutes. "This derivation is warranted", explains Baker's memo to directors of school-age child care programs throughout the state, "in order to allow older school-agers to accept responsibilities appropriate to their ages." The new regulation

does not require centers to extend this newly defined freedom equally to all older children: it applies to those who "have a good understanding of the center's rules and policies regarding appropriate behavior and privileges."

In a separate letter to the eight children, Baker wrote that "this policy was created because of your feelings and your actions . . . please maintain your interest in speaking up or writing letters when you feel your lives are being inappropriately affected. . ."

Many school-age providers across the country have come to recognize that nine to twelve year old children are in a different developmental stage than students in the lower elementary grades, and therefore that programs that wish to serve this older group must be very different from those designed for the younger children. This new regulation makes Vermont the first state to formalize this understanding through the regulatory process. Everyone in the school-age child care field ought to tip their hats to Coleman Baker - and to the eight children and their supportive staff of the Greater Burlington YMCA who made this change possible!

terrible military conflict in Kuwait, unsupervised children skipped back into the open fields in which they had always played—but this time, the fields were littered with unexploded mines. The nature of the physical space had seriously changed, but the uncomprehending children failed to grasp the change—with horrifying results.

Children who attend many of the nation's public schools face daily conditions that aren't very different from those of war zones. Urban teachers lobbying for combat pay wish this were clearer and of more considerable consequence to their funding sources. A popular method for stemming the tide of violence in high-risk areas has been the militarization of schools; armed forces veterans become principals and impose a version of martial law on school operations. This certainly is one way to deal with the problem. However, it hardly creates a climate conducive to SACC.

In other areas, the local school offers the most reasonable, the most comfortable, and the most centrally located facilities for community functions, including SACC. The Fargo Elementary School held together a Georgia lumber-town community of 400, not only by serving as the only K–7 school for thirty miles, but as a town meeting hall, a special event center, and, on occasion, a religious gathering site. Were a SACC program to have been implemented at Fargo, the total community picture might have been reflected.

This type of rural school-centered community may seem exceptional today. Much more commonly, a physical space can only reflect the primary intent of its designers. For example, if a room is manufactured for use as a cafeteria, it feels like and functions well only as a cafeteria. Aside from snacking, such a space can house few curricular activities that will feel appropriate.

The fundamental point is this: *If the children can't tell the difference, then there is no difference.* To be considered wholly appropriate, a SACC program's environment consists of physical space that is planned, designed, and dedicated specifically for the use of the program. This, too, is manufacture for use.

What's Inside

Following a partnership model, adults will want to make certain preliminary decisions about financial matters and state or local regulations. Subsequently, children brought into the process and given the heady opportunity to mold a piece of their own future might readily respond by taking up whatever responsibility presents itself. Children's feelings of attachment to an environment, as well as their behavior in it, will vary in relation to how much that environment is theirs.

Can the children help build and paint their own environment? In the American frontier a hundred years ago, the question wouldn't have even been asked. Children of different ages can participate as seems appropriate to their developmental stage. Program staffers who don't like working with children can be weeded out immediately. Parents who wish to volunteer or donate materials may do so. A shared experience of creation binds everyone more closely together.

In contrast with line-of-sight and manufacture-for-use, two other principles offer more practical guidance to SACC environment planning.

The Modular Motion Principle

Think of the most stimulating, the most interest-provoking environments designed for the child in everyone. What comes immediately to mind? A theme amusement park, with its winding paths and varied attractions? A science museum, with its colorful push-button displays and kinetic discoveries? A miniature golf course? An aquarium? A strip-mall pizza arcade?

What ties all these places together is the way in which their designers have implemented the modular motion principle. Each attraction or activity invites visitors into its own specific and identifiable area, sometimes called a *module*. Each module connects to all the others, sometimes in a determined sequence, sometimes in a random-access pattern, but always in a way that eventually permits any visitor to enter any module. Of course, as anyone experienced around children will attest, the more random the access, the more delighted the child.

Designers of modular environments define space—and motion within that space—for both energy-releasing activity and quieter relaxation. Designers also define the parameters of each module to inhibit unwanted behaviors. In many cases, indoor and outdoor modules lie within easy access of one another, giving the visitor a range of spatial choices. Most important, designers strive for the most aesthetically pleasing conditions they can achieve for each modular series, visually connecting the environment together with spatial harmonies and color complementarity. Under the guiding principle of modular motion, these elements can inform the plan of any child-pleasing environment.

Striking the balance between productive modular utility and the tendency to compartmentalize or "fence 'em in" presents the challenge. Leaving the plan to a few employees with one eye on the clock and one hand in the pocket doesn't bode so well. Bringing the partnership's resources to bear, the modular motion approach can yield a dynamic, varied, exploratory environment that is worthy of designers and visitors alike. The transformation of any given area into a SACC environment must become *every* partner's concern.

The Playhouse Principle

What child hasn't, at one time or another, banded together with one or more friends to form a club? Whether they last just for the afternoon or for hundreds of years, whether spontaneous or extended, chartered or informal, exclusive peer groups and clubs play an important part in millions of peoples' lives. A deeply felt sense of emotional commitment comes with group, club, or gang loyalties. So ingrained can this commitment become that one young boy living in Boston's inner city went on record with the following remark: "Gangs are better than families, because at least gangs can take care of you."

A group consisting primarily of school-age children usually seeks a physical space it can call home—a treehouse, a basement, an attic, a garage, an abandoned building. It's an unalterable aspect of the socialization process, of defining identity in relationship to others, of securing social acceptance and stability. As a physical focal point, the new "home" serves as a base of operations, a place to share experiences with other "family" members.

Many SACC people don't even try for an equivalent sense of "home" in their programs. Instead, from an armload of institutionally approved media materials, they ply the children with educational curriculums "designed for fun and learning." They might give the program a "fun" name, like "KidTime" or "AfterSchool Angels," without asking the children what *they* want to call it. They might not let the children take off their shoes. In basic psychological terms, these programmers are laboring with a severe motivational differential; the desire is strong, but the know-how is absent.

A developmentally appropriate SACC program takes into account children's natural desire to orchestrate their surroundings into a personalized environment. That is, while some children can grudgingly adapt to imposed conditions, nearly all can embrace and care for something that lets them be themselves. Children learn to exercise self-awareness and self-control by doing it *now*, not later when they're "old enough." A developmentally appropriate SACC program gives children a chance to do it now.

Remember, wherever the physical space is located, that space has got to be as home-like as possible. Not warehouse-like, not fishtank-like, not classroom-like—*home-like*. Soft floor pillows. An old armchair. A basketball hoop in the courtyard. A refrigerator with silly-looking door magnets. A tape player. A shoe rack. A couple of potted plants, one of which doesn't look like it's got a chance but stays there anyway. Maybe a rabbit or two. Who knows what else? The children know. It's their home. They live there.

Nuts and Bolts

To mold a suitable environment takes a little vision, a little cash, and a lot of sweat. Pre-fabs and trailers may cut down on physical effort, but they also cut down the possibilities inherent in a school-age child care program. Don't slip into the "all-we-need-is-four-walls-and-a-door-that-locks" mentality without examining the alternatives. Making a place where people *want* to be might be easier than it first appears.

When thinking about the indoor layout, one's own home can serve as a good conceptual framework. In many instances, zoning regulations, building codes, housing association regulations, environmental codes, and a host of other considerations come to bear on the homeowner who is intent on making a personal home out of a tract housing unit. Some work takes quite a bit of preparation, both materially and politically, before the homeowner secures a go-ahead.

The ways in which a house becomes a home apply to the indoor SACC environment plan. For building a program environment that surpasses the lowest acceptable terms, state and local building codes might actually get in the way. Administrators might hold up a disapproving hand. Planners might balk at potential costs. It might do some good simply to remind these detractors that "the old ways" were themselves once new.

• *Comings and goings.* Most homes possess some sort of entry hall or receiving area, a space where people do the things that people do when they arrive or leave: take off/put on coats and hats; put down/pick up mail, books, and parcels; say hellos/goodbyes. Apartment buildings may have lobbies, but each apartment probably strives for its own welcoming area. People tend to require some given space for transitions from one environment to another, sort of like a societal airlock.

In too many programs, children and staff come in through just another institutional entrance, and boom!—suddenly SACC. Settling down for the afternoon in a sterile corridor or getting ready to leave on a parking lot blacktop may be fine for other "service industries," but not for SACC.

Planners and administrators looking to encourage appropriate transitions into and out of the SACC environment can do so by making a specific space for it. Caregivers and children deserve easy access to their personal belongings without having to disrupt SACC proceedings. And, in more threatening neighborhoods, the entry space makes a good last line of defense against undesirable strangers and illegal weapons.

The entry experience sets the tone for every other experience that follows. Why should it be drab, conventional, lackluster? Why not a little more lived-in? Here, between the coat rack/closet and the umbrella basket, might hang some of the latest program art projects or a program team photo. A throw rug for color, a potted plant for growth, today's newspaper for currency . . . the negligible dollar cost for these and other such items earns a significant return in comfort and familiarity.

• *Room for living.* For thousands of years prior to VCRs and fax machines, warring nation-states built their people's loyalty on *xenophobia,* or fear of strangers. From this nearly prehistoric perspective, integration compelled the clash of cultures, or provincialism negated other cultures' value. A quick check of the Roman Calendar tells us that it is now 2,000 years after the dawn of the Christian Era, not 2,000 years before. The multinational society rapidly overtaking the old world of warring nation-states calls not for further cultural repression but for a conscious exploration of world cultures.

When renting, leasing, or sharing a larger space with other groups, PDs and caregivers may find themselves on the short end of a very old stick. One YMCA-based PD tells about the decor in her meeting room, where a huge old-style portrait of General Pershing looms austerely over the proceedings. Though she describes a great deal of discomfort at being stared at by the dead general, this director expresses an even greater discomfort at suggesting the general's portrait be retired and replaced.

Traditional curricula in American classrooms and community organizations entail many such symbols and images, held over from that not-too-distant era when honor paid to military dominators was thought to equate with national honor. Many world communities' leaders still identify more strongly with buried ancestors than with living relatives, and in certain cases this cultural heritage dates back to ancestral practices of Asian, African, Middle Eastern, or European origin. In any event, America today is a country in which Martin Luther King, Jr.'s birthday and the Chinese New Year give rise each year to widespread celebration. Slowly but inevitably, America's tradition learns to reflect *all* of its citizens' traditions.

In line with this natural trend, fondly tagged by Canadian philosopher Marshall McLuhan as "the global village," a SACC environment will endeavor to reflect and examine all of its people's traditions. It will also present children with opportunities to comprehend and embrace the wide diversity of world cultures *without fear and condemnation.*

The central indoor program area cannot help but either enhance or undermine assimilation to world culture. The tiny social microcosm of the SACC program frames an important window through which children form their world views. The central area brings a worldview to the children and, in so doing, acculturates children into that world.

In practical terms, this means an environment that contains many flags, not just one . . . portraits of living legends, not just buried ones . . . unfamiliar cuisine, not just the nationally advertised brands . . . the original patterns, designs, alphabets, and customs from which so-called cultural norms derive. In other words, things that adults, because of xenophobic tradition, may find themselves uncomfortable with but that children may absorb without the slightest difficulty.

Remember, the indoor environment must speak continuously to many interests; pushing sensitive children into boxing rings or cornering roughhousers into a sewing circle often breeds more resentment than character. Experienced caregivers know that forcing children to abandon special interest discoveries simply because "it's not on the schedule" or "you did that yesterday" can trigger the same type of negative emotional reactions. With natural skill and interest development on the line, no appropriate environment forces wholly gymnastic, wholly academic, or even wholly creative agendas on a compulsory basis.

The room for living also contains comfortable and familiar objects. Perhaps a Velcro-ball target board? Some appropriately scaled game tables? Comic-book character wastebaskets? Once again, ask the children. Recognize their right to some measure of environmental control. Not only may they come to regard the program environment with interest and care, but they may more readily learn to recognize the ways in which they contribute to the wider environment around them.

• *Officialdom.* In "Star Trek: The Next Generation," much of the primary action takes place on the *Enterprise*'s main bridge. But occasionally Captain Picard finds it convenient to withdraw to his "ready room," an inner sanctum located immediately off the main bridge, wherein he may conduct more personal or more delicate official matters.

Any organized home contains at least one drawer, one table, one desk, or one room wherein reposes the "official business." It may be as small as a jewelry box or as large as an entire den. In one way or another, this space comes to be regarded as somewhat special, not to be taken lightly, not to be fooled with, not to be gone through or touched without express instruction or permission. In larger homes, several of these official spaces may exist, possibly one for each member of the family.

This principle sets a precedent for SACC program officialdom. Set apart from the central area must lie a protected space for official business. This may mean knocking out a wall, or it may be as simple as setting up a rolling divider. At the very least, here sit the program director's desk, files, leadership materials, confiscated items, reference texts, contact sheets, and whatever else facilitates on-site program operation. Here also one finds consultation space, physical room for others—children, parents, caregivers, administrators, visitors—to meet privately and officially. It may double as the vault for valuable possessions, as a conference area for caregivers to hash out differences or plan upcoming events, even as a safe emotional haven for a temporarily disconsolate child.

Although this space must remain private, it must also lie close enough to the primary space so that the site director can keep an ear open to primary space activities. A more plush or an administrator-dictated space, located down the hall or in another building, defeats the purpose. At all times, the director must remain in close contact to the center of program action . . . unless the director has yielded authority by assuming the mantle of an administrator, in which case program direction stands to slip into hands that are unable or unwilling for the task.

• *"Caution: Keep within reach of children."* Depending on the developmental range of a program's children, probably some of the biggest indoor environment planning bugaboos have to do with storage space. What goes where? How long does it stay there? Who took it? Who's bringing it back? Who can't reach it? How did *that* disappear?

Of course, different programs solve these questions in different ways. Preoccupied with crowd and inventory control, over-enrolled programs tend toward the locked-closet approach. Caregivers in these programs preempt casual access to program equipment and materials. Doling out portioned quantities in assembly-line fashion, they make certain that each child receives the same thing at the same time in the same way for the same purpose. At the other end of the scale, a more exclusive program's dedicated space permits more personalized attention. With the advantage of being able to leave materials emplaced from day to day, caregivers can simply assist children on an as-needed basis. In between, one finds a gamut of rollaway cupboards, sealed trunks, cardboard cartons, shoeboxes, shelf units, and canisters.

Drawing again on the modular motion principle, materials must move in and out of children's accessibility, relative to the children's developmental stages. That is, *staging* materials at various levels of access—easy, less easy, limited, restricted—acknowledges children's capacities and supports caregivers' responsibilities. Over time, the appropriate environment provides varying degrees of accessibility, and materials available in each staging area will vary.

First-graders might require more adult-centered efforts at material rotation, in which caregivers observe and respond to the children's usage patterns. Manipulatives, such as Legos, blocks, jigsaw puzzles, and Cuisenaire rods, offer a variety of uses along the developmental path, so access to these may vary solely by children's interest. More specialized materials, such as sand, watercolors, and construction tools, may move up and down the staging scale as caregiver confidence wanes and waxes.

Fourth-, fifth-, and sixth-graders can more adequately determine their specific relationships to specific materials. In order to exercise greater freedom of choice, they may wish—very rightfully—easy access to more developmentally advanced materials. Arbitrarily denying access to all children under the guise of safety engenders resignation and disaffection, hardly desirable goals for SACC.

Appropriate material staging areas within the given indoor environment often take into account the children's relative physical height. When implementing this prerogative, directors absolutely must account for exceptional and special-needs children. On balance, the natural correlation between chronological age, developmental stage, and height can guide creation and placement of these areas.

Drastic changes in location and content of each staging area drastically alter events and experience of the program. Some kindergartners may want to hold on to that dog-eared coloring book someone just threw out. The fourth-graders may not be able to reach that new shelf. Keep the partnership feel when contemplating such changes.

What's Outside

To the same extent as indoor design, outdoor space layout ideally blends safety and challenge for children. In this regard, such space lies immediately adjacent to indoor areas, allowing for maximum freedom of movement between both. It contains focused and unfocused areas, some explicitly designated for group games or sports, some for multiple purposes, and some simply for relaxing with a friend in the shade.

Outdoor Model #1: The Adventure Playground

Andrew Scott, former executive director of the California School-Age Consortium (CSAC), describes some of the reasoning behind implementation of this option:

Most of the time, children want to create and control their play with a minimum of adult interference or "guidance." Children play wherever they are and create games and situations out of whatever is at hand, in spite of elaborate or no adult planning. Adults have all too often become masters at making simple things complicated when planning the urban environment to accomodate the leisure needs of children and youth. The result is that many of our young people do not have enough opportunities to develop a respect for themselves and others or to develop positive directions as they get older.

This is where the Adventure Playgrounds come in. . . . They have, in their thirty years of existence, had a profound effect on family involvement in the community, on the reduction of vandalism and juvenile crime, by providing a place that belongs to all the children and youth in the neighborhood, a place they have built and that they maintain. . . . Community support develops through the children, so that the playground becomes a true community catalyst.[8]

CLOSE-UP: Mark Twain Adventure Playground, Houston, Texas

The adventure playground at Mark Twain Elementary School opened in February 1986. It is the second playground founded by the Houston Adventure Play Association, a nonprofit agency formed as an outgrowth of the Latchkey Committee of the Metropolitan Organization. The playground is designed on the European model, which provides children with raw materials such as scrap lumber, nails, bolts, rope, sand, paint, seeds, and tools to create their own self-directed projects. Frances Heyck, administrator, says, "You can always tell when you are getting near an adventure playground by the sound of the hammers." (See Figure 4.2.)

Half the children at the Mark Twain site participate as one option in the extended day program offered by the Houston Independent School District. The rest are neighborhood children who attend on a drop-in basis. The school is in a neighborhood in transition and is surrounded by subsidized apartments. No fees are charged. Dr. Tom Matney, board member, says, "The program serves not only latchkey children, but also street children who may have a parent at home but for a variety of reasons that parent is not capable of parenting or meeting the child's basic needs of food, cleanliness, and security."

Children have participated in developing the procedures for the safe

Figure 4.2

At the Mark Twain Adventure Playground, children create their own self-directed projects . . .

. . . and they control their play activity with a minimum of adult interference.

use of tools and materials. They have also helped to formulate the consequences if the rules are broken. Staff consistently discuss safety concerns in staff meetings, and as a result perhaps, not one major injury occurred in the program's first year of operation.

The program provides daily snacks. Occasionally, the children have cookouts, which include foods such as roasted corn on the cob. The children help develop the menu and prepare the snacks.[9]

Outdoor Model #2: Modified Adventure Environment

For some planners, the idea of letting children "own" their environment represents a substantial shift in attitude toward child development. It contradicts a set of preordained dictums—specifically, strong faiths and beliefs in so-called traditional values—that underlie all of their other conscious pursuits. And, factoring in higher liability costs as a function of less conservative environments, these planners find themselves strongly swayed by the pull of traditional ways.

The physical sense of the Adventure Playground, of a world constantly under construction, can often be institutionalized by those who are fearful of an obviously impermanent environment. Pre-approved recreational equipment may be purchased and bolted into immovable positions. Instead of being subject to children's interests and desires, installations may be altered only by acts of the highest counsel. By focusing on outcomes rather than the natural exploratory processes of maturation, planners can easily cut down latitude for adventure and increase the degree of result-orientation. Armed with intentions to achieve pre-ordained outcomes, administrators and directors can then go on to regulate children's behaviors into avenues that may lead to those outcomes.

In these modified settings, strict controls usually prevent the introduction of any stimuli that might lead or encourage children to explore activity that falls outside the predetermined boundaries. Such settings generally are geographically isolated from streams or sources of "undesirable" stimuli. Planners, administrators, and directors are then able to orient the environment as closely as possible to the "correctness" of their beliefs.

CLOSE-UP: Habitat Educare Center, Americus, Georgia

Situated on 2.15 acres of grassland adjacent to an 8,500-square-foot classroom structure lies an outdoor learning environment peppered with a catalogue's worth of equipment: trikes, scooters, and wagons for the hilly riding track; spiral, barrel, and traditional slide sets; swing sets, monkey bars, firehouse poles. It also contains a grassy field for soccer, softball, and volleyball. The program provider, Habitat for Humanity International

Figure 4.3

Safely hidden away in this spacious rural setting, children at Habitat Educare Center powwow over their next move. (Photo: Julie A. Lopez)

(HHI), maintains a ceiling enrollment figure of forty children, although mid-1991 enrollment stood at around twenty-five. As Figure 4.3 depicts, there's clearly room for more.

Program directors Diane and Joseph Umstead describe the relationship between the overall care program and HHI's stated Christian mission to build low-cost homes worldwide for low-income families:

> Volunteers training for overseas work with Habitat participate in a three-month intensive here before going overseas for three years. There is a lot of coming and going, many hellos and goodbyes. We are constantly dealing with transition, change, grief, separation, and firsts for most families. When the families re-enter the States, they return here for debriefing. For many children, there is tremendous cultural shock. We find it very important to develop historical connections for these children and maintain communication with them during their term abroad. . . . We are a support service for the people that make this international organization run smoothly. Folks come here from all walks of life—some single, some married with children, others retired. All profess Christianity and believe in service to God and humanity. Building the center as a benefit makes it easier for people with children to participate in this type of service.[10]

The Educare Center claims to stand alone as the area's only racially and culturally integrated child care center. Scores of HHI volunteers contributed free labor to build the facility, including two mini-scale replicas of the houses that volunteers might build during their overseas missions. Donated building equipment and materials trimmed cash outlay by an estimated 25 percent to $150,000. Only children of HHI employees and volunteers may qualify for no-charge care. When space permits, others allowed to enroll their children are charged on a sliding-scale basis.

Outdoor Model #3: The Partnership Playground

Readers will recall this chapter's introductory point regarding the definition of *curriculum*, that the word itself is severely inadequate for the task of describing the people, events, and conditions of school-age child care. With the goal of bringing life to children and children to life, SACC curriculum must embrace some grander spirit than that of limited workplace concerns or impersonal data transmission. The spirit of togetherness, of the inevitable necessity to co-exist in a many-faceted, ever-changing world, provides the impetus for the Partnership Playground.

In contrast to the seeming chaos of the Adventure Playground and the ordained objectives of its modified cousin, the Partnership Playground provides a living link between the SACC program and the very real community in which it operates. Organizationally, it forms a practical social hub from which stem the spokes of responsive interaction between the children, the citizens, and the so-called pillars of the program's community. Since its genesis calls for the genuine participation of all concerned parties, the success of a Partnership Playground rests on the natural desire—of children and adults—to be included in decisions and events that ultimately affect their lives.

Pipe dream? Hardly. Hard work? Probably. Worth it? Definitely.

CLOSE-UP: Gilpin Neighborhood Park, Denver, Colorado

With varied terrains, hills, grassy areas, climbing rocks, and a selection of coniferous and deciduous trees, the Gilpin Neighborhood Park and playground provides its entire local community with a pleasant alternative to traditional blacktopped schoolyards. Gilpin PD Pat Holliday remarks: "We thought that because the children were spending the majority of their waking hours in the school area, it should be a beautiful place for them to play and grow."

The project developed through grass roots organization, spurred by the Gilpin SACC program. Children were consulted first. They were asked to submit drawings and sketches of their visions for their ideal park and play-

Figure 4.4

The Denver skyline plays second fiddle to the array of activity installations at Gilpin Neighborhood Park.

ground. Adult organizers conducted local meetings at which parents and interested community members discussed the children's input, as well as their own interests.

For practical layout and design, organizers brought University of Colorado–Denver landscape architecture students into the process. Each class member developed a scale model of his or her park design. The completed models were displayed at public exhibit, after which all community members voted for their favorites.

The democratically chosen design was implemented in separate phases, each phase designed so that construction would interrupt ongoing site usage as minimally as possible. With the Community Development Fund in the lead, the project raised $300,000 from both private and public sources. As funds were made available, each successive phase of the five-year construction process became possible.

The completed park contains two playgrounds connected by a walkway, one play area for kindergarten-age children, the other for older and bigger ones. It also includes a soccer field, a running track, a physical fitness course, picnic tables, and even a traditional blacktop area. The whole community has general access to all of the facilities. Figure 4.4 displays just one small part.

Gilpin Extended Day Program regularly utilizes the Neighborhood Park on weekdays from 3:00 to 4:15 P.M. During this segment of the program's curriculum, children may choose between self-directed activity, the "Free Play" option, and adult-guided team activity, the "Sports" option. Both options are available daily throughout the program year.

Meanwhile, Back in Reality . . .

No matter how many models are displayed, the hard fact remains that not all SACC programs can enjoy the luxury of appropriate outdoor facilities. A goodly number of programs operate out of inner-city projects, decades-old fieldhouses, deteriorating de-sanctified churches, and a selection of otherwise neglected or abandoned properties. Never mind the internal finances of these programs; macroeconomic conditions narrow program providers' practical options for safe outdoor space. In many of the neighborhoods where these programs operate, the biggest challenge of the outdoors is to stay alive.

Whether neighborhood risk management concerns run high or low, sanctioned outdoor activity ranks right around the top of SACC environment planning priorities. Alone, an inner-city SACC program planner can do little about local air quality, foot and vehicle traffic, construction zones, gang turf boundaries, and the solvency of a city treasury. These and other obstacles to building a safe and challenging outdoor environment may seem impossible to overcome. But to secrete children away in windowless, characterless basements—that is, *to conditionally equate safety with imprisonment*—can only perpetuate the misconceptions and fears that rule the savage streets without.

NOTES

1. Jim Greenman, *Caring Spaces, Learning Places: Children's Environments That Work* (Redmond, WA: Exchange Press, 1988), p. 5.

2. Sandra Horowitz, "Some Thoughts on Planning for Multi-Age Groups", in *Curriculum Is What Happens: Planning Is the Key,* ed. Laura Dittman (Washington, DC: NAEYC, 1970), pp. 22–23.

3. Jill Ellen Steinberg, *The After School Day Care Association Activity Book* (Madison, WI: ASDCA, 1978), p. 1L.

4. Lillian Katz, *Talks with Teachers* (Washington, DC: NAEYC, 1977), p. 114.

5. Elizabeth Prescott, "Dimensions of Day Care Environments" (Keynote address, Day Care Environments Conference, Iowa State University, June 15, 1979).

6. Ibid.

7. Ibid.

8. Andrew Scott, "What Is an Adventure Playground?" *CSAC Review*, Fall 1988, p. 4.

9. Adapted and reprinted from Nancy H. Beaver, *Somebody Cares: Eight Model Child Care Programs for School-Age Children in Texas* (Austin, TX: Corporate Child Development Fund for Texas, 1987), pp. 49–51.

10. Quoted in "Building a Center—Habitat-Style," *Child Care Information Exchange*, August 1990, p. 16.

FOR FURTHER REFERENCE

Bergstrom, Joan. 1990. *School's Out—Now What? Choices for Your Child's Time.* Berkeley, CA: Ten Speed Press.

Derman-Sparks, Louise. 1989. *Anti-Bias Curriculum: Tools for Empowering Young Children* (pub. #242). Washington, DC: NAEYC.

Elkind, David. 1978. *A Sympathetic Understanding of the Child: Birth to Sixteen.* Boston: Allyn and Bacon.

Hopkins, Susan, and Jeffrey Winters, eds. 1990. *Discover the World: Empowering Children to Value Themselves, Others and the Earth.* Nashville: New Society Publishers/School Age NOTES.

Musson, Steve, and Maurice Gibbons. 1988. *The New Youth Challenge: A Model for Working with Older Children in School Age Child Care.* Nashville: Challenge Associates/School Age NOTES.

SACCProject and the New York State Council on Children and Families. 1990. *Between School-Time and Home-Time: Planning Activities for School Age Child Care Programs* [videotape]. Wellesley, MA: SACCProject.

Winn, Marie. 1981. *Children without Childhood.* New York: Penguin Books.

Chapter 5

FINANCIAL MANAGEMENT (AND MISMANAGEMENT)

Like any other American business, a SACC program flies or dies on its fiscal acumen. More SACC programs fail due to financial ignorance than for any other reason. In principle, it's only the number of zeroes that separates Wall Street and SACC financial matters.

Handling finance with a sure hand means understanding the nature of the beast—and it *is* a beast. Like most beasts, finance can be tamed, trained, and domesticated, but not every partner may have the necessary stamina. Patrolling the economic perimeters takes clarity of purpose, constant attention, and a willingness to be wrong.

Coping with financial matters means coping with *reality*. The reality that guilt-ridden parents who want their children to like them may buy some new "action figures" before they'll pay overdue fees. The reality that those in-kind contributions that were promised a year ago still haven't made their way through the bureaucracy. Reality bites, reality stings, but sometimes, through considered cooperative effort, reality can settle down for a long winter with barely a peep. It all depends on who's handling the accounts.

Financial considerations often lead to the toughest choices a program director makes. Thirty different children may have thirty different fee schedules with the same program, but the mathematical principles used to create those schedules never vary. Neither do the principles used to factor those payments into the program's overall budget. A casual attitude toward financial planning, resource development, and cash management can lead to a situation in which thirty different children have no fee schedule—because the program had to shut down!

Accountants spend years absorbing the formal principles of systematic money management. Most of them trade on their specialized expertise to assist organizations in getting a handle on the beast. To cut down on the cost, a few organizations stay away from professional accountants. These few choose either to hold the financial reins themselves or to delegate the task to well-meaning volunteers. Sometimes this works. At other times, the job requires more than cashing checks and subtracting unexpected expenses. Then, when the tide of red ink rises too high, hands fly up in dismay.

Well-managed finances share some basic characteristics. Whether contracting an accountant, depending on volunteers, or doing it alone, get acquainted with these characteristics. Regardless of administrative structure, size, or mission, it still can't hurt to review them.

- *Checks and balances.* Several people balance all monies coming in and going out in separate running records, then people check with each other for accuracy.
- *Formal systems.* Everybody in the program uses the same basic system to keep their running records. That means everybody who uses the system understands it.
- *Overlapping spheres of responsibility.* Complementary partners team up to keep tasks manageable.
- *Procedural clarity.* Each person understands each other's primary task, so they support rather than duplicate each other's work.
- *Contingency funds.* A cash reserve sits safely out of daily reach.

Successful money-watchers know these characteristics. Parents, outside funding sources, caregivers, site personnel, and the Internal Revenue Service (IRS) all appreciate them. In fact, the line-of-sight principle makes a much better friend in the counting room than in the playroom.

For new programs, one of the first financial management decisions has to do with primary forms of transaction. In *cash basis accounting,* transactions are recorded at the point where funds actually come into and flow out of the program. In *accrual basis accounting,* in addition to recording transactions resulting from the receipt and disbursement of cash, you also record the amount you owe others and others owe you.[1]

The accrual basis option would well serve a program that, for example, depended primarily on in-kind provider contributions and direct-deposit agency reimbursements. This would be a case in which program people handle few or no instruments of exchange. The complexities of this accounting option render it useful for managing "invisible" funds.

Because of its greater simplicity, and because so many SACC programs handle tangible cash or check transactions, this manual focuses on the cash basis option. With either option, a workable accounting system allows money-watchers to keep constant track of funding flow. It makes the numbers work for the program, not the other way around.

ACCOUNTS RECEIVABLE

In the program role of *administrative assistant,* one person bears responsibility for the daily listing of incoming funds. In a book expressly designated for the purpose, the assistant marks dates of receipt next to (1) cash, check, or voucher amount; (2) check or voucher number, if any; and (3) the name to which credit applies.

The assistant passes the cash instruments along to the *bookkeeper,* who records the same information in the program's ledgers. The bookkeeper immediately lists bank-drawn checks on the program's bank deposit slips, *and all funds received are deposited daily.* It may be tempting to "temporarily borrow" cash receipts for program purchases, but no one needs a manual to tell them where this sort of thing leads. Smart PDs won't accept spendable cash in payment of fees.

SACC programs with computer-run accounting cannot forgo manual recording procedures. Hackers can appreciate the principle of hard copy backup to disk-stored data. When the computer is down, those less familiar with computerese will appreciate handwritten records.

Sometimes only one person plays both roles of administrative assistant and bookkeeper. This in no way mitigates the need to adhere to step-by-step procedure. Skipping steps can mean missing money. How important are these built-in checks and balances? In one East Coast parent-run program, the parent-treasurer collected everyone else's fee payments. Unbeknownst to the other parents, he himself paid no fees! Perhaps this inequity could have been avoided had the program implemented a balanced system, one in which the parent-treasurer collected and recorded payments while other parents rotated responsibility for making deposits.

Basic Income

Trying to choose an income system can be like trying to choose a winning system for Monopoly. Some go for the high-rent district, some take up scattered strategic positions, some take whatever they can get, and some just sit on the sidelines waiting for everyone else to bankrupt each other. Each hopes she or he will be the last one left.

Because they are performing a *social* service, many SACC programs hesitate to take a strong stand with regard to their income. To re-emphasize an earlier point, *a SACC program is a business.* In a competitive environment, businesses stay in business by means of sound business practice.

Sound business practice includes offering parents a level of service they can get nowhere else. To offer that level of service, a SACC program brings qualified caregivers and appropriate care to children's lives. When it does this effectively, a program reduces parent anxiety. Things being equal, the program that does this the most effectively will always be the last one left.

Even for that ubiquitous American "service," the IRS, collecting money on the basis of fear, penalization, and intimidation rarely rates the effort. Compare the tenor of a mutual fund manager, stewarding investments to maximize clients' returns, with that of a collection agency, hassling a laid-off worker for a few dollars. The well-planned SACC program emphasizes its service role with a *basic income policy,* which characterizes the program as a steward rather than a collector. A SACC program justifies its basic income by giving partners a chance for another kind of return on their investment.

Businesses whose biggest costs come from human labor are called *labor-intensive.* Since caring labor generally absorbs between 70 and 85 percent of a SACC program budget, SACC is considered labor-intensive. Barring a massive upsurge in tax-supported social program spending, these high percentages will continue to go toward paying caregivers. Given current circumstances, SACC promises to remain labor-intensive for some time to come.

This affects basic income policy in that service to some can mean no service for others. A fair income policy strikes the balance between firmness and forgiveness. With the help of this manual, fair-minded planners and PDs can conceive, create, and put into practice just such a policy.

Income generally arrives in one of these forms:

- Personal payment
- Government voucher
- Foundation grant
- Corporate sponsorship
- School board allocation
- Charitable donation

Successful income management reflects knowledge of these and any other potential form of investment in school-age child care. To this end, the mission statement bridges into the program's "prospectus," the initial tool by which future partners will determine the viability of investing in one or another SACC program. Program brochures usually provide details about basic income policy and procedures.

Each program and each site constructs its own blend of parent and institutional funding sources. When billing institutional sources, successful PDs obtain all pertinent published guidelines and requisite forms. They also strive to achieve cooperative understandings about time frames and billing amounts.

Although government agencies are charged with providing technical assistance to grantees, getting it usually requires more than a phone call. One PD hand-delivers his bills to the appropriate person at the local Department of Social Services. The two are on a first-name basis, and the PD often receives personal calls alerting him to a given bill's processing status. People do more for people they know. Get to know the real people who handle program funding.

Whatever the mix, parent fees constitute the vast majority of programs' income, so tailor procedures to accommodate prevailing conditions at each site. In a multi-site program, income procedures that work well at one site may or may not work at another.

Fees: How Parents Contribute Funding

Most programs receive some portion of income from parents. But simply multiplying the number of enrolled children by the rates of payment, then again by the days of operation, cannot possibly yield a realistic estimate of income. Instead, it yields the *maximum potential income* (MPI), the total amount receivable in a perfect world. How much a program actually takes in—well, that's another story. After a year or two, administrators and accountants can peruse the difference between MPI and actual income. They can even divide the MPI into the actual income figure and arrive at a percentage of utilized potential, which is called the *utilization rate*.

New programs haven't the luxury of calculating a utilization rate. Their PDs can only assume that all children will take every allotted vacation, that some children will be sick for long periods of time, and that no children will ever come along to take the places of those who leave. Even with money set aside in the start-up budget for early months when enrollment may be low, this will leave the program with, at best, perhaps an 80 or 90 percent utilization rate.

There are three main systems by which parents pay. *Flat fees* assign a fixed direct cost of care to every parent. *Sliding fees* work on the principle that each parent contributes according to demonstrable ability. *Discretionary fees* come from one child's parent to pay for something other than that parent's child.

Differences between communities make it impossible to recommend or describe any one "right" parent funding approach. Often, all three types make their way into a program's management base. A successful parent funding blend makes use of the best of each.

Flat-fee systems. Once the precise per-child costs have been calculated, programs may divide these costs evenly between the parents of each child.

If a parent-run program's budget calls for $60,000 of annual operating capital, and if the program serves thirty children, each child's parent(s) would contribute $2,000 annually. In a variation, some planners will discount the cost of two children attending the same program, thereby increasing the relative per-child cost for those parents with only one child.

Imagine a restaurant that derives its daily income from the same thirty diners. If five of those diners decide to eat somewhere else, the restaurant loses 15 percent of its income every day until they return, or until five others decide to come in. To stay in business, the restaurant would have to charge its remaining twenty-five customers that much more. Programs solely dependent on parent funding can experience the same problems. Downswings in enrollment can cause untenably steep direct cost increases to remaining parents.

A flat-fee system works better when (1) in-kind resource contributions, such as program space and utilities, and successful external fundraising efforts serve to moderate program costs; and (2) the program administrator maintains and periodically updates a waiting list, working closely with the relevant resource-and-referral agency. (See School-Age NOTES' *Before and After School Programs* for sample calculations of flat-fee systems.)

Sliding-fee systems. Here, a graduated scale links a parent's direct payments incrementally to that parent's income level. If three families have respective annual incomes of $50,000, $38,000, and $17,000, the first family might pay 100 percent of scale, the second 75 percent, and the third 50 percent. If family income rises or falls into a new scale increment, the amount of the direct payment rises or falls accordingly.

Regarding sliding-scale design, two main approaches exist: (1) Higher-income families subsidize lower-income families, as in a parent-run program funded solely by parents; and (2) higher-income families directly fund the actual cost of their children's care, while lower-income families pay according to ability with the difference being covered by external funding sources.

The first approach keeps a program freer of potentially inappropriate regulatory compliance, and it cuts way down on paperwork and fundraising. However, long experience dictates that when people subsidize their personal acquaintances, it can cause friction and general dissatisfaction. Where parent tensions run high, the second approach can be more effective at maintaining parents' comfort with the funding system.

The task of making a sliding scale that works presents special challenges. Some of these challenges are strictly mathematical, and some concern program logistics. Some require pure sleight of hand. All call for pertinent solutions.

First, *obtain parents' financial and demographic data*. A common planning pitfall occurs when too many families come in at or near the bottom of an arbitrarily designed scale. This would leave the program woefully underbudgeted.

The challenge here is finding a way to get an accurate fix on parents' income. A lot of parents look at school-age care as glorified babysitting. They're not much interested in sharing their most intimate financial details with their babysitter. It's up to the PD—and the board, if there is one—to convince parents that SACC offers them more than they think it does. It means instilling some trust and confidence, not just sending out another questionnaire.

Next, *determine the adjusted cost of care*. Programs just starting up often can't do this. Per-child cost calculations reflect the machinations of fate. This takes some hard budget figures. Unless the PD has previous school-age experience in a comparable location, this could be too tough a nut to crack.

With at least a year of operation behind them, PDs can review actual cost figures. Derive a base figure by dividing the planned number of enrolled children into total projected expenses. Then, to account for under-utilization, bad debts, and other unpleasant surprises, add 15 to 20 percent to this base figure. Finally, divide this sum by the appropriate time unit— week, month, or day. The result represents an *adjusted per-child cost*. In a perfect world, this figure would be the top of the scale.

Go back and *reconcile parent data with the adjusted per-child cost*. What parents can afford and what they're willing to pay are usually two different numbers. Probably neither will match up with the adjusted cost figure. As business operators in the service marketplace, PDs may find themselves promoting one set of figures to their parents, then plotting outside resource development to compensate for actual costs.

Some PDs have reliable parent data. They can compute an *adjusted annual family income,* subtracting from gross income a fixed amount for each child, whether or not all children enroll. Others make a straight calculation using annual gross income and number in family; a family of two earning $10,000 pays the same as a family of four earning $12,000, regardless of the number of children. Subject to local and federal regulation, it's usually the PD's call. Eventually, this reconciliation process yields a relationship between the ideal scale top and an annual family income range.

Crunching the numbers takes some flexibility and imagination. If they stick too closely to government statistics, PDs may try to set the scale top between 105 percent and 115 percent of state median income, even though their local community median calls for something closer to 150 percent. This is a recipe for big trouble. Some directors assume that no program can operate unless at least 50 percent of parents pay at top rate, so they select the parents' reported median income as the scale-top cut-off. This usually doesn't work, either.

Tough-minded PDs assume that child care *deserves* a fixed percentage of family income. For example, with an adjusted annual per-child cost of $1,200 and an assertion that appropriate SACC consumes 5 percent of annual family income, these directors would plan to have families with annual incomes of $24,000 and up fund 100 percent of their per-child cost.

Set the bottom of the scale. In 1980, sliding-fee scales from SACC programs across the country generally set the bottom of their scales in the $5,000 to $7,500 family income range. In 1990, those floors had risen to the $8,500 to $11,000 range. In states that administer federal subsidies, some program administrators set eligibility for these funds as the cut-off. Some aim for a fixed percentage, just as they did for the top of the scale, and apply it to the bottom; but remember, the usual outcome of arbitrary design is a budget shortfall.

To *determine the rest of the increments,* Child Care Information Exchange editor Roger Neugebauer advises following this four-step approach:

1. To obtain the income increment (n), subtract the scale-bottom income figure (b_1) from the scale top (t) and divide the remainder by 9. That is, $(t - b_1)/9 = n$.
2. Work up the scale by adding the income increment to the scale-bottom figure to arrive at the next scale step (b_2). That is, $b_1 + n = b_2$. Repeat this procedure for each subsequent scale step, i.e., $b_2 + n = b_3$, $b_3 + n = b_4$, and so on.
3. To obtain the fee increment (f), subtract the lowest scheduled fee (l_1) from the full-cost fee (h) and divide the remainder by 10. That is, $(h - l_1)/10 = f$.
4. Work up the scale by adding the fee increment to the lowest fee to arrive at the next scale step fee (l_2). That is, $l_1 + f = l_2$. Repeat this procedure for each subsequent scale step.[2]

Properly executed, these steps result in matched income/fee increment pairs—a basic sliding scale. Chances are the first one won't be the one finally used. No one wants huge gaps between income steps or income categories that cover too wide a range. Probably, some fine tuning will still be in order.

Instead of a ten-increment scale, perhaps twelve would work better. To try it, simply adjust the Step 1 formula, replacing the number 9, which yields a ten-increment scale, with the number 11. Then adjust the Step 3 formula, replacing the number 10 with 12. Scales with six, eight, fourteen, or more increments are all mathematically possible.

Ask whether the program can realistically reach a break-even point, let alone a profit, with each possible scale. Decide whether parents at or near the scale bottom receive a reasonable reduction or whether scale-top figures need to be higher. At any rate, make the final scale simple, clear, and

Figure 5.1
After-School Program Sliding Fee Scale

Percentage of Cost	Daily Fees	Weekly Fees	Gross Annual Income
100%	$3.50	$17.50	$26,000–30,000
90%	3.15	15.75	23,000–26,000
80%	2.80	14.00	20,000–23,000
70%	2.45	12.25	17,500–20,000
60%	2.10	10.50	15,000–17,500
50%	1.75	8.75	12,500–15,000
40%	1.40	7.00	under 12,500

Note: The dollar amounts shown are for demonstration purposes only.

easy to understand at a glance. Figure 5.1 displays one program's final result.

For some parents, sliding scales carry a negative cultural connotation. These people find the idea of direct income–based subsidy either embarrassing or disquieting. Yet parents may still want an administrative alternative that permits the program to pick up financial slack in a particular case.

One way around the sliding-scale issue is to hide the subsidy in a separate budget line item. This line item can go by various names: "scholarship," "care cost credit," and so on. It yields authority to subsidize specific children's care on the basis of "hardship" or "extreme need," but only so far as the PD or program board sees fit. This relieves concern or embarrassment about direct financial relationships between funders and scholarship recipients.

The hidden subsidy system gives the PD two main administrative options: (1) in good times, to selectively apply parent payments toward less-well-off children's care costs; and (2) in tougher times, to abandon subsidy in favor of balancing the program budget for the benefit of full-cost funders. The PD also can offer care continuity in actual cases of extreme hardship or encourage cultural diversity by admitting children who might not otherwise afford service.

Though it is practical, the scholarship subsidy has an exclusionary air. It possibly gives administrators too much executive authority.

Some additional thoughts about sliding scales from experienced PDs follow:

- Set a ceiling on projected subsidies.
- Since parents and outside funders will ask (and sometimes complain) about the reasoning, establish a clearly reasonable and defensible rationale for the final scale.
- Remember to factor income tax/child care credit into the scale.
- If subsidy income is highly restricted, a partial scale for at-highest-risk families may have to suffice.

Discretionary funding. The third possible type of parent funding relates to the rather controversial proposition of economic democracy, a system that gives parents more say about where their money goes. This system respects parents' vested authority in the outcome of their children's program experience. It provides funds for specific program components that parents and children themselves deem valuable.

Take the case of a SACC program that offers four different care components: before-school, afterschool, school vacation care, and weekend care. For a variety of reasons, it seems unlikely that every single child enrolled in this program would be present at every single hour of program operation. Some might benefit only from the afterschool component, some from both before- and afterschool, some from before-school and vacation care but not afterschool.

In either the fixed-funded or sliding-scale systems, administrators might calculate per-child costs across all four components and divide by the number of operating hours. Having arrived at an hourly rate, they would set a minimum number of hours each enrolled child must be present for cost-effective care.

But the *specific* cost of before-school care might range much higher than afterschool care. Why? Once again, SACC is labor-intensive, so staff-child ratios for one component might be half again as low as another. And as far as other materials are concerned, even the average dollar cost of before-school breakfasts might stand four times as high as that of afterschool nutrition.

It makes perfect sense for such a program to base fees on the actual cost percentage of the specific components utilized. In this way, each care component consists of a self-contained economic unit, each one designed to support itself on an as-utilized basis. If one component runs into negative cash flow, the other three aren't necessarily threatened or impaired. Another advantage stems from increased capability to determine strong and weak areas of the program's finances. This allows administrators to allocate funds where they are needed.

To put a discretionary system into play, a program might include a list or blank line on its monthly payment coupons, indicating to parents that anything extra they wish to contribute they may assign for a specific purpose. Upon receipt of these funds, the PD then effects the purchase, credit, rental, or additional service indicated. After an option is implemented, parents may choose from subsequent service options.

Single-component programs might wish to expand service hours. Any program might wish to expand its materials acquisition capability, physical space, or daily menu. A discretionary funding system channels funds to the line item that most concerns parents and their children. It makes the program more fiscally responsive, empowering parents to make changes. This in turn earns continuing parent approval and support. What could be more service-oriented than a program that asks parents to decide what they want for their money?

Use or misuse of the term *scholarship* aside, the following item from the Edina Public Schools *KIDS Club News* in Minnesota (Vol. 11, No. 1, November 1990) nicely illustrates the potential of a discretionary funding policy:

> *We Care, We Dare, WE SHARE . . .*
> This fall all Kids Club parents were asked to indicate on your contract if you were willing to allow up to 2% of your fees to be used for scholarships for financially needy families. The response was overwhelmingly positive! (There were only ten families out of five hundred who declined.)
>
> Thanks to this vote of support, we will be able to provide assistance to eligible families who are on the waiting list for the state sliding fee subsidy and to families who are experiencing temporary financial disruption.

Programs that serve primarily low-income and at-risk children may benefit somewhat from federal voucher systems. But who will keep watch? Watered-down or nonexistent state-level oversight can leave parents to choose from unresponsive and inappropriate programs. A discretionary funding system facilitates a resource partnership between parents and providers, thereby instilling a higher degree of self-interest—and, potentially, self-esteem—for children and parents alike.

Would a program benefit from wholly discretionary funding? Probably not. Certain fixed costs remain in place for any program operation, costs that must be firmly ascertained and distributed back to program funders. To base a program's fiscal outlook entirely on its funder's changeable opinions would spell certain disaster.

Even more problematic might be achieving a practical result. One parent might be entranced with the idea of a costly item for which the majority of children have little desire or use. Still, the parent might insist on allocating discretionary funds toward its purchase. This would almost certainly require a little politicking.

However, after fixed costs are met and budgeted line items are balanced, implementing a discretionary funding system can offer all the described advantages. What's more, by increasing fiscal responsiveness, such a system might actually encourage an increase in the funding flow. What administrator could turn up a nose at that incentive?

When Parents Pay Fees (and When They Don't)

Many service businesses demand cash in advance. They do this in order to stem the onset of that most dreaded financial disaster, *negative cash flow*. When debts mount faster than income, that's negative cash flow. When someone has $200 in a checking account, then writes a check for $300, that's negative cash flow. "Buy now, pay later!" . . . *that's* negative cash flow.

For any SACC program to survive, it must avoid negative cash flow. Scheduling prepayments stops negative cash flow before it can start. Beginning the fiscal year with the cupboard full assures any SACC program of healthier operation.

However, preschool child care costs average 20 percent of parents' annual earnings. School-age care costs average only slightly less. Given that parents usually receive only portions of their earnings as a weekly or monthly paycheck, how many programs will be able to collect the entire annual amount all at once?

Programs can hold firm to a policy of total yearly prepayment when they serve primarily affluent parents, whose annual child care costs range around only 5 percent of annual income. Some affluent people accord greater respect to those goods and services that cannot be had on the cheap. They might not think twice about borrowing thousands of dollars for a new car or orthodonture. At the same time, they might gasp in amazement if so "lowly" an entity as a SACC program required them to invest in a comparable fashion.

To command respect—and perhaps thereby heighten its own level of professionalism—a care program must assert, both to itself and to its partners, that their children's emotional, intellectual, physical, and social development are at least as important as a new car or an orthodontic retainer. Multi-site programs that include both upper- and lower-scale neighborhood economies strengthen their overall administrative capabilities by hewing to this ability-to-pay procedure.

A program site that primarily serves children of middle-wage earners can better serve by offering quarterly or monthly participations. One such program provides parents with due-dated coupon books, much like the ones lending institutions use for repayment of loans. The SACC funding thus slips into a parent's monthly bill-paying cycle without causing undue distress.

Understandably, some parents can't handle either the idea or the actuality of prepayments. For them, other arrangements may be made on a case-by-case basis. In some instances, their children could be candidates for the benefit of a discretionary income policy. However, successful operation depends upon timely crediting of fee payments.

Parents who repeatedly ignore their billing, the ones who only get around to writing a check after several reminders from the bookkeeper, director, or treasurer—these chronic late-payers jeopardize a program's financial stability. After months of dunning phone calls to late-payers known to be financially able to pay, a director may have to ask parents to withdraw their children from the program. Of course, if things get to this stage, the children are the big losers. Avoiding conflict means anticipating it, and this holds true for late payment. Prior to enrollment, make it explicitly clear that repeated and unexplained fee avoidance cannot be tolerated. Create a standard sequence of fines and other program responses, and insert this information in the parent handbook (see Chapter 9). In the children's interest, a program funded by parents best benefits children of the timely payers who understand their social responsibilities to caregivers and other parents.

Special Parent Fees

They're not actually so special. In fact, they're pretty common. Most SACC programs deal with them on a daily or weekly basis. What makes them special is that they account for human idiosyncrasies, and what's more special than those?

• *Registration and deposits.* At registration, many programs request a nonrefundable amount of $10 to $50. Some administrators later apply this amount as a credit; others don't. In the latter cases, the fee defrays the cost of time and paperwork devoted on behalf of children who subsequently fail to enroll. Again, it's a method of engendering a little respect for the program.

Believe it or not, some parents withdraw their children from a program without settling their account. To insure against this, many programs set a non-negotiable figure for prepayment. The deposit amount must be high enough to compensate the program and low enough not to inhibit enrollments. Generally, an amount covering two weeks of service will dissuade opportunism.

• *Absences.* Program fiscal health depends on fiscal commitment. Costs are calculated on the assumption that any child may receive regular service on the same number of days each week. Some malls and bowling alleys have "care shops," where parents can pay by the hour, but most reliable programs can't base their budgets on this kind of retail unit pricing. When they enroll their children, parents agree to fund the *continuity of service*—whether or not their child attends on a particular day.

Some programs' policies allow children to take pre-planned absences, or "vacations," at a reduced cost. Some of the same programs also waive a portion of cost in the event a child's illness exceeds a pre-determined number of days. Seek mutual agreement to the elements of these policies, discuss them fully at enrollment time, then stick by them. In fairness to all, make exceptions truly the exception.

• *Whither the weather?* A Wisconsin blizzard, a New Mexico desert scorcher, or a Los Angeles smog alert can keep all the children home for the day. Under such circumstances, one program's parents demanded refunds totaling over $200. The program's administrators fought the demand, claiming its budget didn't allow for such claims. Earning ill will along the way, the program finally returned the money (negative cash flow!).

In such a case, an explicit understanding between SACC program and parents about acts of nature would have alleviated misunderstanding and financial hardship. Whatever the weather, rent costs and insurance premiums continue unabated, and caregivers have to eat, too. Program continuity for the children comes before a few snowflakes.

Programs can obtain their own insurance against earthquakes, lightning fires, tornadoes, and the like. Anything short of these comes under the category of "that's life." Set and publicize this policy accordingly.

• *Late pick-ups.* This trouble-causer joins unpaid fees as the most widespread procedural problem faced by SACC programs. In programs that don't provide group transportation service, parents occasionally run late, and sometimes it's understandable. A tractor trailer really does overturn on the freeway, or the boss really does make someone work overtime. But to keep program doors open for tardy parents can rack up extra operating costs, not to mention the imposition on caregivers' personal lives.

A sound policy speaks to this issue in an even-handed yet firm manner; in many cases, a small fine will remind parents to watch the clock. In other cases, it's program planning that may be causing the trouble. Perhaps a program compulsorily shuts its doors at 3 P.M. every Friday, regardless of parents' job-related commitments. Instead of fining the ones who don't meet the arbitrary deadline, this program's provider might normalize the situation by expanding hours of service, changing the site, or stepping up outside resource development.

When the same two or three parents show up late time and time again, fining them may not resolve the issue. Adults who generally behave in a more-or-less self-serving way won't have too many compunctions about exploiting program people's kindness. Only the most weak-willed directors knowingly allow such behavior to disrupt their programs indefinitely. If fines don't work, give the parent in question some personalized attention. Investigate the possibilities that a parent may be generally disorganized or experiencing some deeper difficulty that causes the chronic lateness. The situation may call for some sympathetic discussion and negotiation. This, too, is caregiving.

ACCOUNTS PAYABLE

The main reason for generating income is to cover the outgo. In addition to caregiver wages and salaries, all school-age programs incur other financial debts. What's the best way to take care of these ongoing obligations?

Probably the handiest device for paying the bills is a checkbook. In fact, one legal requirement of incorporation is that a separate bank account be established. For recordkeeping purposes alone, a checking account makes extremely good sense.

Will the same person who orders supplies and hires caregivers also write the checks to pay for them? Not always, and especially not in large multisite school-run programs. In these, where purchase requests and invoices are daily orders of business, a central accounting office generates payments by computer.

In small programs, it's often up to the PD either to play the role of *checkwriter* or to assign it to someone else. But some directors suffer from "mathaphobia," the irrational fear of rational numbers. In the typical mathaphobic, a temptation arises to leave all checkwriting, bill paying, and bookkeeping details to someone else who seems to enjoy such things. However, it's usually best to resist this temptation. Yielding such authority to one person is a dangerous move and can lead to very unpleasant financial surprises.

Mathaphobic or not, the smart way to go is to split accounts, so that no one person can freely access all program funds at the same time. Large agencies take this precaution as a matter of course, establishing separate accounts and separate books for each of their various service components. Where sizeable cash surpluses exist, account restrictions can help, that is, any check written for more than $200 can require two signatures.

Just as with incoming funds, payment records belong in as many places as seems practical. Canceled checks and the checkbook register alone don't prove sufficiently practical. For the role of checkwriter to run smoothly, create a system wherein (1) all payments get recorded at the time they are received; (2) all credits get recorded at the time they are received; (3) all like transactions get recorded together, that is, paychecks beside paychecks, supplies beside supplies, and so on. These practices can make a mathaphobic experience much less scary.

A payment system fits the scale of the program. A twenty-site program, managed from a central office, could conceivably assign all major payment authority to its central accounting personnel, with each site maintaining a *petty cash reserve* (see subsequent section on account reconciliation) for immediate and incidental expenses. A single-site program might combine all payment procedures into the PD's job description. And an umbrella agency connecting several site-managed programs might divide different types of payment as the partners see fit. In any event, what's right is what's appropriate.

Account Reconciliation

This job is otherwise known as seeing if the balance in the checkbook register matches the balance on the monthly bank statement, and it can't be postponed until someone feels like doing it. For one thing, quick identification of bank personnel error, computer error, or checkwriter error means quicker action; one zero in the wrong place can ruin the whole month. For another, keeping a monthly tab on expenditures aids budget analysis, which is discussed in Chapter 6. If only to ward off possible repetition of error, rotate the task assignment, giving the checkwriter a different account review partner each month.

Mismanaging the petty cash reserve can wreak some serious havoc. A PD might keep a small ceiling of anywhere from $20 to $50 on hand—more likely, in a locked cash box—specifically for small items, emergency purchases, or to reimburse someone for an approved out-of-pocket expense. Normally, if $5 goes out, a register receipt for $5 goes in, keeping the reserve amount constant. When the cash drops below a certain amount, the PD adds up the receipts and replenishes the reserve with an equal amount.

Too many regular excursions into the petty cash reserve can cause problems. If someone buys, say, $20 worth of food with petty cash every week, that's over $700 a school year that *won't* show up on the program food budget. At budget review time, at tax time, at any time, this loss of control won't look or feel good. Whoever regularly handles the petty cash reserve holds the responsibility for preventing such a situation from developing.

Paying the Full Cost of Care

As mentioned earlier, caregivers' pay accounts for as much as 85 percent of program income, which makes pay-out calculations and procedures basic to program viability. To determine annual tax liability, federal and state tax collectors want to know how program monies get spent, which makes these calculations and procedures doubly important. But most critical, caregivers' self-esteem, self-respect—indeed, their very lives—depend on their earnings. How can children—or anyone else—depend on care-

givers who can't depend on themselves? Clearly, pay-out is no trifling matter.

Public and community school-run programs, as well as corporate-run
programs, probably manage SACC people's earnings through pre-existing
computer payroll systems. The PD submits time cards or time sheets to a
central processing office, which in turn generates paychecks. Neither caregivers nor the PD probably have much to say about how this system operates; they can simply cooperate with it.

Either local child care R & Rs or the state's Department of Revenue can
provide information about specific state payroll regulations. For further
reference, see School-Age NOTES' *Before and After School Programs*. Its
"Budget and Payroll" section contains mathematical formulas and IRS form
numbers pertinent to the subject.

State and federal law require certain benefits that add to the direct cost
of labor. These benefits include unemployment insurance, workers' compensation, social security (FICA), and, in some states, paid training. Optional benefits can include paid or unpaid vacation and sick leave, group
medical and dental insurance, and contributions to pension funds.

As with direct pay, large computerized institutions have a big advantage
in putting together benefit packages. For example, if taken as a private
corporation, the Los Angeles Unified School District would easily rank
among the largest in the country. The district's massive personnel base
allows it to offer types and amounts of benefits smaller groups can hardly
match.

Benefits offered by freestanding programs vary with ability to pay. Here
again, the local resource and referral agency may help with suggestions
and options. The insurance company representative who handles program
liability coverage might also serve as a financial consultant. Prior to implementation, *discuss benefit alternatives with all concerned partners*.

In a labor-intensive business like SACC, financial management always
boils down to managing people. Badly managed finance leads to badly
wasted people. "[L]ow pay is also related to . . . staff turnover which, in
turn, undermine[s] the stability of child-adult relationships as well as nul-
lif[ies] in-service training efforts."[3]

POSITIVE CASH FLOW MANAGEMENT

Aside from a sprinkling of charitable contributors, all funding sources
require some type of semiannual or year-end financial report. Programs
linked to umbrella organizations, CBOs, school boards, and like institutions must submit financial summaries. A PD's efficiency often depends on
a financial overview of program operation. For all these reasons, the accountant or bookkeeper prepares a *monthly financial statement*, recording
all program income and expenses.

Properly executed, the financial statement demonstrates how actual income and spending compare with budget predictions. It's a way of presenting all the various entries from checkbooks, ledgers, journals, receipt books, and voucher records in a neat and manageable format. Every business prepares periodic statements, and once again, SACC is a business.

Monthly financial statement analysis aids the process by which program administrators and directors modify resource development as well as spending. In other words, it's how they make ends meet. With the limited total cash reserve of most SACC programs, mismanaged cash flow means unpaid bills, unreplaced equipment, and unemployed caregivers.

Positive cash flow management matches the timing of incoming funds with that of expenses. Putting the financial statement data alongside budget projections (discussed in Chapter 6), make continuous adjustments to scheduled fund intakes, payment of bills, and weekly or monthly caregiver pay dates. That is, create a situation in which available funds will cover costs.

Since 1983, child care management software programs have proliferated, giving SACC program financial managers a computer-age option. *Child Care Information Exchange (CCIE)* features an annual Software Buying Guide that compares functions of all currently available programs. *CCIE* editor Roger Neugebauer has this to say about software selection:

Before you go any farther in the selection process, take time to establish your priorities. Make a list of functions that a program absolutely must perform for you. This is your shopping list—don't be distracted by all the peripheral bells and whistles a program offers. If a program doesn't address your prime needs, pass it by.[4]

Why do so many program administrators and directors let cash flow problems eat them alive? Some try to establish an inflexible or "perfect" system that becomes more important to them than the results they're trying to achieve with it. When parent payments start coming in late, or when agency reimbursements get delayed by some technicality, a quick response in cash flow management procedures can avoid bigger problems. Continuing apace with an attitude that everything's going to be okay won't help the cash flow.

Another common mistake: Instead of making smaller monthly outlays, some PDs spend quite large sums of money all at once. Fearful that funds might dribble away later, they spend perhaps 80 percent of their equipment budget in September. Trying to beat inflation is one thing; tying a program down for the entire year is another. Maybe a little self-discipline can stretch a program's budget over a longer period of time.

Despite all efforts, cash flow problems sometimes arise. Consider this a normal occurrence, like an occasional allergy attack or a bursitis flare-up, and keep some "medicine" handy: a cash flow reserve account. Where feasible, establish a separate savings account with a rolling cash reserve. Like any other rainy-day account, deposit the equivalent of at least 4 to 6 percent of monthly program income. This percentage figures as an indirect cost for break-even programs, which means subtracting it like rent, food, and first aid supplies—*before* getting to zero balance. At the end of the program year, depending on tax regulations, the cash reserve might be rebated to parents or rolled over into the following year's operating budget.

For programs that are more dependent on state or federal funding, reimbursements sometimes take a lot longer than one would like. Voucher deficits have no direct cash management cure. However, using the program's state service contract as collateral, some programs may successfully obtain a short-term cash loan from a friendly lender. Loan application practices vary from lender to lender, but the particular state's solvency will play a big part in the lender's decision. As an "agent" of the state, programs may qualify for lower-interest loans. If pressed into this option, shop around for the best deal, but avoid lenders who are quick to say yes; if repayment problems arise, those same lenders may be even quicker to say, "Close."

The important thing is not to wait until negative cash flow cripples a program. Prepare for it as a cyclical inevitability. When it happens, be ready.

NOTES

1. Malvern J. Gross, Jr., and W. Warshauer, Jr., *Financial and Accounting Guide for Nonprofit Organizations,* 3d ed. (New York: John Wiley and Sons, 1979), p. 15.

2. Adapted from Roger Neugebauer, "Money Management Tools—Sliding Fee Scales," *Child Care Information Exchange,* No. 8 (June 1979), pp. 27–33.

3. Lillian Katz, *Talks with Teachers* (Washington, DC: NAEYC, 1977), p. 29.

4. Roger Neugebauer, "Fifth Annual Child Care Center Management Software Buying Guide," *CCIE,* November-December 1990, p. 53.

FOR FURTHER REFERENCE

Anthony, Robert N. 1988. *Essentials of Accounting.* Reprint. Reading, MA: Addison-Wesley.

Hayes, Rick Stephan, and C. Richard Baker. 1982. *Simplified Accounting for Non-accountants.* New York: Jove Books.

Kamoroff, Bernard. 1992. *Small Time Operator: How to Start Your Own Small Business, Keep Your Books, Pay Your Taxes, and Stay Out of Trouble.* Laytonville, CA: Bell Springs Publishing, Box 640 Bell Springs Road, 95454.

Paulos, John Allen. 1990. *Innumeracy: Mathematical Illiteracy and Its Consequences.* New York: Vintage Books.

Chapter 6

THE BUDGET

> Budget is policy. All our dreams and aspirations for what we want to accomplish for children, for families, for staff are expressed in the budget in the language of money. Every line item in the budget is a policy decision, which directly determines what the program will be. Whoever makes the budget makes those policy decisions.
>
> —Gwen Morgan, Wheelock College

WHICH CAME FIRST: THE CHICKEN OR THE BUDGET?

In the 1980s, for the first time in recorded Euro-American history, people started eating more chicken than beef. Did people suddenly discover they liked chicken better, did they change their diets to reduce cholesterol intake, or was there another factor involved? Perhaps its relatively lower price made chicken more attractive to shoppers on a budget—that is, shoppers trying to cut their costs.

But cutting costs isn't what Gwen Morgan has in mind when she observes that "budget is policy." She's talking about the financial planning tool used by both the wealthy and the struggling. This budget is a document, a well-informed record of somebody's wishful thinking, a prediction of how things might go if there were never any surprises. A budget is also absolutely essential, as it demonstrates that planners and administrators have some idea of what can go right—and wrong—during program operation.

Distressing to Morgan and others is the fact that child care and education budgets have spent so many years on a budget. Keeping costs low has led to low expectations, resulting in low levels of achievement. Too often, what resources have been available have gone to prop up antiquated and sagging institutions, rather than going to fulfill "our dreams and aspirations."

Imagine a SACC program as a vehicle, like a car. The budget represents a seacliff road. The back-and-forth process between making plans and getting money to carry out those plans likens to the car driver turning the wheel. A small curve takes a small correction, a big curve a wide correction. Too little concern for children's care, overambitious program design, failure to draw on every available resource . . . these budgeting mistakes are failures to correct for curves in the road. The driver's vehicle swerves either over the cliff or into a wall of rock.

Planning a drive means planning a route. Planning a SACC program means planning the budget, and vice versa. Neither is more or less important than the other. Both come first.

THREE YEARS AT A GLANCE

All but the most frivolous business operators want to stay in business, which means keeping an eye on the bottom line, not just from day to day but from one year to the next. Unless someone close to the program has a perfect way with tarot cards or crystal balls, the next best future-watching tool is the budget. At the outset, with so many things calling for immediate attention, it may seem handy to cast fate to the wind and hope the program will be around in a couple of years. But a *three-year budget plan* can make the difference between the flash-in-the-pan and the dependable service.

In Year One, programs just starting up incur a wide variety of one-time-only expenses, somewhat akin to a down payment. Building renovation, PD salary, playground equipment, tables and chairs, carpet, brochures, transportation vehicles—the list goes on and on. Sometimes, there's even a fee just to have a licensing agency representative come out and make a list of prerequisite expenses!

The *start-up budget* forms the basis for coping with the substantial initial outlay. It takes into account every conceivable expense a program might incur even before day one of operation. When funders wish to know how the program will affect their own budgets, the start-up budget will tell them.

A SACC program's start-up phase can consume six months or more. Incorporation takes time. Lining up funders and community resources takes time. Obtaining licenses and liability coverage takes time. It's true that in some cases community groups or agencies may offer special no-cost services, or they may select staff to work on start-up as part of their regular assignment. Start-up still takes time, and the budget must reflect this.

As part of the start-up phase, planners also create a *projected operating budget* for Year Two. This predicts the best-case and worst-case results of annual program operation. For example, when a program opens its doors, perhaps only 75 percent of those who registered will actually enroll. Worst-case planning accounts for underenrollment, best-case for full enrollment. This may sound like negative thinking, but a projected operating budget must assume that things sometimes go wrong.

By making it through the first two years, a SACC program has already beaten the odds. The *adjusted operating budget* for Year Three keeps the odds favorable. Over the life of a SACC program, each successive year of operation requires a renewed outlook on post-vacation start-ups and regular annual operation. Initial outlays at the beginning of each fiscal or program year may rise or fall. Program operating conditions may be subject to gradual or radical shifts. Successful adjusted budgets take into account not only immediate necessities or obvious requirements, but also the impact of inevitable change.

Program directors and administrators seeking outside funding have an extra point to consider. Funders don't often finance the whole ball of wax. Foundations may award grants for innovative projects, but they usually expect some other funders to enter the picture later. A local company may help with initial capitalization but balk at having to come up with money for operating expenses. Anticipating this can help in creating a systematic approach to the three-year budget plan.

The following discussion attempts to distinguish clearly between start-up items and those that fit in the operating budget. In practice, some overlap is bound to occur. Practical budgeteers make gentle corrections for curves in the budget road and keep a sharp eye out for oncoming traffic.

Budget Category #1: People

[The] myth is that almost anyone, if friendly, warm and breathing can develop and carry out a good program that meets the unique, complex, individual and group day care needs of school-age children. Of course, school-age children in family day care, group or center care need friendly, caring people supervising them, but they also need to be with adults who have knowledge and understanding of how children grow and develop—adults who can facilitate children's activities, encourage individuality, and stimulate ideas. Children need people who are interested in, feel responsible for, seeing that their day-to-day experiences take place in an environment which promotes growth and learning.[1]

Because SACC is labor-intensive, a good many planners and administrators follow a classic budgeting strategy. They pay their people as little as possible. To implement this strategy, they hire work-study students, interns, unprepared seniors, or inexperienced people right off the street. By keeping these hirees' weekly schedules below 17.5 hours, they save themselves from having to provide benefits or incentives. They invert state minimum regulations regarding staff-child ratios, turning what was intended as a floor into a ceiling. This, they believe, constitutes sound financial planning.

Of course, they are sadly mistaken.

Consider the "invisible" expense of this Scrooge-like strategy. As findings from the 1990 National Child Care Staffing Study indicate, low pay exacerbates caregiver turnover to the tune of a 40 percent national rate.[2] Over the long term, this translates to a marked increase in the costs of recruitment, hiring, and training.

Now consider the strategies employed by other in-service care-and-training businesses. For example, a university-affiliated training hospital maintains a core of competent, well-paid professionals. The hospital employs these knowledgable mentors to encourage and oversee the inexperienced students who constitute the majority of its medical staff. Neither the hospital or the university would dare consider an arrangement in which, without experienced guidance, students arbitrarily perform only the duties that please them. These institutions recognize the importance of and invest in professional caregiving.

What are the duties that SACC salaries are supposed to buy? In the economic sense, the act of caring corresponds with observable manual service, as in "taking care of business": preparing and serving food, helping change wet clothes, removing splinters from fingers. In another sense, the social sense, caring labor depends on an emotional involvement with the outcome of contact: listening to fears, expressing interest, soothing hurt feelings. These two definitions taken together form the socioeconomic role of the caregiver.

To be worthy of success, SACC programs must strive for no less. Budgeting for personnel costs hardly means penciling in minimum wages for whoever will take them. It means creating an economic model in which all the forms of care, be they performed manually or otherwise, are encouraged and reinforced.

A large program's human resource budget might assume costs along the following lines:

Salaries and Wages
1. Caregivers
   a. Primary team
   b. Intern(s)
   c. Back-up team

2. Administrative
   a. Director
   b. Administrative assistant
   c. Secretary
   d. Bookkeeper
3. Social services coordinator
4. Health service coordinator
5. Food service coordinator
6. Maintenance engineer
7. Transportation coordinator

Benefits
1. FICA
2. State unemployment
3. Group health/illness leave
4. Personal/holiday leave
5. Other

Professional Development
1. In-service training
2. Community outreach activities
3. Professional association memberships
4. Performance review and assessment
5. Subscription to professional publications

Budget Category #2: Space and Utilities

Thanks to the debt-fueled spending sprees of the 1980s, upwardly spiraling rental prices resulted in a nationwide glut of overpriced space. Indebting themselves far beyond reasonable limits, many city governments and public schools have skirted or surrendered to total bankruptcy. At this writing, the direct cost of occupancy in any given area can fluctuate dramatically.

Just by virtue of stepping forward as a potential occupant, an independent SACC planner may very well have an upper hand in rental price negotiations. No longer does a limited budget force a program to seek economic refuge in dank basements or burned-out gymnasiums. Many far more attractive physical locations may be standing empty, their owners more in need of a dependable tenant than in the proverbial big bucks.

Budgeting for rent normally plays off against transportation costs, which seem inconvenient and sometimes astronomical when compared with locating a program in low-cost or no-cost public school space. The other part of this trade-off has been a perception that parents would inherently trust the school building more than they would an alternate site. Considering economic conditions, and in the spirit of the partnership model, the cost/reward ratio may actually favor siting a program *outside* the school.

As to whether parents trust a particular school facility, assess the reality from CANARI-based information.

Also in the past, setting down in schools was widely perceived as a way of reducing potential costs of remodeling and state-regulated renovation. A local licensing authority may have specific requirements about exit doors, second-story windows, or number and location of bathrooms. Schools were thought to offer convenient compliance. Again, given the deterioration of many obsolete urban and rural school structures, perhaps the cost/reward ratio of bringing up to par an alternative site outweighs other options.

Rental charges may vary according to time of year and daily times of operation. So may associated maintenance engineering costs, which are often tied to union contracts. Before finalizing this budget category, check with the lessor or site provider for what restrictions may be imposed by less-cooperative third parties.

Rent fee calculations must account for occupancy prior to the first day's operation. It can take anywhere from two weeks to two months or longer to prepare the program site base for daily operation. Naturally, first-year start-ups are looking at higher one-time costs.

Rental pricing options fall into three main categories:

No cash. Naturally, any cost savings that reduces parent payments, increases caregivers' income, or otherwise helps the budget is always most welcome. If a school, church, or other space provider will arrange to waive all rental charges, so much the better. Such an arrangement can occasionally be made with generous building owners, or when space providers sponsor their own activities during SACC hours.

Flat or fixed charges. Some space providers may say they'd like to donate free space but don't have the leverage. Others may not wish to get into tricky calculations but still want some income. Others may just stick to the *market rate,* the same amount they normally charge anyone. Once negotiated, the rate remains constant from month to month—until, like all prices seem to do, it goes up.

Area-based fees. This type of charge usually reflects the cost of maintaining space that the program utilizes. For example, a licensed program that serves a maximum of 26 children might have to provide a per-child minimum of 35 square feet. The school rooms the program occupies may be larger—say, 1,000 square feet—but the school could charge the program only for the space utilized—that is, 35 square feet per child for 26 children, or 800 square feet. With this formula, the program keeps charges within reason and the school recovers its maintenance costs. If more children enroll, the rent increases proportionally.

If this is negotiated advantageously, not every part of the building figures into the area-based formula. Use of areas outside the basic space sometimes takes a separate negotiation. Bathroom and sink space don't count at all.

Area-based fee negotiations call for caution. What initially looks good on paper can end up costing the program its financial stability. In one city, twelve separate groups of parents were running programs in twelve elementary schools. The largest served sixty children. The smallest, at a thinly enrolled school, served only fifteen children in an area much larger than licensing would have required. If the twelve had been linked by a common area-based fee policy, and had they failed to negotiate into licensing standards, the smallest program could have ended up having to charge its children's parents four times what the largest program charged its parents.

Utility costs also affect program base site selection. Each program or program site carries with it a *utility cost floor,* the dollar amount with which adequate lighting, heating, water/sewer service, food preparation, and equipment operation can be maintained. Through applied conservation techniques, these costs can often be reduced. Low-wattage bulbs can replace power-gobblers without sacrificing luminesence. Gas companies often insulate water heaters and pipes at no additional charge to the consumer. If the site under consideration has been occupied previously by another company or group, past utility records can suggest some idea of usage patterns. Utility companies can also provide helpful information about anticipated rate changes.

Whether or not it is required by rule, a telephone represents the program's lifeline to the outside world. So that parents and program people can easily communicate, especially in the event of an emergency, make room in the budget for telephone equipment and service. Those programs concerned about untoward calling practices can contract with the local carrier for lock-out or coded service, but self-discipline costs less.

A CBO-run program might set this category's lines this way:

Site Rental
1. Monthly/quarterly fee due the lessor
2. Start-up preparation occupancy (annual)
3. Water/sewer (if not included)

Occupancy
1. Renovation/construction
2. Electricity
3. Heating fuel
4. Telephone

Budget Category #3: Durable Equipment

All items of a more-or-less lasting nature go into this part of the budget. This includes:

- Food storage and preparation equipment
- Activity materials (such as chairs, tables, couches, playspace equipment)
- Administrative materials (including file cabinets, typewriter, calculator, disk drives)
- Cleaning supplies (such as buckets, mops, brooms)

As the prices of new, used, and borrowed items vary, so will this budget entry.

Create a separate budget sheet for each of the four main equipment line items, then enter the totals for each of them in the overall program budget. This makes for more manageable calculations. Generally speaking, programs incur the lion's share of their equipment costs at start-up. Once a program is up and running, these costs tend to flatten considerably until the time of major expansion or improvement. Ask the program accountant for details about *amortization and depreciation* in regard to durable goods expenses, and consult current U.S. and state tax laws: Over the long run, a single purchase can make the difference between a budget that works and one that doesn't.

Budget Category #4: Consumable Goods

As opposed to the lifetime of durable goods, consumables consist of supplies that may only last a lunchtime. The categories remain the same as for durable goods, but food costs deserve a separate line listing.

Sub-category #4A: Food and Snacks

These can really eat into a budget (pun intended), not to mention their potential for spillage, messes, and the inevitable flying cookie toss contests. To cut fuss and costs, some unimaginative caregivers rely on crackers, peanut butter, and apple juice five days a week. But a variety of colorful, flavorful, USDA-approvable foods can make their way into any SACC program—without constipating the budget or the children.

Parents may not, will not, or cannot supply their children with a day's worth of adequate nutrition. Recognizing this, the USDA provides some meal funding for programs that comply with certain health and nutrition standards. This may be the one program area in which adults have to draw a firm line and ignore children's prescriptions. Heavily sugared foods and drinks have come to totally dominate many children's diets and conscious thoughts, making it absolutely mandatory for SACC caregivers to take appropriate measures.

The USDA child care food program may be of some help. At this writing, each parent's income determines whether their children may receive free, reduced-price, or no subsidized meals, so funding can be obtained even if not every child is eligible. Check with the appropriate local or state agency that administers this program for current eligibility guidelines.

Some smaller programs, especially those with no more than two or three caregivers, seem to like to lump together all the consumable expenses—pepper, pots, paper, and field trip expenses—into one total amount. Some difficult overlap can also occur when a curricular activity, such as cup cooking, happens to involve food preparation. Unfortunately, government record-keeping can't account for the true diversity of a given life experience, so mixing together all consumable costs can cause cash flow problems down the road. For purposes of state and federal reimbursement, keep clearly separate expense records for food.

Sub-category #4B: Non-Food Consumable Goods

As with durables, the initial expense of stocking up on consumables far outweighs the expense of replenishing them during the year. Ordering supplies just before day one can move the cash outlay from a tight start-up budget into the operating budget, but there remains the question of whether the crayons, paint, and tools will arrive on time.

On the other hand, ordering supplies in bulk, well before day one, can offer the dual advantage of a quantity discount and a plank for securing additional start-up funds to cover operating costs. The downside here is less choice and flexibility over the course of the year.

Gerry Loney, a founder of the Thunderburg program in Vermont, describes his very personal experience of budgeting for non-food consumables:

One aspect of independence is related to explore and create, to find out what happens if, and to make mistakes. Both the art room and the shop became places where this kind of freedom existed. . . . For a long time, I was bothered by what I saw in these two areas. The kids would use the materials and tools in vast quantities and not care about what they made. They'd throw their things away or forget about them. I felt that things were being wasted, and I also wanted them to care about what they made. Then I came to realize that they weren't so much making a product as *exploring the processes, the materials, and the tools they were using* [emphasis added]. It became important to have large amounts of cheap or free materials that the kids could use without restriction. In the art room, these were paper scrounged from printing shops, newsprint for the easels, tempera and water color paints, markers, crayons, pencils and popsicle sticks. In the shop, the unlimited materials were scrap wood from lumber yards and construction sites, wonderfully shaped and various small pieces of wood bought from a nearby toy company for one dollar a gunny sack full, nails, and glue.

"Connect Four" is a popular game with my kids. Within two weeks of its purchase, however, the flimsy plastic frame was broken. Philip and Eric, then first-graders, and I made a wooden frame, and the game is now in its third year of use. . . . A press used for book binding and plant pressing was made for about $1.50

worth of hardware. . . . A lacing board which costs over ten dollars cost us less than fifty cents to make, and some alphabet worms which cost seven dollars cost us nothing.[3]

As the Thunderburg experience illustrates, what initially looks like a consumable cost can actually be transformed into durable goods savings!

Typewriter ribbons, stationery, postage stamps, and staples get used up, too. So do bars of soap, sponges, and non-abrasive cleansers. Consumable administrative costs vary with the seasons, higher at annual start-up time or when funding proposals come due, lower during holidays and breaks. Consumable cleaning costs also vary with the weather. Calculate this figure accordingly.

Budget Category #5: Transportation

School-Age Notes' *Before and After School Programs* contains a sample projected operating budget. While the sample is slanted toward school-sited programs, it *assumes* that someone else will somehow handle transportation. It *assumes* that someone else will bear the full cost of getting children to and from the program site. It reflects zero expenditure on program transportation. This sample illustrates the short shrift so many SACC planners give this line item.

Often, a reasonable per-child cost of transportation can be found above this imaginary "ceiling zero." Dollar costs can be redistributed, not only through taxes or increased fees, not only through agency reimbursements, not only through corporate donations, but through all these methods and more. Outright purchase, renting, leasing, factory-financing, bank-financing, borrowing for the day—for as many ways as there are to finance a motor vehicle, that's how many ways a SACC program can budget transportation.

See Chapter 11 for an in-depth analysis of this planning factor. In the meantime, see the similarity here between budgeting personal transportation and SACC program transportation:

Vehicle(s)
1. Direct costs
    a. Outright purchase/down payment (start-up)
    b. Time/lease payments (operating)
    c. Carrying/interest costs (operating)
    d. Up-front repairs/modifications (start-up)
2. Fuel and fluids
3. Vehicular/liability insurance
4. Maintenance
    a. Regular
    b. Exceptional/emergency

   c. Parking/storage
   d. Licenses and operating fees

Event-related
1. Off-site adventures ("field trips")
   a. Event fee
   b. Shared/alternate transport (city bus, tram, etc.)
2. Cooperative/intramural activities
   a. Event fee
   b. Shared/alternate transport

Staff Travel
1. Direct costs (parking fees, etc.)
2. Contingency costs

Budget Category #6: Publicity and Advertising

To stretch an analogy, "publicity" is to "advertising" as "socio" is to "economic." While both are necessary for a business to survive, advertising gets the respect that goes with direct economic exchange, while publicity often goes begging for goodwill. Many large corporations maintain their public relations activities at a marked distance—in space, philosophy, and budget—from their advertising. At its best, a SACC program blends the two with concerted zeal.

Program *publicity*—that is, making others aware of the program—begins with the CANARI (see Chapter 2). No matter how great a community's demand for SACC, new programs' successful start-ups depend on efficient publicity work that capitalizes and builds on the foundation laid by the CANARI. For some reason, building public support often takes a little longer than anticipated, as long as six months or even a year before day one of operation.

Raising public awareness of the program also includes purchasing space in newspapers, renting billboards, and buying broadcast airtime, all of which constitute *advertising*. Ad costs run higher at start-up, as well as any other time a program seeks a new client base, increased funding, or new caregivers.

The ways in which publicity and advertising information ricochets around the various planning factors make it difficult to pinpoint precise, quantifiable outcomes. Even the major multinational corporations have no exact way of knowing how many extra deodorant sticks or cans of beer they sell after a thirty-second spot during the Super Bowl. Instead, they depend on the presumed outcome of viewer exposure. So must a SACC program.

A very basic way to outline this category's costs might be:

Publicity and Advertising
1. Community research

2. Analysis/identification of clients/funders
3. Preparation of publicity campaign
    a. Planning
    b. Materials
4. Preparation of advertising campaign
    a. Planning
    b. Materials
5. Dissemination

Budget Category #7: Legal and Licensing

No SACC program can afford to operate without adequate insurance coverage. Whether a program is covered through an umbrella agency's policy, by lump-sum start-up monies, or through billing as part of the operating budget, *liability insurance must be secured in advance of operation*. There are no exceptions.

Many of those who collect workers' compensation, or work-related injury benefits, mistakenly believe that they themselves have paid for this insurance while they worked. What some states do require is a deduction for a state disability insurance (SDI) pool, which provides a pittance to those who suffer a verifiable injury not covered by any other form of health or major medical insurance. In fact, the employer pays all the premiums for workers' compensation, and payments are legally mandated. An insurance agent can provide cost estimates for program administrators who are not already familiar with the figures.

Some states require fees for inspection and licensing of day care facilities. This may be a one-time-only payment, or it may be an annual expense. Consult the appropriate state licensing agency for specifics.

An annual independent audit of the program's finances may not be required by law, but it's a good idea to do it anyway. Foundations and other grant-making organizations may insist on such an audit for their own purposes. In any event, the audit results will certify the propriety—or reveal the impropriety—of the program's financial management. Private costs for an independent audit can run as high as $1,000. Programs that qualify may seek accounting services as a *pro bono* client, at low or no cost. If no other opportunity presents itself, the local chapter of the American Accountants Association might help identify an appropriate firm.

From incorporation to caregiver contracts, programs can also incur legal expenses. See Chapter 12 for more on these.

Legal and Licensing
1. Insurance
    a. Liability, required
    b. Liability, optional
    c. Workers' compensation

2. License-related
   a. Inspection
   b. Operating
3. Accounting services
   a. Annual financial statement preparation
   b. Tax filing preparation
   c. Independent annual audit
4. Legal services
   a. Incorporation (start-up)
   b. Contract preparation/review
   c. Special circumstance

Budget Category #8: Other Expenses

Any predictable cost that doesn't quite fit into any other budget category counts as an "other expense." For example, a program may encounter negative cash flow. To compensate, administrators might secure a short-term institutional loan for the program's operating fund. The budget must then reflect the periodic repayment of that loan as an "other expense" item.

Membership in the National School-Age Child Care Alliance (NSACCA) or a state SACC coalition requires a payment of dues. Some program materials might "magically" disappear. The program director might apply for defrayment of a personal expense borne as a direct result of a disgruntled client, yet filing an insurance claim may not be a good idea. These are all examples of other expenses.

For budgeting extraordinary costs, the highly arguable rule of thumb points to a figure around 7 percent of program net income. Of this amount, whatever doesn't go to these miscellaneous costs can always be moved at a later date to the program's rolling cash reserve, or to another budget item that could stand some shoring up. Not budgeting for these other expenses may mean leaving an otherwise beautifully designed program up a cash-dry creek without a paddle.

Budget Category #9: Income

To understand the relationship between income and expenses, it may help to consider a technique practiced by the pyramid builders of ancient Egypt. In order to transport monumental slabs of stone across the desert sands, huge wooden rollers were laid out along the intended path. Of course, it would have been impractical to lay miles of rollers ahead of one slab that wouldn't arrive for months. Only a limited number of rollers could be used propitiously at any given time. They had to be quickly removed from behind after the slab had been dragged over them, then quickly moved up ahead to form the future path.

With regard to a SACC program, income represents the rollers that keep the weight of expenses from sinking into the sand. To keep the program moving forward, planners and administrators must first determine the size, weight, and reasonable amount of time the program represents, after which they may formulate "income rollers" of a length and shape appropriate to the tasks at hand. In other words, a successful program requires equal doses of imagination and income.

Of all budget categories, income is probably the least predictable. Expenses tend to vary in accordance with available or anticipated income, but rarely does income conveniently rise to meet expenses. Income can be accurately measured only *after* it has been received. Chapter 5 discusses parent funding, the primary source of most programs' income. Chapter 7 takes up other types of income sources.

MAKING SENSE OF A BUDGET

When numbers have been filled in on a spreadsheet, program budgeteers might believe the process to be complete. True, data has been collected, and projected costs and income laid out. But how is anyone besides a number-cruncher supposed to understand this information?

The math sounds simple enough. Add up the totals from the first eight categories. Subtract that number from Category 9. Nonprofit organizations hope right away for a result that equals zero. Others add a tenth budget category, *profits,* subtract that from income, and then hope for zero. Either way, they're all looking for the financial crossroads of program operation, the breakeven point, where income exactly matches costs. Hoping for it is one thing. Finding it is called *budget analysis.*

An analysis describes the fiscal intents of planners, administrators, and directors. It is the budget's numerical content expressed verbally, and it helps to put a budget's projected results and consequences into concrete terms. It also explains how to arrive at the breakeven point.

Budget analysis begins with understanding the three basic types of *cost variation:* fixed, variable, and semivariable.

Programs always incur *fixed costs,* which remain constant no matter how many children enroll. Even though the prices of electricity and insurance may rise, the necessity of meeting these costs remains fixed. Usually, there is little room for any negotiation.

Administrators sometimes seek to reduce the amount of fixed costs by accepting donated or below-market-cost space, maintenance, and utilities. A school system or sponsoring agency may couch these costs together under the banner of an *indirect cost rate,* which it calculates as a percentage of the program's total budget. By any name, these are still fixed monetary obligations. Transferring the responsibility for fixed costs in this manner generally leads to a program's loss of administrative authority. Overall program integrity depends on the degree to which a program assumes its own fixed costs.

Variable costs derive from specific program characteristics: number of children, hours of operation, food costs, material supplies, and the like. Unlike the impersonal fixed costs, variable costs account for how people actually live during program hours. And these costs can be determined more closely by program people than can fixed costs, with which a program may be "stuck." Failure to address the importance of variable costs often results in heated, well-lit, furnished space in which very little pleasant activity ever takes place.

Semivariable costs straddle the line between fixed and variable. In a SACC program budget, caregivers' salaries and benefits make up the majority of semivariable costs. For example, in the event planners opt for a nominal 1:8 caregiver-child ratio, two caregivers must be on hand for a program with anywhere from twelve, up to sixteen, back down to twelve children. That is, caregiver costs stay the same even when enrollment decreases. In the same example, if enrollment rises to eighteen, might a third caregiver be brought in—only to be summarily dismissed if enrollment drops back to sixteen?

As must be clear, budgeters carry more than a fiscal responsibility when they approach analysis of the breakeven point. They must also consider the human cost of clinging dogmatically to fixed costs or arbitrary ratios. For example, cynically banking on an endless pool of human resources to be had at below-market wages belies any mission statement about human value. Such cynicism will almost inevitably show up in the budget analysis.

From a strictly financial perspective, the breakeven point occurs where income equals cost. From a human perspective, the breakeven point occurs where each program partner's energy expenditure equals the care that each receives. A successful program strives for both.

Income, or *revenues,* usually derives from the number of enrolled children and the amount charged for each child's care. For the purpose of proper breakeven calculation, semivariable costs receive the same treatment as fixed costs. With this in mind, breakeven formulas can be expressed using these abbreviations:

BE = Breakeven Enrollment
CR = Revenues per Child
AR = Average Variable Cost per Child
VC = Total Variable Costs
FC = Total Fixed Costs

One way to express the breakeven point is:

$$BE \times CR = VC + FC$$

But to use this formula, variable cost first must be determined from another formula:

$$VC = AR \times BE$$

With substitution, the first formula becomes:

$$BE \times CR = (AR \times BE) + FC$$

Now solving algebraically, a new equation arises:

$$BE = \frac{FC}{(CR - AR)}$$

If all these formulas seem unsettling, plugging in some actual numbers will help. For example, take a program with a budget based on an assumed enrollment of 30 children. With a total of $2,400 in fixed monthly costs, a per-child charge of $100 per month, and an average variable cost of $40 per month, popping in the numbers comes out this way:

$$BE = \frac{2,400}{100-40} = \frac{2,400}{60} = 40 \text{ children}$$

Clearly, there's a bit of a discrepancy between the assumed enrollment of 30 and the 40 needed for breakeven. Rather than ignore this disaster in the making, planners can pursue alternatives. A few changes they might consider could be:

1. Raise the tuition $20 per month:

$$BE = \frac{2,400}{120-40} = \frac{2,400}{80} = 30 \text{ children}$$

2. Lower the fixed costs to $2,000 monthly:

$$BE = \frac{2,000}{100-40} = \frac{2,000}{60} = 34 \text{ children}$$

3. Lower the variable cost per child by $10 monthly:

$$BE = \frac{2,400}{100-30} = \frac{2,400}{70} = 34 \text{ children}$$

While the budget exists only on paper, every option can receive fair consideration *before* lives are affected. Major decisions can be simulated on spreadsheet programs to the detriment of nobody. While there are no reasonable guarantees of fiscal tranquility, budgets are far more easily analyzed and repaired in advance of implementation. And resource development heavily depends upon a thoroughly reasonable budget.

NOTES

1. Docia Zavitkovsky, "Children First: A Look at the Needs of School-Age Children," *School-Age Child Care, Programs and Issues* (Urbana, IL: ERIC/EECE, 1980), p. 6.

2. M. Whitebook, C. Howes, and D. Phillips (1990), "Who Cares? Child Care Teachers and the Quality of Care in America," final reprint of the National Child Care Staffing Study (Oakland, CA: Child Care Employee Project).

3. Gerry Loney, *Thunderburg: An After-School Program* (Addison County, VT: Addison County Vocational Center, 1979), pp. 25–27.

FOR FURTHER REFERENCE

Hyypia, Erik, and the editors of *Income Opportunities*. 1992. *Crafting the Successful Business Plan*. Englewood Cliffs, NJ: Prentice-Hall.

Neugebauer, Roger, ed. Undated reprint. *The Best of Exchange #2: Tools for Managing Your Center's Money*. Redmond, WA: Exchange Press.

Spurga, Ronald C. 1987. *Balance Sheet Basics: Financial Management for Nonfinancial Managers*. New York: New American Library.

Chapter 7

THE MONEY-GO-ROUND

As evidenced by Figure 7.1 below, parent-sourced money—tuition and fees—finances the vast majority of programs. But between a quarter and a third of these programs meet their budgets by blending in public and private funds. The challenge of balancing a budget in this way goes by the technical name of *resource development*. Some simply call it fundraising.

Becoming an effective fundraiser means becoming knowledgeable about all the various funding sources. It also means learning to play the fundraising game.

But why bother?

Some providers just don't. Some PDs and boards find management easier without the troubles or indignities of fundraising. They opt out of proposal writing, completing endless forms in sextuplicate, and "making nice" with every checkwriter in town. If the occasional bake sale will put them over the top whenever they want a few extras for the children, that's fine. They've already achieved their idea of resource development: paying the bills when they come due.

Probably not too many SACC programs sit in a rooftop garden with a skyline view, treating the children to gourmet cuisine, paying the care-givers top dollar, and investing in income property on the side. In fact, probably none do. When it comes to school-age care, a whole lot less passes for "quality." The fact is that effective resource development can benefit *any* program, no matter how adequate it appears to be.

Some fundraising techniques involve a lot of effort for a minimal return. Everybody knows about school carnivals and car washes. The very lucky

Figure 7.1
Reported Funding Sources of 130 SACC Programs

Funding Source	Used by
Tuition and Fees	95%
Private Contributions	35%
State Government	30%
Child Care Food Program	25%
Local Government	25%
Federal Government	11%
In-Kind Donations	9%

Source: Fern Marx, *SACC in America: Final Report of a National Provider Survey,* Working Paper No. 204, Wellesley, MA: Wellesley College Center for Research on Women, 1990.

ones take in a few hundred dollars. There's the famous get-really-rich-people-to-write-big-tax-deductible-checks method, which only works for someone who knows really rich people. Some local groups and clubs budget a little something for community service out of their membership dues. Put it all together, and a single-site program might be able to pay its December heating bill.

Successful resource development does more than pay the bills. It puts the program on the map, gives the program an economic place in the community. It shows parents, school boards, and local leaders that the program doesn't intend to vanish when times get a little tough. It makes the program a real-life, honest-to-goodness investment vehicle, not only in the eyes of potential funders but for the program's own people as well. When a program's own people take SACC seriously, they get taken more seriously, and that usually means attracting even more investment and support.

A key concept here is *flexibility*. Parents and children may come and go. Political favor may waver. In this day and age, no program can count on a single source for unswerving financial support. Programs that rely too heavily on one source live or die by that source's daily fortunes. The funding mix created by successful resource development spreads the risks, giving programs a cushion against singular adversity.

THE FIVE FUNDING ATTRACTORS

There's an understandable nervousness that goes along with asking some unknown funder a thousand miles away for a few thousand dollars. Most of that nervousness comes from not knowing what might make that person say no, and there's no way around feeling it. However, there are five main reasons why funders say *yes*. Knowing the funding attractors can temper the nervousness and get resource development activities up and running.

• *Poverty has a lock on the neighborhood.* SACC programs aren't the only ones with mission statements. From federal funding acts to corporate foundations, the entrenched underclass usually gets priority consideration. To describe this interventionist policy, some use the term *entitlement*. Others employ the broader concept of *global economic competitiveness*, referring to benefits for American society as a whole. In any event, many funders channel resources toward populations that are at risk from the ills of poverty.

• *The program's agenda matches the funder's.* Aside from intervention, other objectives may appeal to a funder. For example, in 1990, city leaders in Dubuque, Iowa, put into play a courageous drive to attract non-white residents. Theoretically, a SACC program aimed at serving this sought-after population would benefit from city leader support. Such support might involve both political friendship and direct financial contribution. Think imaginatively about how program priorities, goals, and clientele characteristics might fit with funders' expressed interests.

• *Program people enjoy a rapport with funders.* As always, people do business with people they like and trust. Call it personal charisma or political savvy, but whatever it's called, it attracts money.

• *Innovation excites.* Funders often are looking for new approaches, new systems designs, new principles for action. The well-worn term *cutting edge* describes the place where some programs may seek foundation and corporate resources.

• *Proven formulas get proven support.* In contrast to innovation investors, some funders want "the sure thing" on their balance sheets. They look at a program's stability and longevity. They also like to see *outcome studies,* the quantified results of program impact on children's growth and development.

BEWARE THE WINDFALL SYNDROME

At any given time, some funders want to get involved in a big way. They want to make a big splash on behalf of a narrow purpose. So, rather than distributing smaller amounts of money to many programs, they focus their funding on a few. For instance, to show how a SACC program can promote literacy, the U.S. Department of Education might allocate several million dollars for five or ten demonstration projects.

Pursuing special project funds takes time. Some program providers regularly employ sophisticated grantspeople who scan the *Federal Register* and foundation reports for these types of grants. While this gives them an edge, it doesn't rule out a smaller provider's chances.

The "big" grant sounds good. With that much money, programs can add new service components, expand hours of operation, increase enrollment, remodel, and update durable goods. It's a little like winning the lottery.

As with any windfall, there's a downside. Suddenly given the opportunity to spend like the wind, programs expand to unsustainable proportions. It seems like the funding will never end—*but it will*. No grant lasts forever. As the expiration date approaches, a mad scramble ensues. Can the grant be renewed? Can another funder be interested in maintaining the new levels of expenditure? Entire programs have been built out of thin air around such grants. When the grants end, they disappear into the nothingness from which they came.

So, in practice, big grants don't normally strengthen the foundations of solid program service. The usual net effect—one of rapid expansion and sudden painful contraction—hardly justifies the time, cost, and human resources that getting such grants involves. Though it may seem hard to believe, there can be such a thing as too much money.

THE PUBLIC SECTOR

At all levels of government—federal, state, county, and local—certain agencies administer funding that can go for school-age care. Some funding can go directly for care, some for caregiver training, some for building maintenance and repair. It all depends on the funding source, the agency that administers it, whose children the program serves, and how soon the next elections are.

Finding a path through the public funding sector can be a daunting challenge. SACC people who remember that their involvement with a program is a political act always stand a better chance of getting funded. They maintain a constant political presence, use public relations strategies, engage in information sharing. What they don't do is roll over.

State and Federal Funding

The Tenth Amendment to the Constitution reserves to the states all rights not expressly granted to the federal government. That goes for child care, too. Federal funding may originate in Washington, but the state governments administer it along with their own state's monies.

Each state's allocation of federal funds differs according to U.S. Census statistics, primarily population and income levels. Most federal sources, though not all, invoke eligibility requirements as well. These generally address risk intervention among the disadvantaged and the young, with drug use, drop-out rates, and transmittable diseases ranking high on the list. Some state administrators don't like eligibility requirements, matching fund policies, or red tape, so they choose to administer only particular federal funds.

In the child care universe, school-age care is only one little star cluster. When a state government decides how and where to spend child care money, it might not allocate substantial funding for before- and afterschool programs. Because of the scarcity of new child care dollars, fierce competition always arises. It is indeed ironic that the people charged with teaching children how to share haven't yet learned the lesson themselves.

Government funding agencies solicit inquiries in two ways. When federal monies are being made available, the news appears in the *Federal Register*, a weekly publication from the U.S. Government Printing Office. Federal and state agencies also put out a clarion call in the form of a *Request for Proposal* (RFP). Each RFP details one or more public funding opportunities and invites organizations to submit proposals.

In 1992, some SACC programs were technically eligible for these well-known federal funds:

• *The Federal Dependent Care Block Grant Program (DCBG)*. States distribute the grants primarily as seed money for providers seeking start-up capital. DCBG funds may also go toward program expansion, new sites, technical assistance, and professional development for SACC caregivers. If not administered directly through the governor's office, DCBG monies come by way of a state agency (e.g., Department of Education, Department of Social Services), that is responsible for children, youth, and family policy.

• *Social Services Block Grant (SSBG)/Title XX*. These funds provide major support to low-income families seeking school-age care. Each state receives a lump sum and then allocates dollars as it sees fit. Each state also sets eligibility according to income and employment levels.

• *Child Care and Development Block Grant (CCDBG)*. The 1991 U.S. budget legislation authorizes the CCDBG, which distributes nearly $2.6 billion for center-based and family child care. It also earmarks money specifically for caregiver training. So that eligible parents may choose any licensed, regulated, or registered provider, states offer them vouchers. States may also contract for service or make grants directly to providers. The same legislation also expands the Earned Income Tax Credit. At this writing, parents can receive a maximum credit of $1,852 for one-child families and $2,013 for others.

• *Social Security Act/Title IV-A at-Risk Child Care Funds*. This provides for families receiving Aid to Families with Dependent Children (AFDC) who work outside the home or who enroll in approved education or training programs. When their earnings increase beyond AFDC thresholds, certain families can qualify for one year of transitional child care assistance. Because it's believed that child care assistance can help keep some families from becoming AFDC recipients, they too can be eligible for these funds.

• *The USDA Child Care Food Program.* USDA reimburses SACC programs on a per child, per meal/snack, sliding-scale basis. USDA asks SACC programs to adhere to USDA nutritional guidelines, post copies of menus, keep records of expenditures and attendance, and fill out monthly forms. It's a great deal of paperwork, but quite a few PDs depend on the assistance.

The only way to obtain public funding is to identify the proper agency and apply for the money. Here's where the confusion starts. The agency that administers DCBG may not be the same one that handles CCDBG. Each type of funding comes with a different set of regulations, reporting procedures—even different eligibility standards!

A few states are moving toward a civilized "seamless" system, such as Indiana's Step Ahead. Indiana puts its child care funds from all state and federal sources into a single basket. But in most states, people who want public funding have to devise their own continuity. To that end, they're likely to have to scurry around from agency to agency, seeking answers to such questions as:

What is the reimbursement rate for each source?

Are sliding-fee scales used? Are they reasonable?

How will vouchers or grants be distributed?

What are the licensing or registration requirements?

Are there funds set aside specifically for SACC?

How much is available for the cost of training?

How does the state plan to address compensation?

Are there any existing ways to coordinate funding?[1]

Federal funding doesn't end with the well-known sources. Deep within the bureaucratic labyrinth there may lie hidden resources, money that SACC people can put toward specific projects or target populations. Unearthing those often-untapped sources takes more research, more time, and more patience. Among other places, the quest might lead to:

• The Community Services Block Grant (CSBG)
• The Federal Office for Substance Abuse Prevention (OSAP)
• The Drop-Out Prevention Act

- The McKinney Act–Homelessness
- The Federal Office of Indian Education
- U.S. Department of Veterans Affairs
- U.S. Department of Housing and Urban Development

Some states, such as Kentucky and Texas, also administer their own funds for before- and afterschool programs. These states' initiatives can serve as action models for SACC advocates in other states.

Kentucky: The Education Reform Act went into effect July 1, 1990. It mandates the creation of a Family Resource Center (FRC) in each elementary school where 20 percent or more of children qualify for free/reduced lunch. While an FRC itself is not required to act as provider, it is required to coordinate SACC in its community if care is otherwise unavailable through the schools. Some FRC directors are former SACC PDs, which makes them very attuned to SACC demand. While FRC funding primarily takes the form of salaries for directors and their assistants, some centers' start-up grants partially fund SACC start-up costs.

Texas: The 71st State Legislature passed a bill that requires each school district with 5,000 or more students to hold two public hearings annually to consider the before and afterschool, holiday, and vacation care needs of its constituency. The bill also established a School Child Services Fund (SCSF), supported by state employees' pre-tax donations. The state matches each dollar donated to child care with another fifty cents for the SCSF. Money accrued in one fiscal year is budgeted for allocation the following year.

State and local SACC coalitions can provide more details about these types of initiatives. See Appendix 2 for contact information.

City and County Funding

Crumbling infrastructures; understaffed police and fire departments; school and library shut-downs. Sometimes, civic governments have their hands full and their pockets empty.

If there's any money left after essentials, or with the help of an occasional bond issue, cities and counties can make direct dollars available to child care systems. Much of local public funding comes from local tax revenue. Cities sometimes administer federal or state funds, such as the *Community Development Block Grant (CDBG)*. (Admittedly, in the wake of the Reagan Era, most of that revenue has dried up.) Some include child care in their housing development fund administration. But often, local government support takes a non-monetary form.

A growing number of municipal leaders take action on their own school-age care initiatives. Cities seem to function best as funding coordinators, lending credibility and administrative muscle to school-age care projects, then spinning them off to schools, YSAs or CBOs. A good example of this full-on civic commitment can be found in the city of Seattle, Washington.

The city's Division of Family and Youth Services received $8,860 from the DCBG. With this, it leveraged another $38,000 in matching contributions and in-kind donations. These monies were used to finance the development of the School's Out Consortium, a SACC advocacy group. Billie King, Seattle's child care coordinator, describes the city's role as that of "incubator."

One of Seattle's recent efforts, the Day Care in the Schools Project, addressed developing dedicated space for SACC. Providers with programs sited in elementary schools were getting tired of "The Schoolhouse Shuffle." School districts were touchy about giving programs the run of the house. The city stepped in, bringing together school district representatives and providers through a regularized proposal process.

Once again, the city facilitates. Neighborhood meetings play a part in site development. So does a professional review panel, which visits, interviews, and confirms each provider's arrangements. The city's General Fund kicks in with subsidies for low-income children. CDBG funds pay for a nurse/consultant and caregiver training.

The city of Cincinnati, Ohio, uses its administrative authority to tackle the cost-of-care issue directly. There, the Recreation Commission is the main provider of school-age child care. Although the Commission charges fees to parents in more affluent areas, it charges no fees at those sites located in areas with high concentrations of poverty. Because the Commission basically operates through tax support, it simply allocates a higher proportion of those staff positions supported by tax dollars to the poorer sections of Cincinnati. Other sites fund positions wholly from parent fees.

For local funding possibilities, look to mayors' offices, county boards of supervisors, city planning departments, human services agencies, and school districts. The National League of Cities (1301 Pennsylvania Avenue NW, Washington, DC 20004; 202-626-3000) publishes helpful information about city-supported child care.

THE PRIVATE SECTOR

What often makes public funding tough to swallow is all the agenda-busting that goes on. Priorities get set and re-set at the drop of a hat. SACC programs look forward to the promised funding only to find it's already been allocated for another sector entirely.

Governments in general have been latecomers to SACC funding, but the private sector has long been a source of capital. Efforts to blend SACC function and finance have fit with the movement toward so-called public-private partnership. For example, in Dade County, Florida, American Banker Insurance (ABI) Company concocted the concept of *worksite schools*. At several ABI workplaces, employees' children take their classes from Dade County public school teachers. They use publicly financed materials and curriculum. ABI foots the bill for classroom space, maintenance, utilities, and security. And they have an afterschool program, too.

A fuzzy distinction between public and private operations may ultimately imply less government involvement. It may mean more private decision making. It could end up meaning more of everything for some people and less for everybody else. Public-private partnership goals involve shifting cost management into the private sector—something a national health and child care policy would also do nicely. In the absence of such a policy, many SACC fundraisers look for financial stability from direct private contributions.

Private funding usually still refers to investments by foundations, corporations, small businesses, community organizations, and parties of one. In other words, everything that is *not* government funding is private funding. An exhaustive review of the private sector is obviously beyond the scope of this book. What follows is an overview designed to familiarize the reader with the primary private funding sources.

Foundations

More than 21,000 foundations in the United States administer funding to encourage various forms of social action. National foundations tend to fund projects of broad national significance. With regard to SACC, their support usually comes with an expectation of statistically based research. They often want studies that show how children benefit from participation.

Community and local family foundations make likely sources of private SACC investment. They typically focus their giving in specific geographic areas. Their administrators take greater interest in meeting local imperatives.

In any given year, one foundation can offer significant support for the direct cost of care or capital improvements. However, it would be unwise to count on the same foundation year after year. Anticipate by making proposals to different foundations every year.

Foundation administrators prefer to feel that they aren't the sole source of support for a particular project. Going in with a commitment for additional support from other non-parent sources can make a real difference. Where possible, collaborate with other community agencies and groups to achieve this.

The United Way (and Other Charitable Organizations)

When a product or service becomes a household word, like Kleenex, it can literally blow away the competition. The household name in charitable giving is the United Way. By swallowing up or elbowing aside smaller organizations, it made itself *the Way* to give at the office and in the school.

By virtue of its unchallenged dominance, United Way stood for years as the nation's largest private school-age care funder. It contributes direct operating capital to its member agencies. It also funds community-wide surveys to determine unmet need for SACC services. Its agencies convene task forces, conduct conferences, and write reports about latchkey children.

By virtue of its huge top-down bureaucracy, United Way's funding procedures make application lengthy, complex, and often anti-competitive. It uses the data it gathers to determine its priorities for a given geographic area. Only when *it* deems school-age care an area priority may a provider successfully apply. Even then, review panels evaluate proposals using a predetermined set of criteria having to do with agency size, political presence, longevity, and reach. Single-service entities, such as independent SACC programs, don't often meet the criteria.

The Way organizes its membership around *funding cycles,* periods of time between priority determinations. In any given regional cycle, the Way funds a finite number of agencies. Generally, new applicants must wait for the next "window" in the cycle, and several cycles may pass before that window opens. Even then, the Way may fail to evaluate school-age care in and of itself as a local priority. In this event, it might be effective to join with other SACC providers and present the Way with a case for formal reconsideration.

Another tactic involves what the Way calls *Targeted Community Care.* In some areas, givers can earmark their United Way donations for a particular agency or group of agencies. A strong public relations campaign might influence decisions at the donor level.

Somehow, other charities continue to survive in the shadow of the Way. Some, like Catholic Charities and Jewish Fund for Justice, thrive on their religious affiliations. Others, such as the Soroptimist Club, maintain a secular presence. SACC fundraisers would do well to investigate possibilities at local chapters of these less dominant—and possibly more accessible— organizations.

The Business Sector

Multinational or mom-n-pop, many companies don't know exactly what to do about SACC or how to get involved. So they generally look to child care professionals for information and advice. Many seek linkage with reputable agencies that they and their employees trust.

Without convincing documentation, most companies will have a hard time making anything more than a token commitment. The Way's community-wide surveys and focus groups help fill the gap, but conducting an inside survey will reveal more immediate concerns. Along with independent consultants, SACC providers themselves can suggest strategies to employers. The trick is figuring out to what degree a company is likely to commit itself to SACC—low, medium, or high?

Low-level commitment:
- Scrap material for art and construction projects
- Tax-deductible in-kind donations of
  —office supplies
  —company-made goods (paper, lumber, food)
  —administrative, legal, accounting, technical, printing, or maintenance services
- Shadowing, or apprenticeships in learning work environments for children aged 10 and above

Medium-range commitment:
- Tax-deductible cash contributions to
  —training programs
  —resource and referral agencies
  —program self-evaluation studies
- Partial cost coverage or reimbursement for regular SACC, employees' children only
- School vacation and holiday care program funding, employees' children only
- One-time gifts or grants designated for a special purpose
- Lunchtime seminars for parents

High-level commitment:
- Cost-of-care coverage, including other resident children as well as employees' children
- Public relations campaigns to raise awareness of the latchkey syndrome and school-age care solutions
- Creation of company position for full-time work-family coordinator
- Direct investment in SACC consortia that address the cost-of-care issue
- Low-interest loans for construction or renovation
- Personal collaboration with other high-level funders on future school-age care improvement

When seeking corporate funding, underutilized programs can take a page from the air carrier business. Airlines operate on a slim profit margin of 2 percent. To achieve a profit, they need to maximize their utilization while managing to sell as many full-cost fares as possible. As a result, they sell a certain number of discounted seats on certain flights.

SACC programs can and do negotiate discount rates with corporate employers. In exchange for regular referrals, a child care center typically lowers its fee by 10 percent. The program's apparent loss of revenue is offset by the upswing in utilization. The employer may choose to further subsidize employee costs, making an otherwise expensive care arrangement much more affordable.

In tax year 1992, a company could make up to 10 percent of its gross taxable income tax-exempt through charitable contribution. To take advantage, some companies have set up their own foundations for this express purpose. Gifts to nonprofit R & Rs or child care centers qualify for the deduction. Even when a company can't contribute, perhaps its foundation can.

How to Identify Prospective Private Funders

Information about foundations is fairly well organized and accessible to almost anyone. Much the same can be said for charitable organizations. The business sector is vast, diffuse, and not as easy to penetrate. Research into each of these areas will yield the broadest possible list of prospects.

The Foundation Directory. This reference is published by The Foundation Center, an information clearinghouse that maintains a nationwide reference network. Libraries often have a copy, as well as other useful foundation reference guides. Look for foundations with mission statements that include child care, informal education, youth services, at-risk children, drug or school drop-out prevention.

Some foundations may not have funded school-age care before, but that may be because no one ever applied. If a program serves economically disadvantaged children and families, plan to approach foundations that share this particular interest. Also target those that have funded child care projects in the past. For a referral to a nearby network member, call The Foundation Center at 800-424-9836.

Corporate Foundation Profiles. This is another major reference, also published by The Foundation Center. Corporations don't always like to reveal the names of contribution recipients, so identifying prospects here may be a little more challenging.

More focused is *The Corporate Reference Guide to Work-Family Programs,* published by Families and Work Institute (330 Seventh Avenue, New York, NY 10001; 212-465-2044). It's a savvy source listing of progressive companies known to invest in child care.

Look into back issues of Resources for Child Care Management's *BusinessLink* (16 South Street, Suite 300, Morristown, NJ 07960; 201-267-9100), The Foundation Center's *Foundation News,* and various publications from Catalyst (250 Park Avenue South, New York, NY 10003;

212-777-8900) and the Bureau of National Affairs (1231 25th Street NW, Washington, DC 20037).

At the local level, the Chamber of Commerce usually has information about major companies and employers in the area. People there may also have ideas about which companies could be willing to donate services or scrap materials.

Simple as it seems, check the "Charitable Organizations" listing in the local phone company's yellow pages. And don't forget the people at the local R & Rs. The growing network of child care resource and referral agencies across the United States provides information and technical assistance in the search for funds. If their phone numbers don't pop into mind, the National Association of Child Care Resource and Referral Agencies (NACCRRA) in Washington, DC, should be able to help.

Narrowing the Field

Unlike public funders, foundations only issue RFPs when they get particularly excited about an issue. At all times, their areas of interest appear in prospectuses or annual reports, which are readily available on request to anyone in the world who wants one and, therefore, not too informative. Foundations and charities often couch their funding imperatives in generalized terms. Corporations play their interests *very* close to the chest. A face-to-face conversation can give program fundraisers a chance to learn how to read between the lines. The added insight helps them tailor their proposals to a private funder's particular focus.

Not all funding officers will agree to meet prior to a proposal submission, but most will. Several strategies for arranging the meeting can pay off. One way is to make a straightforward phone or mail inquiry. Another is to find out if an acquaintance, a SACC board member, or an associate personally knows someone on the funder's staff or board of trustees. Perhaps that person can help set it up. If a meeting can be arranged, go prepared with detailed planning elements, costs, and reasons. When the opportunity arises, take a few moments to discuss transition plans for the time when funding ends.

THE PROPOSAL: Ask and (Perhaps) Ye Shall Receive

Almost every funder requires a formal written proposal. They'll also want letters of support or other objective testimonials. Funding officers use these as indicators, of both a project's viability and the proposal writers' competence.

Each funding source uses a different format for proposal submission. Government funding applications are detailed, specific, and numbers-oriented. Some foundations want proposals to include evaluation plans; others expect a detailed time-and-task plan. Companies tend to prefer the short form. One may want a three-page letter simply stating desires and objectives. Another may want an explicit ten-pager, a comprehensive three-year budget, and a list of board members.

Whatever the variation in format, most funders ask the same essential questions about prospective recipients:

Why is our funding necessary?

What do these people plan to do with it?

What qualifies these people to do what they say they will?

How and when will it be done?

How much will it cost altogether?

How much of the total cost are they requesting from us?

Does any other funding tie in?

They want all of this information in a style that is brief, clear, free of jargon, and personal. Scores of books and articles about proposal writing are readily available through The Foundation Center, libraries, and bookstores. Perhaps the single best guide is *Program Planning and Proposal Writing,* published by The Grantsmanship Center (1125 West 6th Street, P.O. Box 17220, Los Angeles, CA 90015; 213-749-4721).

As part of the proposal process, some funding officers will gladly accept an invitation to see the program in action. Such visits make the human connection between funder and children. They can bring lively imperatives to an otherwise distanced concept.

Funders turn down proposals all the time, even good proposals. A turn-down could be because of stiff competition. Pleas for economic assistance have hit a forty-year high, so all forms of funding support are under withering siege. Don't take a turn-down too personally, and try to learn from the experience.

THE REAL COST OF RESOURCE DEVELOPMENT

Talking about child care resources almost always connotes money, but there's a hidden cost to that thought. If the child care field has flourished at all, it is thanks to the *human* resources that have fueled its development. All SACC people, but primarily caregivers, provide the unseen subsidy that keeps school-age care businesses going. Their wages and working conditions almost never reflect their personal and professional contributions.

Financial resources provide the basic skeleton of a school-age care program. SACC people give it a life.

NOTE

1. Adapted from Joan Lombardi, "New Federal Dollars: How Are They Being Used?" *Child Care Information Exchange,* December 1991, pp. 56–57.

FOR FURTHER REFERENCE

Carnes, Kevin, and Connie Hine. 1988. *Kids and Companies: The Employer's Guide to Child Care Solutions.* Carson, CA: Lakeshore Curriculum Materials, P.O. Box 6261, 90749.

Flanagan, Joan. 1982. *The Grass Roots Fundraising Book.* Chicago: Contemporary Books.

Morgan, Gwen. 1991. *The Hitchhiker's Guide to the Child Day Care Universe.* Boston: Wheelock College.

Neugebauer, Roger, ed. Undated reprint. *The Best of Exchange #6: Guide to Successful Fundraising.* Redmond, WA: Exchange Press.

Steckel, Richard. 1989. *Filthy Rich and Other Nonprofit Fantasies: Changing the Way Nonprofits Do Business in the '90s.* Berkeley, CA: Ten Speed Press.

Stern, Gary. 1990. *Marketing Workbook for Nonprofit Organizations.* St. Paul, MN: Amherst A. Wilder Foundation, 919 Lafond Avenue, 55104; 612-642-4025.

Chapter 8

SACC PEOPLE

In highly competitive fields, education and expertise often command a job with top pay, generous benefits, flexible working hours, performance incentives, company cars, expense accounts . . . the list could go on. There may be a hundred candidates for just one such position, each candidate struggling to be chosen out of the crowd. With prestige and financial security at stake, top performers from a variety of disciplines present their credentials for consideration.

In school-age child care, education and expertise often command a minimum wage, part-time hours, few benefits, and tight budgets, with the incentive of seeing a few children safely through another day. There may be a hundred programs desperately seeking one bright, caring candidate for the position of caregiver. Under these conditions, people actually select themselves as caregivers long before someone else gets around to hiring them.

Some argue that it takes a certain type to do a certain job, that only someone who prefers playing with children to doing "real work" would choose the child care profession.

Others say the low pay and part-time hours repel all but the least qualified applicants, that SACC programs are nothing more than way stations for people on their way to something better.

Still others claim that these stigmas deter confident people from entering the field in the first place.

While these points may have some basis in truth, none of them change the fact: *Some people simply care more about children than they do about material gain.* These are the people on whom SACC thrives. They are also the people whom SACC providers can most easily exploit. This chapter examines ways to identify them, attract them, train them, excite them, and hold on to them. It also explains how to respect them, rather than exploit them.

WHAT MAKES SOMEONE A SACC PERSON?

One pioneering expert in the child care field says:

Adults are needed who respect and listen to the children, who know which activities are appropriate, who challenge their curiosity, who are flexible and who inspire confidence, who do not talk down to them, and who are available.[1]

True enough. Unfortunately, the same holds true whether the subject of conversation is SACC recruitment or democratic citizenry. If human civilization is to survive, such adults are needed everywhere.

Turning to a newspaper's classified section, one can sometimes find dozens of child care employment opportunities. Most ads describe only where the job is, the ages or grades of children to be cared for, and the minimum experience or education required. Occasionally, they add a telling phrase such as, "Should be good with children."

Having your master's degree doesn't mean that you are going to be able to take a group of eighteen kids and one adult to the swimming pool and make it. It doesn't matter how many books you have read.

—A SACC Person

Interdepartmental memos or staff handbooks contain formal job descriptions. They may ramble on about implementing, organizing, recordkeeping, maintaining, reporting, and lots of other -ings. Every mechanistic duty may be listed.

You want people who are willing to do more than is expected, who know that there are going to be times when a parent may be late and we need to stay a few minutes . . . someone who sees beyond what the job description says.

—A SACC Person

State licensing standards and regulations set forth restrictions on who may or may not work with children. Employment applications and interview formats revolve around these governing rules. Applicants' acceptability depends on their compliance. Interviewers assign point values to peoples' verbal responses, then calculate peoples' total numerical value.

The sort of thing I would look for is a person who can be warm and authoritative. And can be simply matter-of-fact about kids getting out of bounds, and that it's okay to set limits, and that you don't have to get grim about it.

—A SACC Person

As the contrasts suggest, SACC people resist the notion of *result orientation,* which places such great importance on final products and final scores. Human relations are frail, fragile, funny, and sad. They don't fit into a box. All too often, androcratic result orientation toward human behavior gets rid of the "human," leaving an empty shell of behavior.[2] What truly distinguishes SACC people from others has much less to do with measurable criteria than conventional thinking might suggest.

After all, childhood is a process through which young people learn and grow. Real SACC people tend toward *process orientation,* which allows for skill building, personal achievement, and dynamic daily experience within firm but flexible limits. They take genuine pleasure in that tough-to-measure process. Anyone else is just looking for results.

Most successful directors take a skeptical view toward hiring education majors and elementary school teachers. With few exceptions, people trained in the old-style industrial methods of elementary education don't work out very well in SACC. Their prior experience, with its emphasis on controlling children's behavior, runs contrary to SACC precepts. Letting children play and socialize as they please takes a good deal more self-restraint than these people can usually exercise.

What Else Makes Someone a SACC Person?

Many high schools qualify a teenager's verifiable off-campus job as a transcript item. Colleges and universities promote internships for degree credit, putting students' job experience on the same level with classroom instruction. And any number of American postsecondary educational institutions now grant course credit for the knowledge people have acquired by actively pursuing their own interests. All these institutions recognize that *a dynamic life experience actually is an education.*

In order to bring a sense of caring control to SACC, people must already have some idea of what's going on. Most of the child care ideas they read about in books such as this one will seem like second nature. Their informal education (many refer to this as "common sense," a personal characteristic that, at its best, never seems common) naturally aids them in taking appropriate care with children.

These people have few problems sorting out issues of authority . . . they kind of assume that the world, and all of its objects and arrangements, is a really fascinating place—and how could anybody possibly resist getting involved?

—A SACC Person

For a brief review of these issues of authority, please refer to the discussion of PAVEWAY in Chapter 2.

Long-time SACC people can list personal character traits they have observed in themselves and have looked for in other SACC people. They boil these traits down to one-word labels, such as *warmth, enthusiasm, maturity,* and so on. But these labels are relative terms, subjectively defined and difficult to express. That's why whoever hires SACC people had better be SACC people themselves.

My ability to spot the dreaded "need to be needed" is almost instinctual. . . . A person who [expresses dislike for] children's habit of growing up and going away is revealing the need to be needed. She (I'm sorry, but it's almost always a she) will be always "saving the day" by doing things for children that they need to be learning to do themselves. She will be trying to ingratitate herself with them by putting away their toys to save them from discipline. . . .

Children are universally ungrateful for these favors. They accept them, of course. But they never say more than a gruff "thanks" as they rush out the door. And so this woman not only sabotages your program, she also becomes very unhappy.

Don't hire her. Suggest that she apply at an infant care center, maybe. But don't inflict her upon school-age children.[3]

Some Concrete Things to Look For

Let the following blended comments of children, parents, caregivers, and other SACC people explain just a few of the things to look for. In no particular order, look for:

- Commitment
  Children are [negatively] affected by staff changing every six months. Parents want people who are going to stay in the job, and they don't mind paying for it.
- Organization Skills
  She is here every day with the comings and goings of the program. She is so involved. . . . I have to trust in her ability, decision making, et cetera.
- Physical and Emotional Well-Being
  No back problems, for example. This is important . . . to be able to get around with the kids. I would say our most successful [caregivers] have been happy with themselves, haven't had a lot of problems, and can relax.
- Communication Skills
  You have to be able to work as a member of a team and be able to get along with others. I look for people with a sense of humor . . . someone who's willing to learn something from children. . . . I want someone I can talk with.
- Cultural Awareness
  In our home, we don't want to get into staring contests, and I don't want

someone teaching my kids that this is okay . . . You have to respect and appreciate differences, not punish them.

- An Accent on the Positive

  If people are glad to come to work, then they feel good about themselves, and then about the job. You want [children] to trust you when they're feeling good, frightened, hurt.

- Flexibility

  You have to understand how children grow and develop, and the meanings of different behaviors. [I want] someone who can let kids be in on decisions . . . and who knows kids are really going to be able to handle it. [But] after you've given all the reasons, you have to be willing to say, "You can't jump off the roof of the shed, and that's it."

THE ROLE OF THE PROGRAM DIRECTOR

The basic characteristics just described help identify people who can fill the role of caregiver, driver, or bookkeeper. But a PD has to have more. Much more.

Strong candidates for program director know everybody else's job well enough to do it themselves. Otherwise, how can a PD know if things are going according to plan? Not only that, but how can a PD even forge a plan without a practical understanding of each role?

At various times of the day—and night—PDs may find themselves handling:

Overall program planning

Board liaisoning

Caregiver supervision and development

A broken swing set

Cash management

A bloody nose and a sprained wrist

Parent conferences

Negotiations with school personnel

Somebody trying to hop a fence

Food purchase and supply

Field trip notices

Interagency relations

Not enough paint brushes to go around

Government regulation

Body lice

Transportation arrangements

Resource development (non-parent funding)

And that's only a partial list. Sounds like a typical $15-an-hour part-time job, doesn't it?

Don't forget "the dreaded 'need to be needed.' " Envision a PD who actually tries to do everybody else's job at the same time. Not a pretty sight. That's why PDs have to know how to delegate.

• *Delegating in small programs.* When only one person plays most of the roles, an ability to delegate may not seem too important.

Nothing could be further from the truth.

The less people there are to pick up the slack, the more important it becomes for the PD to determine which role to play at which time of day. Responsibilities sometimes come fast and furious, dovetailing one into the other. A director-caregiver has to know how to delegate responsibilities to her/himself. Planners and providers must realize that to be effective, a director-caregiver must be employed and compensated as a full-timer. Anything else portends complete inadequacy.

• *Delegating in larger programs.* Where more people are spread out across a wider span, time and space lengthen the lines of answerability. This means finding ways of understanding between each person along the line. If people carry out policies more readily when they see the reasons behind them, part of the delegation process must involve building commitment through comprehension, and that takes some up-close, one-on-one contact.

Chief executive officers (CEOs), board members, or district coordinators typically use memoranda, but these photocopied directives from on high miss the partnership spirit. *Site-based management* helps mitigate some of this ivory-towerism. It downloads administrative authority to the people on the spot, imparting to them more of a sense of vested authority. Program people might then take a greater interest in outcomes, which in turn improves chances for successful performance of delegated responsibilities.

This authority transfer generally won't achieve desired outcomes all by itself. Effective site directors possess the personal confidence to delegate, as well as the administrative authority.

So, a site director candidate can enter the picture with proven expertise, solid references, a demonstrable track record, and educational experience. Combined with a show of personal confidence at interview time, all this can easily engender CEO or board confidence. Once assigned, this candidate can either be held accountable to the wage authority—*or* mutual confidence can be fostered and reinforced along the lines of the partnership model.

But here's the rub. To be truly effective, the director also has to have confidence in his/her team's ability to accept responsibility when it's delegated. And what about the caregivers? They may have some postsecondary education or not. They may have worked with preschoolers or even raised a child, but not necessarily for a market employer. Their only personal reference might be a family friend. How are *they* supposed to earn a director's confidence, let alone a board's or a CEO's?

Some larger programs answer this dilemma with the sneaky market manuever of *headhunting*. They steal SACC people from smaller or less well-funded programs. Because of this competition, weakly funded programs stay weak, and this hurts the children.

At this writing, it remains unclear as to how much caregiver turnover stems from burnout, how much from performance failure, and how much from headhunting. What *is* clear, however, is that the high turnover rate demands a fundamental field-wide approach to building SACC people's confidence.

THE HELPING HANDBOOK

Smiles, hugs and handshakes can go a long way toward sealing understandings between SACC people. But when directors run their programs too informally, the resulting disputes and disagreements put a huge and unnecessary strain on everyone involved.

Successful PDs provide a written document that clearly describes their people's rights and responsibilities. The idea here is to anticipate and mediate conflict before it happens.

I. Mission Statement
Consists of the provider's intents and purposes, as well as basic tenets of child development. See Chapter 1.

II. Establishing and Amending Personnel Policies
A. Describes how a board of directors or personnel committee works with program people to develop policy.
B. Indicates minimum frequency of policy reviews (how often do they take place?).

Building partnership means building a climate of respect for each partner's personal position. It takes a terrific amount of commitment to people, not simple obeisance to the administrative shell that surrounds them. Effective policies require negotiation between program people and administrators. Describe here the terms and conditions by which this negotiation formally takes place.

III. Employment Status Designations
A. Defines what constitutes a permanent employee, a probationary employee, an independent contractor, a substitute, and so on. Indicates the terms and methods of internal promotion and transfer.
B. Gives a statement regarding equal opportunity employment.

C. Describes the process by which vacancies are filled.

D. Defines acceptable separation procedures, including the requested period of notice.

IV. Basic Employment Conditions

Covers every critical aspect of regulated performance standards, including but not limited to:

- certification requirements;
- health testing;
- descriptions of clothing that is considered hazardous or that might impede dynamic experience;
- parking and transportation alternatives;
- how full-time days and full-time weeks are measured, and how time is documented;
- when and how paychecks are delivered;
- areas for breaks/smoking/prepping.

V. Wages, Salaries, and Benefits

A. Wages and Salaries—includes information about how they are established and reviewed, as well as how increases are determined.

B. Benefits—describes workers' compensation and unemployment insurance, as well as applicable data regarding health, dental, vision, and life insurance; explains retirement fund, reduced-cost care for caregivers' children.

VI. Authorized Leave

A. Defines medical and personal leave—describes accumulation, carryovers, and effect on wages; explains lead time for vacation requests; sets conditions that require confirmation from medical practitioner; lists family members whose illness qualifies for use of medical leave.

B. Defines and explains effect on wages of special purpose leave, including that due to jury duty, electoral activity, funerals, inclement weather, and the like.

C. Defines education and professional development leaves.

D. Defines parental leave.

E. Gives preferred procedures for notifying program people in the event of lateness, illness, or other unusual absence; explains policy regarding failure to notify.

Few traditionally structured SACC programs pay their people as much as they would like. Limited income and high material costs put a double whammy on pay scales. Budget compromise in so labor-intensive a business as SACC generally means that caregivers take it on the chin.

Pay disparities in traditional programs complicate matters. A 1988 SACCProject study revealed the range of these disparities. Based on responding providers' reports, the following table projects average annual salaries based on average hourly wages, hours worked per week, and weeks worked per year.

Figure 8.1
Approximate Average Annual Salary, by Position, in School-Age Child
Care Programs, 1988

Center director	$18,879
Program director	$15,996
Teacher	$ 9,431
Group leader	$ 5,630
Aide	$ 4,960
Assistant teacher	$ 4,858

As Figure 8.1 shows, caregivers titled "teacher" earn on average nearly twice as much as those titled "assistant," and a center director's salary equals that of two "teachers." With these figures in mind, is it any wonder that among frontline caregivers, commitment and confidence run low while transiency runs high? Opportunity for substantial advancement or for making a living wage comes only on the infrequent occasion when a director moves on. Typically, caregivers hunker down under low wage ceilings.

Paying hourly wages works best for programs with several part-time people who are caregivers for different numbers of hours each week. The director sets up methods for recording each person's hours daily and for approving the record weekly. Most people will want their wages weekly, but some directors can improve program cash flow by negotiating with their people to take paychecks on a biweekly or monthly basis.

The Handbook explains what the program management considers a paid hour. Of course, this includes time spent in direct caregiving. But what about planning sessions? Certification workshops? Parent conferences? Shortened days due to bad weather? Overtime? Anticipate and also explain forseeable unpaid time that people might spend in program service.

Paying salaries means both asking and making broader commitments, because regardless of a person's hours, the weekly or monthly pay remains the same. Directors almost always receive salaries, since their roles practically put them in a 24-hour-a-day on-call position. Some program people's personal situations may prevent them from accepting salaried responsibility; others may strive for it.

Most programs combine wage and salary systems. For example, a particular program pays new full-time hires $5.50 an hour for 37.5 hours a week. That's 30 hours of direct caregiving, 7.5 hours of planning and meeting time. Over a full year, this comes to a total of $10,725 per person. With a biweekly pay system, each paycheck comes out to 1/26 of the annual figure. See the section on paying the full cost of care in Chapter 5 for more on payroll management.

By virtue of their designation as full-timers, people earning reasonable salaries usually "qualify" for added benefit packages that substantially increase their effective compensation. To subsidize this practice, employers often hire people into part-time positions, usually no more than twenty hours a week. SACC hours being what they are, it's easy to keep people under the limit. This effectively redlines low-paid people out of hours that would qualify them for these benefits. So these people perform services that generate income that pays for someone else's benefits.

Treating qualified SACC people like unskilled transient day laborers utterly ignores the difference between a knowledge-based service business and assembly-line or construction work. Don't qualified SACC people deserve at least what they could get for stuffing mattresses or pouring concrete? After all, they're directly molding people's lives.

Some confusion can arise from the interchangeable usage of the terms *fringe benefits* and *benefits*. The way it usually works, *fringe benefits* begin and end with the mandatory ones—social security, workers' compensation, unemployment insurance, and the like. (On the budget sheet, they show up as payroll-associated or program insurance expenses.) Government agencies administer program payments and paperwork for fringe benefits. If necessary, consult the local R & R, Small Business Administration (SBA), or appropriate government office for current procedures.

In contrast with legislated fringe benefits comes the wide variety of *voluntary benefits,* options left to administrative discretion. Structuring a voluntary benefits plan so that it cares fairly and equitably for program people takes no little planning. However, it is *the* essential inducement for attracting and retaining qualified SACC people.

Paid personal leave. Here's a wonderful way to recognize the human worth of program people. When personal emergency strikes, they can resolve it without worrying that it's costing them their wages or their job. Full-timers may receive a fixed number of paid personal days per annum, or they may accrue leave relative to accumulated service—say, 2.5 personal hours per 140 service hours.

At this writing, California leads the nation with a progressive law that permits people up to sixteen weeks of unpaid leave for parenting and related family matters. Of course, the nation trails the rest of the industrialized world, most of which supports paid family leave. In discussion, consider the meaning of a policy that penalizes SACC people for caring for their own families.

Paid medical leave. This highly practical benefit can prevent people from bringing contagious illness to the program simply because they couldn't afford to stay home. Full-timers receive twelve or more paid medical days per annum, but everyone in the program can benefit from better health if part-timers get a few, too.

Paid professional leave. Successful programs invest in their people's professional growth and self-esteem. Who stands to gain from improved literacy, critical thinking, and managerial skills? Everyone. If major corporations spend millions training their people to specification, certainly a SACC program can afford a few days' wages.

Paid vacations. Some programs deem administrative duties to be more taxing and, therefore, more deserving of this recognition. They automatically give directors up to double the vacation time that others may earn—that is, if the others receive any at all. Still, many year-round SACC programs provide full-timers with at least one or two weeks of paid vacation per annum. As an additional incentive, their systems allocate vacation time according to tenure—say, one week the first year, two weeks the second year, and so on to a plateau.

A policy of fixed-length vacations deters cries of favoritism. Being fair and equitable also means understanding each person's particular situation and evaluating on a case-by-case basis. Picture a part-time caregiver who is trying to stay with the program but also trying to make ends meet. The caregiver takes another part-time position elsewhere. Perhaps by combining the two positions' wages this person can earn a living. But between the program and the other position, this person is putting in forty-five hours a week. That's a full-time week. Policies that prohibit this person from taking vacation, paid or otherwise, would mean burnout and/or separation in no time at all.

The previous example illustrates the consequence of implementing blanket policies at the expense of long-term health, both the person's and the program's. With fewer people, most smaller programs can afford to personalize vacation policy. They can easily include the subject in the pre-hire negotiations.

Paid holidays. Like paid vacations, administrators' ideas about which holidays merit pay may not automatically match their people's ideas. It's easy to fall back on school, state, or national holiday schedules, but cultural sensitivity calls for recognition of holidays that are important to each program person. More often than not, a combination of fixed and optional holidays can balance out the paid holiday time each person receives. For example, this gives someone in Massachusetts a chance to "trade in" Bunker Hill Day for Chinese New Year . . . or vice versa.

Health insurance. While the nation waits for a health care policy, program people not covered elsewhere might never see the inside of a doctor's office after they take their TB tests. Honoring a SACC program mission statement means providing caregivers and other program people with a chance to maintain their own well-being. Assure program people an opportunity to stay well by offering group health coverage.

Many programs pay only a percentage of their people's premiums; some pay the full cost. Disparities stem from variables such as group size, types of services covered, and family member coverage options. Naturally, a school district with 100,000 employees can obtain cheaper coverage and contribute more to costs than can an unaffiliated single-site parent-run program with two co-directors and eight caregivers. To increase a smaller program's coverage options, investigate coverage offered to members of professional groups, such as the National Association for the Education of Young Children (NAEYC). Here again, the SBA or a local R & R may also have some helpful information.

VII. Program People Development
    A. Describes planned in-program practices related to care and performance improvement, involving:
      • regularly scheduled meetings;
      • special-focus and case conferences;
      • one-on-one supervisory interaction;
      • independent consultants.
    B. Describes available outside opportunities, including:
      • community-based health and safety instruction;
      • multi-site support and technical workshops;
      • continuing education and extension courses;
      • caregiving development institutes;
      • professional associations and conferences;
      • credentialing opportunities.

The term *training* often brings to mind visions of formal courses and expensive seminars. Consider as well the idea that it can be any opportunity to learn school-age care skills—formal or informal, in or out of a program, from independent speakers or just from each other.

Some of the most effective SACC "training" isn't training at all: It's *mentoring* by experienced program people. Their ability to communicate their grasp of child development and group skills makes them the most cost-effective learning resource a program can tap. By giving these mentors opportunities to expand their knowledge and confidence, by helping them share approaches, content areas, and levels of difficulty, programs put themselves on ever-stronger footing.

By drawing on people from diverse educational backgrounds and professional experiences, school-age care gains as an interdisciplinary field. Great promise lies in these people's willingness to *develop* their own intrinsic sense of childhood and to *adapt* that sense in a practical setting. Some students and graduates of early childhood courses will have sought this out beforehand. Being already familiar with child-centered concepts, with multiple skill-and-learning layouts, and with free play movement patterns, they might develop the more complex skills that can help them guide school-agers. But development relies on the desire to learn new things, and in this sense, anyone may be ripe for SACC training.

A commitment to appropriate school-age care takes an equal commitment to program people's development. Often, the PD facilitates this commitment by planning and coordinating development functions. For example, as the result of a one-on-one supervisory session, perhaps a PD and caregiver agree that the caregiver's activity planning for nine- to twelve-year-olds lacks creativity. Shortly thereafter, a local R & R queries the PD about possible workshop topics for an upcoming day care conference. In this case, the PD might suggest "Can't-Miss Games for Older Kids" and encourage the caregiver to attend.

Goals of development. Each one feeds into and supports the next: deeper understanding of school-age care; increased competence; strengthened communication skills; improved caring relationships; personal growth, self-awareness, and feeling connected; the ability to accept wider responsibility. Each forms a link in the chain of personal and program betterment.

Building in development. Active administrative and parent support—or the lack thereof—can substantially affect a PD's success in this respect. The development process mostly flourishes beyond normal program operating hours. It's important that the budget provide ample paid time for supervision, meetings, workshops, and the like.

With development practices written right into the handbook, people get a much clearer idea about what to expect. Some people who don't wish to spend time developing their caregiving abilities may opt out of the program before they begin, thereby saving the director the trouble of replacing them later. Conversely, people who see themselves as learners and who wish to partner into a learning environment will find the program that much more attractive.

Built-in development also furthers the realization of specific goals. As particular conditions arise, program people can meet both to tackle questions and to track results on a continuing basis. The less scattershot the approach, the more coherent the resolutions.

Local resources. Most places offer learning opportunities from outside the program's walls. A Red Cross staffer can train people in CPR. A mental health professional can discuss attention deficit syndrome. A social service counselor can give updates on street gang trends. Anyone with a vested or professional interest in children's health, safety, and development may have something to offer. That shared interest between program people and the local resource makes an excellent point of contact.

Community and junior colleges, always centers of practical knowledge, frequently offer evening courses in appropriate subjects. Programs connected by the CANARI process with a college or university can sometimes keep that affiliation alive and well through continued training and evaluation of program people. Staff and students from the college or university might even come to the program site to observe program life.

Development facilitators keep apprised of new opportunities in and around the community. One way to do so is by keeping in touch with a local

R & R. Another, more proactive way is through direct association with other local SACC and child care providers. A single-site program can't always supply the time, money and logistical support that some development functions require. However, as part of a state or regional coalition, programs can offer their people otherwise impracticable opportunities. Not only can a broad-based provider coalition arrange more expensive development activities, it can also:

—exert stronger political influence;

—set joint agendas for issues of common concern;

—mitigate feelings of isolation;

—share and reinforce strengths with cooperative workshops.

State resources. Through September 1992, each state and eligible territory will have administered its share of the Federal Dependent Care Block Grant. Certain states will have backed up these monies with a variety of supplementary and matching funds. The following samples illustrate the range of SACC professional development activities that states may sponsor or co-sponsor in a given year.

Alabama: four regional extended-day workshops for caregivers, offered quarterly; one conference for directors.

Illinois: the School-Age Network, a consortium of three state agencies, which in turn sponsors two annual statewide conferences as well as a variety of local training activities.

Kentucky: the annual SACC Leadership Institute for Directors at Berea College; start-up/planning workshop for school administrators; grants to R & R systems for training and regional conferences.

North Carolina: grants to five SACC programs to finance provider training; state-wide conference for providers and directors.

Pennsylvania–Northeast: annual SACC conference; Basic School-Age Child Development workshop series; "Tattletales, Tantrums and Tears" workshop series; management seminars for directors; SACC activity fairs; site visits.

Even when states conduct no development, their licensing requirements may compel SACC program people to demonstrate a minimal development effort. The requirement may be as low as three hours of certified instruction annually. A state will usually contract with an established agency to provide this obligatory training session at specified times and locations.

National resources. Major YSAs such as Campfire Inc. and the YMCA provide training and guidance materials to their affiliates. In addition, both NSACCA and NAEYC have a stake in all program people's development.

Formed in 1988, NSACCA functions as the premier U.S. peer support organization for SACC professionals and friends. Its membership derives from the many regional and state SACC coalitions. Once each year, it holds a three-day conference for members. Formal conference activities consist primarily of information workshops, which are designed to advance providers' and directors' awareness of recent developments in the field. Prominent experts and local practitioners take this opportunity to exchange perceptions and research, as well as to form new bonds and strengthen existing ones.

NAEYC's National Academy of Early Childhood Programs has developed an accreditation system. Although NAEYC designed the system for overall program accreditation, a major element of the self-study process seeks to help determine caregiver competence and effectiveness. The self-study focuses on a variety of qualifying factors, such as hiring procedures, supervision, continuity of care, and in-service training.

VIII. Evaluation Procedures
    A. Explains purposes of formal review, including:
        • assessment of personal accomplishment
        • advancement and salary increase
        • viability of program policies
        • method for improving careplace satisfaction
        • conflict resolution
    B. Identifies frequency of and procedures for evaluation

IX. Child Abuse and Neglect
    Gives appropriate legal definitions; explains responsibilities associated with knowledge or observation of abuse or neglect of any enrolled child.

X. Conflict Resolution
    A. Lists possible acts that could lead to summary dismissal, such as:
        • use of physical force against a child
        • falsification of employment file information
        • failure to comply with licensing regulations
        • repeated failure to abide by program policy
        • incompetence
        • violations of confidentiality
    B. Describes steps leading to summary separation; defines classifications for probation, suspension, and dismissal.
    C. Describes personal and group appeal procedures.

The preceding outline touches on only the most common topics. Some centers are subject to federal laws that prohibit their people from engaging in certain political activities. Some have policies regarding reimbursements for out-of-pocket expenses incurred during the caring day. This kind of information also belongs in the Handbook.

TAPPING THE WELL OF HUMAN RESOURCE

To different people in different ways, hiring methods reflect administrators' philosophies about human value. They can celebrate or denigrate. They can imply confidence or desperation. They can invite or repel.

Hiring practices make up the administrative membrane through which program people enter. As such, each of these practices has a dual purpose: to gather information from prospective hires *and* to give it to them as well. Often, a program's wages, benefits, and immediate environment offer little incentive. Bringing in qualified, caring people can depend entirely on more subtle inducements such as training, education, community involvement, and personal advancement. To bring in the best people, SACC hiring practices had best focus on these subtleties.

Some funding sources or umbrella administrations impose strict hiring guidelines. The given intent of these guidelines is to ensure fair hiring practices. Force of law aside, don't confuse discretion with discrimination. Reach out to women and men of all ages, cultures, and ethnicities. Diversity enriches the dynamic daily experience.

With so much at stake, hasty judgements based on limited or purely personal perceptions can lead to irreparable damage. Develop hiring procedures that take into account the very special nature of a SACC program, and keep developing them as befits that special nature. Put them in writing for clarity's sake, but review and revise them regularly for children's sake.

Phase 1: Recruitment. Printed announcements are the program's calling cards. They ought to embody the very qualities that administrators want to find in applicants: creativity, dynamism, sensitivity, and commitment, to repeat a few. As mentioned earlier, SACC people actually select themselves long before administrators ever know about them. Plain old photocopied job listings probably won't attract the people who are likeliest to energize a SACC program. Use colorful paper, cartoon characters, varied typefaces—anything that says, "This isn't just another job, and here's the proof!" Always include information about the position, its general requirements, and application procedures, but sell the SACC spirit first.

Advertising a lively profession in dull block paragraphs does a disservice, but don't trick or mislead people into believing the program offers more than it does. That may be all right for Madison Avenue, but not for Main Street. An announcement that fairly represents the program screens out frivolous inquiries and saves valuable time for valuable applicants.

Many programs successfully use these general avenues of distribution:

- College and university placement offices
- Resource and referral networks

- Cultural centers
- General circulation newspapers
- PTO and community newsletters
- Child care professional magazines
- Seniors' centers
- Service agency communication channels
- Store windows and bulletin boards

To attract people with specialized skills, strengths, and backgrounds, a more target-specific outreach effort becomes essential. In California, for example, a program seeking bilingual caregivers might spend more of its advertising budget with the local Spanish-language newspaper. Or it might be able to cut its ad expenses by connecting with the National Council de La Raza district office.

Another invaluable recruitment method, *word of mouth,* reaches into people networks that printed notices can't reach. Current program people, parents, and others with an interest in building the best possible SACC team often gladly spread the word among their friends and acquaintances. Even where strict administrative codes stipulate preconditions to employment, word of mouth sends the message across a wider spectrum.

Phase 2: Pre-screening. When recruiting goes very well, it brings in stacks of letters, resumes, and applications. A typical effort yields somewhat less than a stack and sometimes only a handful. But whether it's five or five hundred, allocating valuable interview time depends on how closely each applicant appears to meet some basic criteria.

Some large administrations driven by equal employment opportunity (EEO) concerns, such as urban school districts, have established systems for pre-screening. Working from checklists, administration staffers sort through various positional requirements with each applicant. These staffers operate a general buffer zone that passes people along to an interview only after every standardized application requirement has been met.

In these same administrations, the next screening step consists of a panel interview conducted by designated professionals. Often using a point system, the panel evaluates the applicant's general character, background, problem-solving ability, and appearance. The panel then assigns a total point score. If it is high enough, the applicant gets the chance to interview with someone who actually does the hiring.

The whole process can take many months. It's a highly bureaucratic and political approach to pre-screening. Bureaucrats like it. Applicants don't.

CBOs, parent boards, and some YSA administrators can take EEO precepts in hand and still move people more quickly from recruiting to interviewing. They can more immediately recognize the value of life experience.

They can more easily design pre-screening methods that reflect the SACC spirit.

CLOSE-UP: YMCA Kids Club, Vero Beach, Florida

If they'd been planning to hire basketball coaches, they might've held a dribble-and-shoot contest. To hire Nautilus training instructors, perhaps a weightlifting competition would've narrowed the field. But program director Tom Manwaring was looking for eight adventurous school-age caregivers.

Under typically tight budgetary restraints, Manwaring realized the low wages offered would probably deter experienced professionals. That meant the pre-screening process had to focus on enthusiasm, sense of humor, energy, and personality fit. Candidates who demonstrated an *aptitude* for SACC could then be initiated into more formal training.

The big question was how to test for SACC aptitude. It had to be simple but engaging, casual but concentrated, and it had to work with a large group. It had to be Jam-A-Quacks.

Manwaring set a date and time, then invited all the applicants, advising them to wear comfortable clothing appropriate for SACC. Once everyone had arrived, he asked them to return in thought and deed to the age of eight as he explained how to play the Jam-A-Quacks game: Six "quackers" squat down, grab their ankles, close their eyes, and quack like ducks, while everyone else forms a close circle around them. The circlers open a space just wide enough for a quacker to escape, and the quackers waddle backwards, looking for the opening. The next thing they knew, everyone of a mind to was Jam-A-Quacking.

After the game, applicants took ten-minute turns as "the grown-up" leading the others, still as eight-year-olds, in some spontaneous song, game, or activity. No one was compelled to participate, but Manwaring took a refusal as a signal and eliminated those who refused from consideration.

How well does this kind of pre-screening work? In this case, it produced so many excellent candidates that Manwaring upped his hiring limit from eight to twelve. The new hires, ranging from high school seniors to a retired schoolteacher, received forty hours' training and bonding: overnight workshops, pizza parties, action presentations, swimming, and instruction in developmentally appropriate activities. On the strength of the newly hired caregivers and their training, Manwaring was able to expand program enrollment from 80 to 120 children.

Source: Michelle Seligson and Dale B. Fink, *No Time to Waste* (Wellesley, MA: SACCProject, 1989), p. 59.

Phase 3: Interviewing. An administrator has plans for the program. So does someone who's thinking about joining the program. The point of an interview is to find out what personal and professional plans each one has, then to try to figure out if these plans fit together.

Choosing partners is accomplished through a discovery process. By the time an interview has been set up, both parties have already discovered a certain amount of surface information about each other, at least enough to satisfy them that sitting down together could lead to more. It's generally up to the interviewer to create proper conditions for this deeper discovery.

Some advance preparation will smooth the experience for both interviewers and candidates. Take steps to:

- standardize interview location, format, and length;
- formulate a list of both fixed-response and open-ended questions;
- plan comparable opportunities for candidates to learn about the program and to elaborate about themselves;
- standardize evaluation methods.

With these elements in place, everyone can concentrate more clearly on the important aspects of an interview: looking, listening, and intuiting.

On the day of the interview, set an appropriate environmental tone. Putting someone on the edge of a hard-backed chair surrounded by ringing phones and whooping children won't usually bring out someone's best. Give each other a meaningful chance to get to know each other.

Welcome people into interviews as guests, for that is still their due at this point. Don't just point to a seat and shoot off a question. Especially if there are several interviewers, give people a chance to get introduced and acquainted. Relax for a minute, and let them have a chance to do the same. Offer something to drink, touch on a few casual subjects, then ease yourselves into the formal interview.

Start off with a short recap of the discovery process. Indicate how a candidate's performance in the pre-screening phase led up to this interview, and explain how the interview fits into the process. Make all this as clear and candid as possible.

Appropriate Q & A catches qualitative information from a candidate. Rather than interrogate for answers, encourage responses with friendly conversational inquiry. Almost everybody's favorite conversation subject is themselves. Aim to discover things about the candidate that only the candidate knows.

Hiring people is like mining for gold. After shoveling for a while, the miner stops digging and checks to see if there's actually any gold. After asking a question, a good interviewer *stops talking, looks, and listens.* An interview is already a short enough time to find out about someone, so why shorten it even further?

A good rule-of-thumb ratio is 1:4—that is, for every one minute that the interviewer talks, give the candidate at least four minutes to respond. Turn the tables—and the ratio—at the end of the interview. That's when

---

Sample Interview Questions

Please describe your understanding of differences between a six-year-old and a nine-year-old.

I see you've listed several hobbies on your resume. Would any of these lend themselves to program activities? (If yes) In what way?

Let's imagine a situation in which a couple of children keep ganging up against the others. How would you handle this?

Do you believe school-age care differs from the regular school day? (If yes) In what ways?

In general, what do you *least* like about children?

Have you ever been on a team of any kind? (If yes) What was that like for you?

Would you please describe your experiences as a group facilitator? (If any, follow up.) In what ways do you think this experience can be adapted to school-age care?

What in the foreseeable future might prevent you from staying with us for five years? (Follow up.) Where do you see yourself five years from now?

As a caregiver, what do you imagine your typical day would be like?

---

it's the candidate's turn to ask questions about the children, the program, overall organization, and the position itself.

Immediately after seeing the candidate out, complete a written record of impressions from the interview. This record is sometimes called a *numerical evaluation form,* because many administrators observe Affirmative Action guidelines by using a formulaic scoring system. Of course, the problem is how to accomplish a highly subjective task and, so as to avoid lawsuits, pretend that it's actually objective at the same time. A numerical evaluation form pretends this beautifully.

On the other hand, *descriptive evaluations* call for some thought, consideration, effective communication skills, and a more conscious understanding of human characteristics. They're not as easy, impersonal, or defensible as a punch card with numbered holes. They call for the interviewer to have some ideas about the exchange that has just taken place, and they leave the interviewer to express those ideas *in his or her own words,* without the number crutch. Literacy-based evaluations may carry greater liability risks and may not be suitable for administrators who are considering state and federal funding sources, but isn't that always the way?

Phase 4: Selection. Even with the results of the pre-screenings and interviews in hand, smart administrators will want to:

• verify employment and education data, if any, from the application;

• obtain at least two written character references *and contact the referents.*

These two steps help ensure the accuracy of information obtained from the earlier phases. If an applicant has no previous paid experience, references can help immensely, but only if they are checked for authenticity.

When the time for decision arrives, the subject of hiring standards comes back into play. If the standards are too broad or ill-defined, no candidate will seem any more desirable than another . . . except on the like'm scale ("Didja like'm?"). Overly idealistic standards cause the same problem. To identify candidates who seem best suited, it may become necessary to formulate a new set of questions and conduct a second round of interviews. Administrators who conduct ongoing recruitment tend to fare better in the selection phase. Remember that 40 percent national average turnover? Trying to shift in and out of hiring gears every time a position opens or gets filled can really strip away effectiveness.

For caregiver openings in existing programs, there's a less time-consuming and highly effective tie-breaker. Invite candidates to spend a supervised day inside the program. Observing potential program people right alongside the children can give everyone a splendid idea of who may fit the program and who may not.

Eventually, this entire process will reveal the likeliest candidate(s). Offer the top pick(s) the position(s) right away, perhaps by telephone. Make certain the candidate agrees to either accept or decline the position within a fixed period of time—for example, by the end of the week. To help candidates make their decisions, clarify once again the conditions of the position and of accepting the offer. If for some reason the top picks decline an offer, don't just take whoever's left unless they meet comparable standards. Although it could mean starting all over, don't be discouraged. Successful recruitment is an ongoing process: Keep things rolling, and there'll be more applications on the desk tomorrow.

Many programs like to have new hirees sign contracts. A contract is one way of making the new hiree responsible for knowing the program handbook's contents, and it takes away the "how-was-I-supposed-to-know?" defense. School-Age Notes' *Before and After School Programs* contains some institutional samples.[4] Still, one might just as easily draw up an agreement that reflects the mutual commitments inherent in a partnership program.

Phase 5: Private Screening. Interviews may yield any number of likeable candidates who appear to possess both aptitude and appropriate personal demeanor. But, unfortunately, appearances can sometimes be deceiving. For peace of mind and legal compliance, further discovery remains necessary before someone becomes a full-on SACC person.

Over the years, a great deal has been made about the right to privacy. It is shamefully discriminatory—though not always illegal—to use someone's age, marital status, family size, or sexual orientation to prohibit employment. Some states have enacted enlightened legislation that redresses such discrimination. If a program's funding sources include public monies, asking questions about such personal matters can lead to Equal Employment Opportunity Commission (EEOC) action and cash judgements. Privately funded programs can choose to take the low moral ground at the risk of inviting civil suit.

However, when children's lives hang in the balance, some aspects of a person's background do demand consideration. After a formal offer has been made—and *only* after this—administrators may:

- require evidence of vaccinations and medical treatment;
- perform a criminal records check (forms are available from state child care licensing agency).

Remember, the hiring doesn't depend on the results of these checks, but it hinges conditionally upon satisfactory results. Some programs like to assign people a probationary status while waiting for their final screening results. In this way, programs can save certain valuable program benefits— and small mounds of paperwork—for the people who make it all the way through the process.

ANOTHER WELL TO TAP: FRIENDS OF THE PROGRAM

Besides all these wonderful employees, I also have a wide circle of friends. I cannot overemphasize the value of friends, particularly unemployed friends. There are about four people on whom I can count in such emergencies as an employee's sudden contagious illness.[5]

From the posses of the Old West to the public action groups of New England, American life abounds with examples of unpaid people joining forces with paid ones in a common purpose. In light of recognized crises in drug consumption, communicable disease, poverty, homelessness, education, hate crimes, urban infrastructures, toxic waste, global warming, and ozone depletion, it sometimes seems that clear and present dangers have become too commonplace for a response. Yet somehow, because of rampant apathy—or perhaps in spite of it—thousands stand ready to befriend the coming generation, to help care for and guide it into the world that lies ahead. These thousands give their goodwill, their affection, and their support simply because they have it to give. These are the Friends of the Program.

The world at large truly is a dangerous place. Rocky realities of child rape, sidewalk shootings, and missing children have reinforced the fearful perception that anyone may be an enemy. But this view causes many to lose sight of the fact that the opposite is also true: Anyone may be a friend. Just by virtue of its focus on children, a SACC program can be a powerful vehicle for awakening others' empathy and compassion, fueling the program partnership.

The primary purpose of SACC is to undo children's isolation and the accompanying dangers. How well can programs serve that purpose when they shunt children into en masse isolation, surrounded only by paid watchers and snack servers? Yet hundreds of existing programs play out this scenario day after monotonous day, their administrators unaware of how they perpetuate the very isolation they are charged to undo. Opening the program to Friends can break this cycle by bringing fresh energy and vitality to daily experiences, by offering caregivers perspective on their interactions with children, by offering children a window on the world beyond the walls.

Friends of the Program come in all shapes and sizes. They may be the director's personal acquaintances. They may belong to a group such as Foster Grandparents. They may be children's parents or other relatives. They may be skilled professionals who are between assignments. They may be ballet instructors or furniture makers. They may be in wheelchairs. They may be anyone with some time and understanding to share.

Identifying Friends always calls for more than a little discernment. Friends will offer up their assistance freely, asking only for the privilege to help. If their attitude is that they're doing someone a favor, if they arrive with strings attached, if they're trying to drum up sales, they are definitely *not* Friends of the Program.

Returned friendship, not money, is the currency between Friends and the program. How each director accomplishes this exchange, as well as how it affects the overall program, depends entirely on the director. It simply follows that a director's capacity to run a successful SACC program depends on a capacity to make and build friendships.

THE LAST RESORT: PAID SUBSTITUTES

Extraordinary circumstances may arise when, for a day or two, neither regular caregivers nor Friends of the Program can supply a proper caregiver-child ratio. A well-run program won't experience this very often, but when it does, a director may have to resort to a paid substitute. If a director occasionally chooses to compensate a Friend of the Program with cash, that doesn't automatically classify the Friend as a substitute. For whatever reasons, a substitute can only afford to show up for a promise of pay.

The most appropriate method for cultivating substitutes derives, naturally enough, from the partnership way. Sharing resources between programs can mean setting up a substitute pool from which several programs may draw. Where a single-site program can't support another qualified caregiver, perhaps a multi-site program and/or a partnered network of several single-site programs can.

Shared substitutes benefit from more caring hours, becoming more familiar with caregiving and perhaps more likely to continue. The continuity gives them a better opportunity to become more intimate in their caregiving. There's always an outside chance that this intimacy might transform them into Friends of the Program.

The sharing pool also creates a built-in "Caregiver Exchange Program," which enhances the flow of cultural information between sites and programs. And the advantage to the director? Less time gets wasted on substitute hunts or on orienting people who never come back.

Prior to assignment: Substitutes can pretty much charge whatever they can get. Be prepared to pay the price. So that everyone has a chance to see what they're getting into, ask potential subs to visit the program sometime during normal operating hours. Print up an information sheet for them that includes basic program goals, regular schedules, first aid kit location, site and materials layout, and special information concerning particular children.

On assignment: Ask a regular caregiver to help the sub and to introduce her/him to the children. A familiar face can ease the strain between strangers.

Post-assignment: Get feedback from the children, caregivers, and the sub. Rate the various responses to help determine future substitute procedures and practices. Reinforce positive feedback by contacting and thanking the sub.

FOLLOWING ALONG IN SINGLE FILES

Application forms. Interview forms. Health forms. Orientation forms. Certification forms. Evaluation forms. Every single step of the way creates another piece of paperwork. That's why they invented file folders.

In a well-organized program, a file gets opened for every program person—and that means *everyone*. Potential hirees' files open with application and reference forms. Friends of the Program start off with availability and contact information sheets, agency partners with fact sheets, and so on.

To keep track of the myriad documents, directors will find another form handy: *the checklist of required forms.* Especially for paid program people's files, an itemized rundown helps keep the paper flow under control. School-Age NOTES' *Before and After School Programs* contains one such basic checklist[6] and recommends attaching it inside the appropriate folder. This is a good idea.

• *Orientation.* Becoming accustomed to a new place and new people takes time. In brand-new programs, everyone can find themselves learning to swim together in strange waters. But after a while, successful new programs develop their own rhythms and patterns, senses of what works and what doesn't. "Veterans" of only a few months can give newcomers valuable assistance in their orientation, and well-established program people have even more to offer. Each orientation sheds fresh light on what might otherwise become stale routine.

Orientation basics—Handbook familiarity, evacuation procedures, medical emergencies, and other surface contingencies—can be standardized. This can spawn yet another form: *the orientation checklist*. The important thing is to make sure that new program people have time to ask questions, time to absorb relevant printed matter, time to get truly oriented.

• *Personal Evaluation*. The stereotypical evaluation procedure arouses all kinds of anxiety. Being dressed up on best behavior before a stern-faced critical administrator or panel isn't much fun. But evaluation needn't take this result-oriented form nor induce these threatening effects.

An *ongoing performance evaluation* brings things back into synch with process orientation. It's daily invocation of critical thinking among program people that makes such a process possible. For the director, it means staying receptive to observations from every sector—children, parents, other program people, Friends of the Program, site support people. There's no sense waiting till the last minute (the formal review) to take action.

A person's file can often show that person something she/he might not have realized otherwise. It might contain unsolicited letters of commendation . . . or complaints from the maintenance crew. It stands as a visible record of a person's impact on program partners, and it can carry added weight when mere words lose their meaning, as they sometimes do.

The danger here lies in using the file as a sword of Damocles instead of as a friendly developmental tool. Threatening someone that "this is going to go in your file" has a nasty Orwellian ring to it. For this reason, with the exception of confidential references, give people open access to their own file's contents. They deserve to see how their paper profile is shaping up as time goes on.

When it is part of an ongoing performance evaluation, a formal review punctuates rather than defines. Areas for improvement and goal-setting flow from even-handed mutual perceptions that are arrived at over a period of months. Talking points for the formal review will have been examined and explored beforehand, through applied use of the personal evaluation. The reviewer can help the program person measure performance and progress in a meaningful context. What might have been a rite of judgement has been transformed into a step of personal growth and program betterment.

At subsequent formal reviews, written records can help recall earlier objectives and goals. These records can point up interim achievements, reinforcing people's confidence. Written records of all reviews belong in the personal file.

• *Separation and Dismissal*. Every person who regularly joins the SACC environment brings some kind of energy to the daily experience. Some bring youthful liveliness for just a year, others a decade or more of comfort. However long or short their stay, a person's departure can deeply affect the lives of children and other program people, even more deeply than their arrival.

In the most benign form of departure, *voluntary separation,* program people reach a natural or previously agreed upon point in time when life's many alternatives beckon them onward. Most directors ask for written notice of decision no less than two weeks before the intended date of departure. This notice goes into the personal file prior to closure. Where appropriate, time can then be arranged for the person who is leaving to help orient someone new.

A voluntary separation presupposes that most everyone has been happy with this person, that they might not wish to lose this person from their daily experience. Though they are somewhat adaptable, school-age children may be hard pressed to understand why someone they like has to go away. Depending on how it is handled, a separation can cause children undue behavioral problems or it can be an excellent opportunity for them to deal openly with fear, anger, and sadness about being left behind.

Special events help mark important turning points in a program's life. It might be a nice idea to promote a bon voyage party on this person's last day with the children. Leave it until later to close the personal file.

More problematic are the two types of *involuntary separation.* The first type arises from circumstances that in no way reflect on a person's performance: budget cuts, a change in management, merging of programs, and so on. No one may wish to separate; the director may have to make an unpleasant command decision.

Personal file data may be of some use in regard to these painful decisions. Directors may later be asked to justify their actions with the paper trail, so a private review of files seems in order. Other political and legal considerations beyond the scope of this text may also affect the final decision. However, in most cases, extreme differences won't show up in the files.

In the event of involuntary separation, apply the same standard that is requested of program people. Use the same minimum period of notice, and put it in writing, with a copy for the file. Programs with any resources available at all provide severance pay, at least one or two weeks' typical wages or salary. And, again, the children's responses deserve consideration. Unless children are already jaded by people's comings and goings, trying to make it quick and painless often results in behavioral patterns of denial and sudden shock.

After the separation, keep these people's files open. Further contact and correspondence may come in regarding COBRA (extended health insurance), unemployment insurance, and a variety of other post-employment concerns.

The second type of involuntary separation is *dismissal for cause,* otherwise known as getting fired. Sometimes people suddenly go over the top in front of witnesses, which can justify firing on the spot. Much more often, dismissal is the culmination of a series of events, all of which had best be recorded in the personal file.

NOTES

1. Docia Zavitkovsky, "Children First: A Look at the Needs of School-Age Children," *School-Age Child Care, Programs and Issues* (Urbana, IL: ERIC/EECE, 1980), p. 6.

2. The socio-political implications of the term "androcratic" are discussed extensively by Riane Eisler in *The Chalice and the Blade*.

3. Sue Lawyer-Tarr, *How to Work with School-Age Children and Love Them* (Tulsa, OK: Clubhouse After School Caring and Sharing, Inc., 1980), p. 70.

4. Mary McDonald Richards, *Before and After School Programs: A Start-Up and Administration Manual* (Nashville, TN: School-Age Notes, 1991).

5. Lawyer-Tarr, *How to Work with School-Age Children*, p. 74.

6. Richards, *Before and After School Programs*, p. I/25.

FOR FURTHER REFERENCE

Bellm, Dan, and Marcy Whitebook. 1986. *A Good Sub Is Hard to Find*. Oakland, CA: Child Care Employee Project.

Bellm, Dan, Marcy Whitebook, Peyton Nattinger, and Carol Pemberton. 1988 reprint. "Special Stresses of School Age Child Care Work." Oakland, CA: Child Care Employee Project.

Child Care Employee Project. 1990. *Who Cares? Child Care Teachers and the Quality of Care in America*. Oakland, CA: Child Care Employee Project. (Final report of the National Child Care Staffing Study.)

Jorde-Bloom, Paula, Marilyn Sheerer and Joan Britz. 1991. *Blueprint for Action*. Lake Forest, IL: New Horizons, P.O. Box 863, 60045.

Lawyer-Tarr, Sue. 1991. *School-Age Child Care Professional Training: A Workbook for Teaching Staff*. Tulsa, OK: Clubhouse Press, 1906 South Boston, 74119.

Neugebauer, Roger, ed. Undated reprint. *The Best of Exchange #1: Enhancing Your Professional Growth*. Redmond, WA: Exchange Press.

———. Undated reprint. *The Best of Exchange #3: Fostering Improved Staff Performance*. Redmond, WA: Exchange Press.

Chapter 9

INTERNAL POLICIES AND PROCEDURES

To illustrate the origins of a nation's struggle for identity, traditional American histories often point to the Boston Tea Party. They tell how tax-weary American colonists boarded a British ship and heaved an importer's cargo of taxable tea into harbor waters. Visual renderings of the event often sport the motto of these supposed revolutionaries: "No taxation without representation." It certainly makes for a wonderful democratic legend.

Modern texts seek to reveal the actual motivations behind such legends. Some reasonably suggest that those who boarded the ship were merely company thugs, hired by another tea importer who wished to improve his own immediate position. To throw off suspicions against him, this unscrupulous competitor disguised his thugs as the "terrorists" of the day, American revolutionaries. In point of fact, the Boston Tea Party, long heralded as a turning point in American independence, may well have been nothing more than business as usual.

Planners of a school-age child care program may state their purposes and put together an administrative/financial structure. They may site, stock, and staff a program accordingly. They may assert what they like about this program. But will it provide families a meaningful alternative to the status quo? In the penetrating gaze of potential clients, the whole thing may seem to be nothing more than business as usual.

Who finally determines whether or not a SACC program successfully serves? Its clients. In areas where parents hold tight rein over their children's lives, they will wish to see that standard upheld by any SACC program they patronize. In other areas, where children exercise greater degrees of physical freedom and access, they will vote with their feet. Like any business, school-age child care relies for survival on its clients' faith.

So, where conditions approximate that of a war zone, SACC planners cannot blithely proceed along conventional paths and hope to serve. And communities with finely trimmed lawns and white picket fences are unlikely to accept revisionist programming. As marketing and education professionals have debated for years, there's a fine line between giving people what they want and enlightening them about what there is to want.

POLICY COMPONENTS

SACC policies, procedures, and regulations all properly stem from a recognition of parents and children as a distinct special-interest group. In a special-interest group, one common condition or understanding between all group members unites the group in a common cause or purpose. Here, the special interest is "quality time" for school-age children. In addition to income policy (see Chapter 5), there are nine other policy components that make up SACC "quality time."

Child eligibility and/or *parental eligibility* determine admission procedures and describe who may avail themselves of a particular program.

Group size and *caregiver-child ratios* reflect the result of administering these procedures.

Health practices and *physical risk management* are determined not only by city and state regulation but also by an informed understanding of how people live . . . and die.

Food and nutrition standards vary between economic classes, but nutritional requirements don't.

Behavior standards and discipline are co-determined by city-state regulations, parental disposition, and children's particularistic natures.

Parental partnership derives from internal family dynamics and workplace demands. For the most part, these exist—and belong—beyond the dictates of program policymakers. However, some policies engender greater parental participation than others.

ADMISSIONS

What happens when many people seek the same limited resource? Usually, egalitarian precepts about age, ability to pay, infirmity, intensity of desire, and other relative factors go right up the chimney. A SACC program site can only accomodate so many children at a time. The first criterion for admission usually boils down to who gets there first.

Unregulated programs that pile children one on top of another miss the point altogether. In effect, they have no admission policy. To circumvent an involuntary shutdown, they may have to go through an entire series of remedies: replacing the director, relocating the program, initiating a detailed expansion plan, or surrendering authority to another partner agency— all for the want of workable enrollment limits.

Programs just starting up usually experience the opposite problem: underenrollment. Rather than flocking in, parents and children may take a wait-and-see position before committing themselves to something new. In fact, most start-ups cater primarily to what are known as *early adopters,* people who are generally more willing to accept unfamiliar goods and services. Early adopters possess a vested authority in the community as public opinion leaders. An admission policy that embraces their interests clears the way for subsequent enrollment.

In some cases, underenrollment may be due to some other planning factor oversight: poor CANARI evaluation, lax administration, or inappropriate site selection. But it can also result from too-restrictive admission criteria, which keep out people who might otherwise be well served. From the very beginning, admission policy profoundly affects program viability.

Children's Eligibility

Chronological Age

A 1988 SACCProject study, *SACC in America,* confirmed that children between the ages of five and nine constitute the vast majority of those attending programs. Fully 93 percent of the programs studied included kindergartners in their scope of service, while only 9 percent admitted children older than age twelve. Even these latter programs reported that in the main, enrollment dropped off considerably above age nine, the point at which societal expectations of self-care start to kick in.

In most states, the number of children enrolled from each age group corresponds to a regulatory caregiver-child ratio. More caregivers are legally required for children aged five and six than for those over age six. At this writing, for example, Minnesota requires a ratio of one caregiver for every ten five-year-olds, or 1:10, but at age six, the ratio goes up to 1:15.

Legislators intend these state-set ratios to be absolute rock-bottom floor levels for licensing. Unfortunately, many a cost-cutting program takes undue license from the state and makes these minimums standard operating procedure. To avoid running a least-acceptable program, some criteria other than age must be considered.

School Grade Level

SACC eligibility frequently ends for children before they even complete their elementary education, that is, after fifth grade. This practice sharply contrasts with state licensing standards, which permit admissions up to ages thirteen or fourteen. So, although nothing in the regulations prevents programs from serving children through ninth grade, providers have a harder time planning and managing appropriate service components for the middle or junior high school set.

As discussed in the statement of mission section in Chapter 1, planners face challenge enough as they strive to organize new programs. For them, limiting admissions at the start to kindergartners or below a certain grade level helps keep the focus on mission and service. It's easy to imagine that, after a few years of successful operation, upping the grade level limit might seem too risky, too much effort, or too unpredictable.

Even so, providers of well-established programs, rich in goodwill and resources, have met the initial challenges and have prevailed. For these providers, it may very well be time to consider filling the service vacuum that lies between the end of SACC and the start of teenage youth programs.

Neighborhood of Residence and/or Location of School Attended

A school-run program may limit admission to enrolled students. A corporate-backed community program may set geographical boundaries relative to its zip code area. Projected program capacity, number of sites, planners' philosophies, and funders' agendas all will affect the use of these two criteria.

For multi-site programs, *cross-registration* admits a child who lives or attends school outside a site's usual service area. Cross-registration prioritizes admission for children (1) whose primary site has reached maximum enrollment; (2) whose primary residence area or school has no program; and (3) whose circumstance administrators deem "special." Since a usual program goal is to make care arrangements safe and sensible, the most common stumbling blocks to a policy of cross-registration are transportation logistics and liability concerns.

An *open enrollment policy* ignores these two criteria altogether. At programs with open enrollment, children who live one block outside what might have been a limit line get the opportunity for care. Planners who are concerned about underutilization might best adopt this more inclusive policy.

CLOSE-UP: Greenwood Family Life Center, Dorchester, Massachusetts

In hard economic conditions, it's also hard to start a new adventure. But that's exactly what one church organization set out to do. In September 1990, with the help of several religious students, the Center's Rev. Bill

Loesch, a United Church of Christ pastor, volunteered to plan, start up, and seek initial funding for a drop-in afterschool program.

The Center, located in Greenwood Memorial United Methodist Church, operates entirely through volunteer assistance. The church's pastor and congregation support the effort by providing the necessary space at no cost. The volunteers include a former nun, an Australian lay woman, and a young woman seeking ordination in the Presbyterian Church.

Joined in purpose, these caregivers recruited teens and parents to operate the program, which, in its first six months, served up to thirty-five children from sixteen different schools. With pottery work, arts, group games, and informal recreation, they have sought to offer these children a chance to develop their self-esteem and cooperative skills in a family-style setting.

Source: Rev. Bill Loesch.

Family Size and Income

Government-funded programs inherit their admission policies from their funding agencies. Priorities are set according to (1) agency-assessed degree of family crisis; and (2) sources and levels of income.

The following priority list for one state's Title XX day care programs is illustrative:

1. Referrals from the Department of Family and Children's Services for children who are in danger of neglect or abuse.
2. Employed parents who are receiving Aid to Families with Dependent Children (AFDC).
3. Income-eligible parents who are employed, but who are eligible for aid because of level of income.
4. Other income-eligible clients.
5. Former clients.

Religious Affiliation

This de facto qualification often applies to programs operated at parochial and religious school sites. Being a member of the parish/church/temple and a student in the school, a child qualifies for admission. Before getting involved with restrictive policies, consider the livelier alternative of multidenominational enrollment.

Physical/Medical/Emotional Condition

Every child has his or her own special nature, but some have personal qualities that make them even more special and demanding than most. Historically, family support service for these children has suffered from inadequate funding and organization. For the most part, these children's SACC options are, in the word of one director, "abysmal."

Martha Ziegler of the Federation of Children with Special Needs once put it this way:

The length of the school day and a lack of after-school activities prohibit many mothers of handicapped children from participation in employment or educational opportunities. Such women, especially low- or moderate-income women ineligible for welfare support, are thus in a double bind. Because their children often require costly special services and equipment, they have a great need to earn income; however, they cannot earn that income unless after-school care is available for their handicapped children.[1]

Not every special child is "handicapped." Less overt conditions can make a child special, too. Attention deficit syndrome, hyperactivity, severe depression, immune system weakness, unrevealed abuse—any number of things can impact a child adversely, taking that child beyond the range of so-called normal care. In fact, any maladaptive trait that heightens a child's demand for care and attention makes that child special.

Special or average, all children deserve consideration of their strengths, abilities, and potential benefit from SACC. A special-needs school in Fairfax County, Virginia, serves mentally retarded and physically disadvantaged children aged five to twenty-one. The school also offers afterschool SACC. As for any other SACC program, admission was initially age-restricted to children five through eleven. It soon became clear to the school principal that in this case such a restriction made no sense. He realized that "special" means special in more ways than one, and he opened the program to all of his school's children, regardless of their chronological age.

Superior or average, a PD can still meet with each child's parent(s) to discuss pluses and minuses. Will a particular group setting benefit from the child's inclusion? Can the child actually benefit? Does admitting the child fit snugly into other service and work responsibilities?

Consulting with the caregivers most likely to take responsibility for a child's daily experience also makes good sense. Some social service coordinators can provide important elements for decisions based on experience, not simply fear or speculation. Make every possible effort to overcome ingrained prejudice against someone special. Any child deserves at least that much.

Tenure: The Hidden Eligibility Requirement

In a parent-run program, it would come as no surprise that board members' children receive admission preference over other children. With most other administering bodies, a standard of contiguous care seems to apply. Once enrolled, children may remain in care until they opt out, their parents remove them, or the program bars them for cause. Children who attended previous care segments get priority over newcomers.

Tenure also favors children's brothers and sisters. Solely by dint of blood relation, younger siblings get priority over other children . . . and at reduced rates to boot! Of course, it's good service practice to include two or more children from the same family. It's also good marketing strategy, since it capitalizes on an existing relationship.

As the pitfalls of political and academic tenure have become the targets of public inquiry, so it behooves SACC administrators to examine their own program's tenure policies. Without question, stability within a social group can create a sense of confidence, safety, and freedom to express oneself. On the other hand, a dysfunctional family can often benefit from the presence of a new face, new thoughts, and new perspectives. Tenured admissions certainly limit the program's exposure to "unknown" forces, but they can also precipitate staleness, predictability, and institutionalized dysfunctions.

Families with an inside track will want to keep it, but is that always best for everyone involved with the program? The tenure category belongs as an equal consideration for admission, not an overriding one.

Qualification or Discrimination?

All programs that incorporate as nonprofit organizations must file a policy affidavit of nondiscriminatory admission. For example:

ClubTime makes no discrimination in admissions or determination of enrollment on the basis of race, sex, religion, creed, color, or national origin.

Naturally, Affirmative Action policies in effect for schools, local agencies, or municipal and county governments also apply to SACC programs that these entities fund, administer, or host.

Generous program planners have been known to add further to the previous statement. To wit:

It is our policy to register families without regard to race, creed, color, physical or mental disability, sex, national origin, or income.

In this example, planners make even more clear their commitment to the principles of Affirmative Action. At this writing, few programs can marshall the resources—or, for that matter, the personal resolve—necessary to fulfill such goals totally. However, making such a statement from the outset bodes well for an inclusion-minded clientele.

Parents' Eligibility

Anti-discrimination policies only express what programs will *not* consider in their admission reviews. The matter remains as to what criteria can equitably qualify one child more highly than another. At its inception in 1973, The Hephzibah Children's Association SACC program in Oak Park, Illinois, took the following position:

The requirements for admission are:
• The child must be in kindergarten through fifth grade;
• The child must be a resident of Oak Park or River Forest, or go to school in Oak Park or River Forest;
• The parents must be working or students.

Hephzibah selected three children's eligibility categories (school grade, neighborhood of residence, and school attended). But what about the last requirement?

In its wording, this policy presupposes a particular—and untowardly exclusive—family circumstance. Note the presumption of a two-parent dual-income household for each enrolled child. The admission policy makes no concession for a single-parent family in which the parent is currently seeking employment. Under this policy, a child whose parents divorce and whose custodial parent does not immediately work or study could theoretically be barred from the program.

Hephzibah has long since amended its admission policy, which no longer implies that it will restrict or exclude children because of their parents' divorce, job loss, disability, or illness. Its more proactive policy better responds to changing social realities.

BRIDGE OF SIZE

Only so many people can fit into a given amount of space. Somewhere along the line, the square footage designated for SACC comes to a finite end, and so must the total enrollment size of the program. Even where green rolling fields stretch for hundreds of yards, 300 school-age children wandering around in all directions would cease to resemble anything akin to SACC. In terms of enrollment, site-based school-age care has to stop somewhere.

Fortunately for site directors, total site attendance falls well below 300, but not always well enough. Some sites carry in excess of 100 children. In a small program, a lone caregiver/director might—just *might*—collect tuitions, order supplies, cut checks, prepare food, and directly care for children—but only at the risk of a quick burnout.

For single or multi-site programs, total enrollment depends on standards and requisites of any partner agencies, but most state and city regulations also call for a minimum square footage allowance per child. These regulations include caveats such as this one: "Work areas, unused space, and areas which are not exclusively used for child care center purposes shall not be considered when computing minimum space."[2] So, technically, the total allowable space creates a legal limit to total enrollment size.

Never let financial difficulties precipitate an increase in total enrollment. If the law allows a ratio of 1:28, legal limits and desirable limits rarely coincide. When they enact child care laws, legislators don't have any particular groups of children in mind. An appropriate maximum enrollment figure takes into account the appropriate number of children who can receive attention and care. The job of fixing a reasonable, responsible figure rests with the PD and partner administrators.

Regulating population figures may seem a difficult task, and it is. Entire nations wrestle with notions and methods of population control. China sets a legal limit of two children per family, a law that at times translates into serious social dilemmas. In the United States, families may become so large as to run into double digits without any legal proscription, which translates into other types of social dilemmas. Setting a program's size limit answers a disturbing question: Who may benefit from available resources, and who may not?

Group Size

Program size refers to the total number of children served at all sites at all times. *Group size* describes the number of children for which one or more caregivers take direct, on-site responsibility. The smaller the group, the more individuated the attention to each child, and the more successful the program.

Group size can ebb and flow in relation to time of day and type of activity. For example, in one single-site program with fifty children, all may arrive at a common meeting point, and group size may open at fifty. As children move off into more specific areas of interest, they create varying smaller group sizes.

For lack of imagination, many PDs seek to regulate lines of caregiver responsibility by pre-ordaining group sizes. In the example, the PD might arbitrarily "bundle" the same five groups with the same ten children every day. According to program regulations, children must stay with their group, caregivers must stay with their group, and everyone must do the same thing the same way at the same time.

What's developmentally appropriate for one third-grader may be boring for another. One nine-year-old might like to re-visit a sensory experience deemed appropriate for six-year-olds. Just like other human beings, children have their own ideas about desirable social groupings. On paper, locking them into groups without giving them some choice in the matter may *seem* to make internal regulation easier. It can even be argued to put some predictability into at-risk children's lives. But when administrative authority overtakes the precepts of child development, be on the lookout for a whole new crop of behavioral problems.

The Tribes process advanced by Jeanne Gibbs[3] offers a more people-focused means by which to arrive at group composition. By virtue of children's innate social bent, by their daily selection of different experiences, group formation itself becomes a meaningful activity. It better reflects the SACC mission of social development, and it makes a much better indicator of which adult-directed activities children appreciate and which they resist. Most of all, it gives children the chance to explain just exactly who they are and who they'd like to be.

Don't be afraid of different group sizes. Maybe one day it's fifteen for kickball, twelve for reading, two for rocket science, seven for dramatic play, and forty for an excursion, then tomorrow it's something else again. Help it happen.

Caregiver-Child Ratio

How many caregivers have direct responsibility for a group? Texas requires only a 1:28 ratio, meaning that directors may assign only one caregiver to each group of twenty-eight children. This would be considered a serious violation in California, where the legal ratio—1:14—requires twice as many caregivers for the same number of children.

Due to the impact of group size on people's lives, most states have some regulatory laws that address the issue of caregiver-child ratios. For children who have spent the rest of the day in large classrooms, an all-afternoon group size of thirty, fifty, or more can hardly afford an opportunity to wind down or engage in quiet solitary activity. And when burdened by overwhelming group sizes, caregivers more closely resemble cattleherders.

Balancing the affordable with the humane makes program practices more manageable. With appropriate ratios, caregivers don't just sit and watch, calling out warnings from a stationary position. Nor do they go about all day directing traffic. They actively facilitate children's dynamic experiences, stepping in when the situation demands, stepping back as the children get oriented to the experiences at hand.

A FRONTLINE HMO

All concerned parents want concrete assurances about their children's health, safety, and well-being. Such assurances rest on policies regarding nutrition, illness, accidental injury, emergency conditions, and purported abuse. In this sense, a SACC program actually functions as a health maintenance organization (HMO), and that means: (1) helping prevent the spread of disease; (2) supporting behaviors that maintain existing personal health and hygiene; (3) intervening when conditions threaten illness and injury.

Most parents with children in school have seen and filled out emergency cards containing their day-and-night contact information. SACC directors also maintain just such an emergency file. Keep this file apart from any other records and easily accessible to program adults. Also keep it close to the nearest available telephone, and update it regularly. Make all caregivers aware of its presence and purpose. Don't run SACC without it.

Health Practices

Prior to formal admission, ask parents to provide proof of their children's immunizations, medical and/or dental forms, and special authorizations for dispensing medications. Despite paperwork precautions, children occasionally fall sick. Caregivers and directors must agree on exactly what formally constitutes an "emergency illness," then decide how to proceed if one arises. Put these procedures down in writing. One program's policy illustrates:

MEDICAL EMERGENCIES

For children who become ill while at the Center, parents will be contacted and the child sent home for the following:

1. Oral temperature 101 degrees or greater
2. Vomiting once
3. Liquid stools
4. Uncontrollable and persistent cough
5. Appearance of acute illness or complaint of severe pain

In the event a child exhibits any of these symptoms, that child's parent will be phoned. . . . Unless other specific arrangements have been made previously, when the coordinator deems a child too ill to remain in the program, parents have the responsibility and will be expected to pick up their child as soon as possible.

Until the parent arrives, the child will be excluded from activities with other children. The child will rest in the "quiet area" secluded from the main program area, supervised by a staff member. Health situations of general import will be brought to the attention of the Health and Safety Committee. This committee will have a role in determining Center policy in dealing with the staff and the coordinator of the Center. Parents will be personally notified about outbreaks of:

1. Streptococcal pharyngitis
2. Impetigo
3. Measles, mumps, chicken pox, rubella
4. Pinworms
5. Lice

No policy describes every possible response to every possible condition. A child exhibiting, say, all five emergency symptoms, and severe bleeding besides, probably can't wait the time it takes for a parent to drive forty miles from work. Only a fool would leave a child in this condition waiting for that parent. Don't live by policies. Just allow them to guide responses to the more typical situations.

Obviously, a child with chicken pox, measles, pink-eye, or some highly contagious airborne disease ought to remain home for the duration. Unfortunately, not all parents will be able to identify the onset of such illnesses. Directors and caregivers who can spot and separate contagious children certainly serve better than those who can't tell the difference.

For the parents who can figure it out, their part includes keeping their child or children at home, as well as notifying the program about the cause of absence. The people at the local board of health may stipulate that PDs notify them about cases of contagious diseases, so PDs have to know. One more piece of contagious paperwork: Before allowing a child back, require an "all clear" note from a doctor.

Here's how an illness policy might look:

Parents may *not* bring a child to the Center if the child has:

1. A strep throat or impetigo that has not been treated with antibiotics for at least 24 hours;
2. Any rash of acute onset associated with fever or symptoms of illness;
3. An oral temperature of 100 degrees or greater;
4. Persistent vomiting and/or diarrhea in the previous 12 hours.

If a child has been diagnosed with any of these, we must receive a doctor's signed note indicating that this child may safely return to the Center.

If a child's absence lasts five or more consecutive days due to a contagious disease, common colds excepted, parents must bring in a doctor's signed statement indicating that the child and any enrolled siblings have passed the communicable stage.

In addition to the doctor's statement, the following limitations apply: (1) Chicken Pox—a child may return 5 days after the last blister has scabbed; (2) Pinworm—a child may return after being on medication for 48 hours.

Physical Risk Management

Accidents can happen. Windows can get broken. Children can get hurt. Caregivers can get hurt. Programs can get sued. As one social service executive from Chicago puts it: "City park regulations require the ground to absorb a fall from eight feet. You can't just put in the sod, put a swing down, and call that a playground."

Some concerns are real. In Massachusetts, a badly anchored shelf unit collapsed on a young girl and crushed her to death. In North Carolina, a young boy was entangled in a makeshift climbing structure's steel bars and fractured his skull. Similar stories abound. Casual attitudes toward physical risk inevitably result in either preventable injuries or death.

Other concerns are less real. Filled with visions of mangled limbs and million-dollar lawsuits, some programs shift into overprotectiveness. Their liability-driven mentality hangs "no," "don't," "can't," and "stop" like sullen clouds over the children. No children may sit on the floor; not a drop of liquid may be left to evaporate. By eliminating chances, these programs also eliminate incentive, expression, and initiative.

Bumps, bruises, scraped knees, and a little spilled blood naturally occur in the course of normal energetic child's play. Video game training aside, children aged five to nine still haven't perfected small-muscle motor skills or eye-hand coordination. Girls often begin to develop these abilities at an earlier age than boys, but both are subject to other impediments—undiagnosed vision problems, biochemical imbalances, and so on—that interfere with grasping monkey bars and judging distance from a height. So building in reasonable safety precautions means recognizing the general nature of childhood.

Risk management takes more than simple preventive oversight. Children themselves can proactively conceive and fashion risk avoidance strategies. When it comes to intimate dangers, children's strategies may in fact turn out to be superior to those of adults. Here's a case in point:

Dealing with the issue of touching, children in a SAC program brainstormed all the ways that they could think of to "let someone know that you like them." This included, "ask them to sit by you," "ask them to play with you," "invite them to your birthday party," "write them a note," "give them flowers," "tell them," and several other strategies. But it also led to a recognition that you need someone's permission if you want to kiss them: intimate expressions of affection, it was agreed by the group, are only by mutual consent.[4]

The highest risk of injury stems from adults' failure to ensure social respect and physical safety. Even the most controversial SACC activity formats, such as playfighting, come with sets of guidelines designed to maximize prosocial impact and to minimize physical risk. The following guidelines can serve equally well as playfighting ground rules or as a general precautionary checklist.[5]

1. Define and clear area for activity.
2. Use mats, carpet, and pillows to soften indoor area.
3. Use grass or sand area for outdoor activity.
4. Set flexible time limit for activity.
5. Take off shoes, belts, or other impinging articles.
6. Discuss rules for activity.

7. Involve minimum of two adults.

8. STOP activity if injury occurs. Restart only after injured child is cared for.

9. Remind children (and adults!) that this is meant to be a FUN activity, not a time to hurt or be angry.

10. Forbid kicking, biting, hair pulling, choking.

11. Respect one's face, eyes, and genitals as sensitive areas.

12. Settle untoward conflict verbally, with adults as arbitrators.

13. Signal the nominal end of activity five minutes in advance.

14. Allow fifteen minutes as transition between one activity and the next.

Ideally, to respond to injuries that are not life-threatening, caregivers will become well versed in first aid, but at least one properly trained adult ought to be available throughout the day. In any event, local health regulations—not to mention common sense—make a first aid kit mandatory SACC equipment. Familiarize caregivers with its location and contents. A proper kit contains *at least* the following items:

Red Cross First Aid Manual

adhesive bandages

sterile gauze

adhesive tape

liquid antiseptic

scissors

tweezers

syrup of ipecac, single dose container

thermometer

Life-threatening injuries can cause shock and panic not just for the injured party but for everyone else as well. To forestall confusion and panic-induced amnesia, the PD would do well to post a clearly visible list of emergency telephone numbers and basic instructions. To wit:

SERIOUS INJURY RESPONSES

STOP THE BLEEDING

ADMINISTER ARTIFICIAL RESPIRATION

CALL 911

If injured is—

    a child: CALL PARENT OR GUARDIAN

    a caregiver: CALL CAREGIVER'S EMERGENCY CONTACT

General emergency procedures for evacuation can depend on lessor regulations, city codes, and/or other pre-existing conditions. Some programs

Figure 9.1

FIRE ESCAPE PROCEDURES

Close windows and classroom door upon leaving room.

Take roll book from file cabinet.

Children Inside
    Line up with staff member and move outside through
      exit doors in playroom.
    Proceed to the ball field adjacent to parking lot.

Children Outside
    Line up with staff member and proceed to the ball
      field adjacent to the parking lot.

Staff member in charge, immediately check roll of students
present.

* Fire extinguisher is located to the left of the playroom
  door exit.

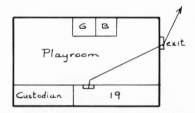

---

may have to generate their own appropriate procedures. Figure 9.1 illustrates the Eugene Latch Key Program's evacuation plan (Eugene, Oregon). Note that the plan includes taking a head count to see if everyone has evacuated safely.

If SACC programs existed in a cultural vacuum, the concerns and guidelines described to this point might complete the discussion of safety. However, severe risks to children's well-being also arise from the mishandling of alcohol, other drugs, and firearms. To promote physical safety in these areas, caregivers might find themselves stepping by proxy into the role of law enforcement agent.

Prohibitions against smoking, drinking, taking drugs, and carrying lethal weapons in a SACC program are self-evident. Tangential effects of these risks may be less obvious, but PDs have no business burying their heads in the sand. Impressing intervention procedures upon children, parents, and caregivers, as well as encouraging them to be situationally responsive, can save lives. Most likely, such procedures will address situations in which

—a parent arrives to pick up a child, and the parent is clearly under the influence of narcotics or alcohol;

—children are discovered to be in possession of narcotics, cigarettes, alcohol, lethal weapons, or unusually large sums of cash;

—anyone other than a registered parent attempts to remove a child from the program site;

—reliable information about imminent and exceptional street violence in the area of the program site becomes known.

Feature relevant procedures prominently in parent handbooks, and make them conditions of caregiver employment.

Food and Nutrition Standards

Time and time again, informal surveys of school-agers confirm a sad fact: The types and availability of nourishment in an average SACC program are simply horrendous. Nearly one in five programs makes no regular provision for children's hunger, counting instead on parents to send along something. Of the rest, most seek only to stave off starvation with a couple of saltines and a three-ounce cup of juice. What could possibly account for this critical failure?

Once again, convenience and expedience are the main culprits. A lot of program people seem to regard snack time as something to hurry up and be done with. "Real" food doesn't fit the scheme of institutional mass feedings. It takes time to select and prepare. Keeping it fresh takes refrigeration and storage capacity. Making it available means having to do more than just ripping open a cardboard carton and handing out plastic-wrapped packages. An objective observer might see little difference between the way in which some program people handle food and the way a zookeeper hurls a bucket of fish to the seals . . . except that the seals eat better.

"Real" food in reasonable quantities can also get pretty messy. Some program people worry more about having to wipe up a spill than just about anything else. For them, maintaining neatness and order takes precedence, so they force school-agers to remain seated while they serve each child in place.

Finally, there's the cost factor. Bottom-line consciousness and shoestring budgets can often barely account for a caregiver's minimum wage. Where, then, can PDs find the money for food?

SACC people don't originate these attitudes toward eating, they simply perpetuate them. Assaulted for a generation by fast foods, junk foods, microwaves, and drive-throughs, few American homes witness anything like what was once the cornerstone of the nuclear family unit: the sit-down family meal. If the only style SACC people know is hand-to-mouth gulp-and-run, how can they promote anything else?

On the positive side, more and more Americans have begun to become aware of the connection between what they eat and how they feel. Tapping what it sees as a trend toward healthier eating habits, Madison Avenue promotes what it calls "high-fiber" and "fat-free" products. Even the world's biggest fast-food chain has come out with salads, carrots, and celery sticks.

Snacking is indeed a program activity like any other. It can be handled in a manner that meaningfully addresses the SACC mission of children's physical, intellectual, and emotional development. It can convey warmth, comfort, and caring. Appropriate food and nutrition policies incorporate the following guidelines.

• *Limit intake of salt, fat, and refined sugars.* The American Cancer Society recommends that children have five daily servings of fruits and vegetables. That's *daily.* If children don't see a carrot or an apple in the program, they may not see one at all. Smart PDs also pay heed to the well-known connection between children's sugar consumption and hyperactivity. Wholesome food not only promotes health but also reduces the incidence of behavior problems.

• *Emphasize recyclables.* A little environmental awareness can't hurt. Many public and private schools have initiated recycling efforts, so programs sited at these ought to have no trouble linking up. Organic wastes like orange peels and eggshells can be turned from garbage into a composting project. And 40 percent of all solid waste produced in this country consists of paper and paper products: paper plates, paper napkins, paper towels, paper cups, paper wrappers, and so on. Reusable items set a more appropriate standard. Program people who feel they must use disposable products can at least use those made of recycled materials.

• *Vary the choices.* This doesn't mean offering a different-flavored cracker every Friday. Central supply warehouses may buy huge quantities at bulk discounts, but living by the economy of scale concept is no way to plan a menu. Children can actually enjoy new textures and flavors along with their familiar favorites. It's one of the easiest ways to put a little diversity into even the most unimaginative program.

• *Make snack time fun, but treat it—and the children—with some dignity.* Of course, it's simpler to stick a piece of food in front of a child and say, "Here, eat this." An equally unpleasant opposite is the food bar concept, in which children are given play money to "buy" their food at a concession stand. Ancient cultures had long-standing rituals of respect and gratitude surrounding their meals. Although the Thanksgiving holiday stands as the last widespread vestige of this in modern America, food is still considered by many as something not to play with. It's pointless to expect children to appreciate their food without showing them *how.*

• *Give children a hand in food preparation.* Like adults, children take more interest in something they themselves create. This principle informs a successful program's meal time. Instead of a rushed mouthful of some factory-made substance, children in these programs get a chance to explore another art activity: culinary art. There's just as much creativity to put to use with bananas, peanut butter, and popcorn as with any other project, and it's okay to eat the final product.

See Chapter 10 for tips about scheduling snacks and meals.

ACTING UP, REACHING OUT

Think of all the stereotypical cliches about children who misbehave. Affluent children are said to be spoiled. Poor ones are said to be deprived. Some say talkative children crave attention, and others say violent ones have no vocabulary to express their feelings. Intelligent children are branded as smart-asses, younger children escape blameless when older ones are near, and compliant quiet ones receive the highest praise. On the verge of the twenty-first century, all of these cliches still flow freely, exerting their untoward influence on adults and children alike.

But cliches are dangerous crutches, designed to relieve people from the burden of having to engage in original thought. Especially when it comes to children's behavior, even when something is often true, rarely is it always true. Special circumstances and conditions lie behind a child's most trivial antisocial behavior, and to ignore them is to deny that child's humanity. Few would expect SACC people to come across as full-on social psychologists. But they are in positions of trust and intimacy with certain children. Being in that position demands at least some effort to understand the factors that influence those children's behaviors. And that may require some original thought.

Behavior Standards and Discipline

Some of the simplest daily events in life rely heavily on computer systems. When something goes wrong, it's become typical for CRT operators to blame their computers. Since everyone knows a computer has no will of its own, they mean to place the blame on higher-level programmers and system maintenance engineers, the people who design and oversee the system.

When one or more children in SACC seem to be getting out of hand, the first thing to look at is the hand. Many of children's typical behavior problems arise from failures in the systems that surround them. Only after correcting every potential system failure will a wise SACC person think about correcting children's behavior.

Successful PDs address the issue of caring behavior from day one. They put into effect and visibly post normative concepts to be observed by children and caregivers in their relations with each other. Jeanne Gibbs' process for social development and cooperative learning depends on just such a set of norms.[6]

ATTENTIVE LISTENING—paying close attention to one another's words and feelings; giving another caring respect and consideration

APPRECIATION/NO PUT DOWNS—avoiding negative remarks, name-calling, hurtful gestures and behaviors; instead . . . treating others kindly and stating appreciation for their unique qualities, value and helpfulness to others

RIGHT TO PASS—choosing when and to what extent one participates in group activities; recognizing that each person has the right to make choices within a group setting; practicing how to say "no" within a peer group

NO NAMES/NO GOSSIP—honoring the confidentiality of a group's discussion; being confident that what we say here stays here

Some system failures are more obvious than others. *Overt system failures* are like flashing red lights: Anyone can recognize them fairly easily. Children who consume high amounts of refined sugar can't help getting hyperactive and sometimes running wild. Even without sugar, children have a naturally high amount of energy that developmentally appropriate activities can tap. Trying to repress this natural exuberance by confining too many children into tiny little classrooms inevitably leads to problems. So does treating most ten-year-olds like five-year-olds. Much of this manual's text goes toward taking care of overt system failures.

Subtle system failures won't jump up and bite. Spotting them takes a little more sensitivity. That's because they have less to do with physical conditions and more to do with human understanding.

One common subtle failure relates to the discussion of gender-related activities in Chapter 4. Gender stereotyping causes program people to punish children, especially girls, for perfectly natural behavior. In many places where boys may evince active, vocal, physically demonstrative behavior, girls may not—unless they wish to be branded tomboys, troublemakers, or worse. Boys may normally prefer to join in gentler activities unduly reserved for girls. It's sometimes tough enough gaining peer acceptance, so some children can become extremely petulant or uncooperative when program people also exclude them.

Another common misunderstanding has to do with the difference between child-directed activity and actual misbehavior. Take the example of two young girls playing with a checkers set. Instead of playing by the rules, the girls are moving the checkers sideways, making geometric designs, making up their own game. A program person happens to see the girls playing "the wrong way" and tries to impose the official rules of checkers on their play. Almost immediately, one girl picks up some checkers and starts throwing them, then knocks the board on the floor and walks away.

As far as the girl is concerned, it's the program person who misbehaved—and she's right.

As these instances demonstrate, subtle system failures generally stem from an institutional mindset on the part of program people. When a child won't placidly give in to mental authoritarianism—what *1984* author George Orwell dubbed *rightthink*—it's hardly a sign of a problem with the child. Program people had better first examine the ways in which they impose their own preconceived notions of right and wrong on otherwise healthy children.

A great many behavior problems fall under the general heading of *mimicry*. Being able to act out or copy someone else's behavior is actually a human survival mechanism. But young children don't critically differentiate when they mimic; their very perception of a particular behavior automatically validates it. This can account for anything from foul language to jumping out of trees to sexually aggressive actions. It's pure hypocrisy to encourage children to emulate adult behavior and then discipline them for succeeding. Psychology experts agree that it's also a common source of childhood neuroses and erratic behaviors.

Sensitive caregivers won't take immediate disciplinary action against children who might be mimicking. They will instead try to find out who or what is being mimicked and seek to resolve the problem with information. Caregivers who think they don't have time to find out about a particular child's external influences only spend that much more time dealing with the results during program hours. They also risk overlooking a clear and present danger to children's emotional and physical well-being.

After thoroughly exhausting systems failure responses, it's time to look at child guidance techniques, only one of which is discipline. Just as with many parents, taking disciplinary action may say more about a caregiver's exhaustion, inflexibility, or lack of imagination than it does about a child's behavior. The old technique of separate-and-isolate can make an adult's life easier, but only occasionally does this punishment fit a particular "crime."

Make no mistake: Sooner or later, children find ways to get what they want. If a program's concept of discipline is to put a child in the "quiet corner," children who don't like being compelled to take part in group activities can easily get out of them by purposefully misbehaving. Program people on ego crusades can try any variation of reverse psychology they like, but as soon as they enter into a power struggle with a child, they've already lost.

Like all program practices, even discipline is a program activity. As such, the most successful strategies invite the children themselves to devise their own discipline. Early each program year, caregivers and children can come to terms with the consequences of norm violations, then contract to abide by those terms. Any child who agrees, then later reneges, runs the terrible risk of being a "liar, liar, pants on fire." Seriously speaking, this kind of self-enforcement imparts a degree of fairness and equity no adult-imposed punishments can possibly hope to match. And children will be more apt to cooperate with censures they themselves have created, thereby reducing the number of later conflicts.

Only the most extreme cases of non-cooperation, violence, or destruction justify arbitrary discipline. Occasionally, children will wreak such havoc without warning. More likely, a behavioral pattern will have emerged over a period of time, and observant caregivers already will have employed a wide variety of mitigating techniques. When a PD makes the difficult decision to suspend or discontinue SACC due to behavioral problems, it usually comes from the urge to protect the other children and caregivers. These children simply require a greater degree of care than a center-based program can reasonably offer.

Parental Partnership

Without even realizing it, people are constantly entering into contractual agreements. When they park their cars, buy sporting event tickets, or spend the night in a motel, there's always some fine print that explains exactly what they're getting for their money. And generally speaking, the service provider doesn't ask them for anything other than their money.

In these types of transactions, neither party really wants any more obligation than is absolutely necessary. Naturally, people accustom themselves to this sort of marketplace mentality in which money buys time. One gets a service, the other gets some money, and that, as they say, is that.

When people enroll their children in a SACC program, when they arrange to render money or vouchers for child care service, they also enter into a contractual agreement. Workplace responsibilities, personal disposition, or something else leads them to believe that a SACC program can and will provide child care when they cannot. Since they have become accustomed to the marketplace mentality, many of these people feel that their signed check or voucher takes care of their end of the contract.

When asked, many PDs express ongoing disappointment that more parents don't get actively involved with their children's SACC programs. PDs try all kinds of ways to engender more parent involvement: monthly or biweekly newsletters, late afternoon general-invitation meetings, PTO-linking, special social events, and so on. Some parent-run programs go so far as to set mandatory requirements, threatening to suspend child care if the parent fails to help out.

But all the pleading in the world can't change the ways people live. With so many other real—and imaginary—demands on their time, parents don't usually opt for SACC because they want more responsibilities. What they do tend to want is less uneasiness about their children's overall well-being. Once the uneasiness has been lessened, parents' motivation to do anything more than write a check will also decrease . . . hence the parent-run programs' threats.

Why would a particular parent choose a particular SACC program for his/her children? All parents have formed mental images of their children. One sees his as a "genius." Another sees hers as a "dear." Still another sees hers as a "go-getter." With these examples in mind, the first parent might choose a SACC program for its enrichment potential, the second for its protective capacity, and the third for its outdoor activity. Tapping into and understanding each parent's image of his/her child also tells program people something about the parent. This knowledge can lead to overall program policies that encourage parents to get involved.

The *parent handbook* constitutes the general terms of agreement between parent and program. It summarizes the pertinent aspects of program policies that affect how parents conduct their own behavior. This normally includes payment schedules, transportation notes, general operating hours and conditions. It also describes required forms, absence and illness procedures, insurance, meals, and discipline practices. Usually, when parents sign registration forms, they are also acknowledging receipt and acceptance of the handbook's contents.

The handbook strongly contributes to first impressions of a program. It is the primary public document of the program, and every parent receives it. If it reflects dominator-style thinking or institutional rigidity, it will actually repulse many parents. In some rare instances parents may appreciate a handbook that bullies them, but not as a general rule. In an effort to make their handbooks "formal," many PDs omit the sweet breath of humanity, ending up with stale and alienating pamphlets. They lose their chances for parental participation before they've begun.

A poorly written handbook furthers parents' *notions of trespass.* Especially in regard to school-sited programs, many parents possess a built-in fatalism. Their experience of school, both as children and as parents, has taught them about the uselessness of questioning teachers and principals. Many have no stomach for the bureaucratic confrontations or the one-note righteousness that characterizes such meetings. They have learned that even as taxpayers, they can exert no direct authority on school practices. So why bother?

Appropriate program policy doesn't simply serve parents' vested authority, it *shares* it. It can begin with a suggestion box for rushed parents. Some programs go on to set up a comfortable area where less-rushed parents can sit and talk for a few minutes before they take their children home. Some highly advanced programs even plan day's-end or weekend activities that encourage parents to participate.

In both small proprietary and large public programs, group transportation arrangements often imply that parents rarely, if ever, appear in person at the program site. And PDs discover that a transportation policy that keeps parents away from a program really does keep parents *away* from a program. This puts the child in the middle as a means of communication between two distant adults—almost the way an unpleasant divorce does. With the parent saying, "You tell them I said . . . ," and the PD saying, "You tell your parents I said . . . ," the child becomes an unwilling pawn in the back-and-forth of it all. It's not exactly a developmentally appropriate situation.

Especially in these kinds of programs, direct communication between program people and parents becomes an essential factor. In all programs, the reason for it relates back to behavior standards and discipline. Conditions or adult behaviors in the home powerfully affect a child's behavior in the program. Admittedly, it remains outside the scope of many programs to act in the capacity of a social service agency. However, to identify problems stemming from mimickry, abuse, and neglect, program people find direct contact with parents absolutely essential.

PRIMARY PROCEDURES

Simple enrollments involve at least four hours per child. Phone inquiries often require eight to ten hours a week. And dealing with potential [program-served] parents can take well over five hours every week. Peak enrollment times often demand the full-time attention of the director.[7]

Who applied for admission when? Whose parent paid how much? Who didn't get permission to go to the museum? Who missed half a day last week? Which children aren't insured? Who's taking medicine when?

Before and during a child's official enrollment, scores of questions like these are going to come up. Putting policies into practice takes informal understandings between parents, children, and program people. It can also take an armful of forms.

Registration forms. The first step toward matching a child with a program is to get some basic information. This can be as simple as the child's name, age, and school attended, along with parent name(s), address, phone numbers, and preferred days/hours of care. If the child meets basic eligibility requirements and the program has room, everyone can move on to the next paperwork stage.

Waiting lists. Programs operating at maximum enrollment can't admit everyone they'd like. Their registration forms might add an optional question: "If your child cannot be enrolled immediately, would you like to be placed on a waiting list?" To keep waiting lists trimmed to sincere applicants, some programs charge a nominal registration fee, usually between $10 and $25. To keep them organized on a first-come first-served basis, it's also a good idea to record dates of receipt. In any event, keep waiting lists up-to-date and confidential.

Pre-registration. Another way to handle waiting lists is through full pre-registration. This means taking advance deposits, as well as

requiring all paperwork such as medical forms, enrollment forms, etc., to be completed and in the child's folder in order to place a name on the waiting list. When a vacancy comes up, the first family with a complete folder would be considered first. Directors who use this method say that the list is self-limiting and that those on the list have shorter waits, since only very interested parents will bother to complete a folder. This method may not work if the wait exceeds six months, since medical information about young children may become obsolete.[8]

Pre-registration aids PDs in determining how many children might be expected for each service component. Make clear the purposes and procedures for pre-registration, as illustrated in Figure 9.2.

Notification of admission status. When waiting lists and pre-registration procedures stand between application and enrollment, interim acknowledgments keep parents informed. Multi-site programs will want to let parents know which site can admit their child(ren). See Figure 9.3 for an example.

Enrollment. Here's where the form count really goes up. In addition to internal forms, state licensing bureaus and other legal bodies require programs to obtain certain documents, such as medical histories, within a mandatory time from date of enrollment. Some programs wisely package every form requiring a parent's signature into a single enrollment packet.

The number of forms can be reduced by requesting most pertinent information with a single form. School-sited or school-run programs can often get most of the information they want from school files. In other situations, a form like the one shown in Figure 9.4 can fill the bill nicely.

Enrollment contract. Most programs ask parents to sign a form that stipulates they have read and agreed to program policies and procedures. Figure 9.5 shows a sample of such an agreement.

Health records, including immunization records. These are required by law and must be updated periodically. Figure 9.6 from the Latchkey Program of Community Day Care, Inc., of Lawrence, Massachusetts, is one example.

Dental examination forms may be required by law, if not taken care of by regular school procedures.

Developmental history. Some programs don't take formal histories, but others have very detailed ones, including personal information that the program feels will better help it to serve the child: an inventory of the child's interests, habits, any special home and family situations, and so forth. In agencies, a social worker or other person—or sometimes a team of professionals—may do this "intake." Programs that are genuinely committed to filling children's needs will want to obtain this information. The example in Figure 9.7 is from the Santa Monica Children's Center in Santa Monica, California.

Figure 9.2

PROCEDURES FOR PRE-REGISTRATION

May 30-June 7, only families currently in Extended Day Care may pre-register for the 1979-80 school year.

Beginning June 8, pre-registration will be open to all special ed. children. Pre-registration will be handled on an individualized basis and total enrollment will be determined by the specific needs of children pre-registered.

Spaces will be strictly limited, and we recommend early pre-registration. Our receipt of pre-registration forms does not guarantee placement in EDC.

A. Complete the pre-registration form attached, detach it from this brochure, and bring or mail it with your registration fees to the EDC office, 4100 Chain Bridge Road, 10th Floor, Fairfax, VA 22030. (This is the Massey Building behind the County Court House.)

B. Make checks or money orders payable to "Fairfax County." Write on the bottom your child(ren)'s name(s) and center.

C. Allow 3 weeks for notification by mail either that space has been reserved for you or that you have been placed on a waiting list.

D. Final registration forms and further information will be sent during the summer to pre-registrants.

E. We strongly recommend that new families call EDC's Special Ed. Program Director (691-2924) for guidance in pre-registering your special ed. child.

 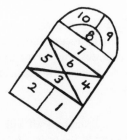

Figure 9.3

AFTER SCHOOL DAY CARE ASSOCIATION, INC.

Dear Parent(s):

We have received your completed enrollment forms, and would like to inform you of the status of your application for your child to attend the After School Day Care program that you requested:

ADMISSION STATUS:

_____Your child/ren has/have been officially enrolled in the _____ program and may attend the program on the date that you requested.

_____The program to which you applied is full, and your child/ren's name(s) has/ have been placed on a waiting list. We will contact you as soon as there is an opening.

_____Full-time enrollments are given priority over part-time enrollments until _____. Since your child/ren is/are scheduled to attend on a part-time basis, we will inform you immediately after _____ whether or not there is space available for your child on the day(s) that you requested.

_____other _____
_____
_____
_____

PROGRAM LOCATION:

_____

We look forward to having your child/ren in the program.

The After School Day Care Association

3200 Monroe St.
Madison, Wi 53711
233-9782

enc: Registration agreement copy
     Enrollment form copy

Authorizations, permissions, and waivers of liability. This form (or forms) delineates *who* is accountable for *what*. It is the authorization for child care and stipulates the hours that the center is responsible for the child. The wording on the authorization form used by a Milwaukee, Wisconsin, program is:

The After School Program staff will assume full responsibility for a child from the time he/she arrives at the program until dismissal time. Dismissal time is 6:00 P.M.

Figure 9.4

ENROLLMENT FORM
AFTER SCHOOL DAY CARE ASSOCIATION

Today's date_____ First date of attendance _____ Program _____

Child's name	School	Age	Date of birth	Sex	Circle days of attendance	Did child attend ASDCA last year?
_____	_____	___	_____	__	M T W TH F	__Yes __No
_____	_____	___	_____	__	M T W TH F	__Yes __No
_____	_____	___	_____	__	M T W TH F	__Yes __No

Parent(s) or guardian(s) with whom child resides:

Name_____Address _____ZIP _____ home phone_____

Name of business _____work address _____work phone _____work hours_____

Name_____Address _____ZIP _____ home phone_____
(if different from above)

Name of business _____work address _____work phone _____work hours_____

Person responsible for payment, if different from above:

Name_____Address _____ZIP _____Phone_____

DEPARTURE PROCEDURES: What do you wish the departure procedures to be for your child (Example: Walk home, take a bus alone, wait to be picked up by parent or authorized person, etc.) If you make a change in these procedures later, please inform the staff *in writing* of any new instructions.

PERSONS AUTHORIZED TO CALL FOR YOUR CHILD: Any changes in this list must be received from you in writing.

1. _____Phone_____ 3. _____Phone_____
2. _____Phone_____ 4. _____Phone_____

CHILD/REN'S PHYSICIAN
Name_____Address _____Phone _____

EMERGENCY NUMBERS: Please give the name, address, and phone number of two people that may be notified in case of emergency or illness, when parents or guardian are not available. These people should live in Madison. Please provide a telephone number where these people may be reached *during program hours*.

_____Address _____Phone_____
Name and relationship to child

_____Address _____Phone_____
Name and relationship to child

EMERGENCY MEDICAL RELEASE
If emergency medical care is deemed necessary and I cannot be contacted, I authorize the day care staff to act in my behalf in granting permission for my child to receive emergency treatment.

_____
Signature of parent or guardian

PHOTOGRAPHIC PERMISSION
I DO   I DO NOT   (circle one) give permission to have my child appear in any media coverage approved by the After School Day Care Association. I understand that the lead teacher, in conjunction with the Coordinator, has been given the authority by the ASDCA Board of Directors to determine appropriate requests.

_____
Signature of parent or guardian

Figure 9.5

REGISTRATION AGREEMENT
Family After School Program, Inc.

---

1. I understand I am enrolling my child for a total of 36 weeks.
2. I understand that during vacation periods and days school is closed because of bad weather there will be no program.
3. I understand that I am responsible for monthly payment of contracted fees, paid in advance. I will give two weeks notice of withdrawal from the program.
4. I agree to pay_____per month for_____days a week.
5. If my child is having problems adjusting to the program, a conference will be arranged between myself and the staff.
6. In the event of illness, vacation, or other absences such as Scouts, music lessons, and other out-of-school activities, the After School Program staff will be notified and I am responsible for my child and tuition payment. Communication with the After School Program staff can be made through the After School Program's main office (964-5545).
7. The After School Program staff will assume full responsibility for my child from the time he/she arrives at the program until dismissal time. Dismissal time will be 6:00 P.M. or earlier upon my written authorization. The child must sign in upon arrival and sign out or be signed out by an authorized person.
8. I give my permission for my child to participate in hikes and field trips.
9. If a medical emergency arises, the After School staff will first attempt to contact me. If I cannot be reached, the After School staff will contact the child's doctor. If the emergency is such that immediate hospital attention is necessary, the After School staff may take my child to the hospital.

I agree to adhere to the Family After School Program registration policies and give my child permission to participate fully in this program.
Signature _____ Date _____
Send registration packet accompanied by the first month's fee and the $7.50 registration fee to Family After School Program, Inc., 2717 E. Hampshire, Milwaukee, WI 53211.

---

or earlier upon parent's written permission. The child must sign in upon arrival and sign out, or be signed out by an authorized person, upon departure.

Emergency medical care. The program should obtain a signed statement from each parent authorizing it to provide emergency medical treatment, including the administration of anesthesia by a physician. This form usually includes a statement by the program that it will notify the parent

Figure 9.6

LATCHKEY INTAKE

Policy Re: Medical Physicals and Immunization Records

We are required by law to maintain current medical records for each child enrolled in the Latchkey program. An immunization record must be on file for each child within two weeks of your child's enrollment in the program.

If your child has had a recent physical, we need a copy of this information, signed by the doctor within two weeks of entry. If your child has not had a physical during the last six months, you must make an appointment with your child's physician at the time of your child's entry into the Latchkey program. The physical must be completed within eight weeks of entry in the program for day care to continue.

I understand the above policy and am aware that if I do not comply, my day care services will be in jeopardy.

Signature: _____

Date: _____

Immunization record will be received by _____

Date of scheduled physical (if necessary) _____

Statement of physical will be received by _____

11/29/79
mkn

---

before the child is treated, if possible. Some programs ask the parent to indicate his or her preference for physician and hospital, or tell them which hospital they'll take the child to. This form also includes a statement that the parent is responsible for any expenses incurred, including an ambulance. It makes sense to request a statement of allergies to medications or anesthesia, although this may be on the health form as well. The example in Figure 9.8 is from the Eakin Care Program in Nashville, Tennessee.

Some parents, because of religious or other reasons, refuse to permit the center to provide their child with medical treatment. Some programs require that this refusal be stated in writing. Similarly, if parents refuse to allow their child to be immunized, some states require a signed statement to this effect; in such cases, programs have to follow state licensing regulations. They may also choose to make their own policy about whether to refuse admission to a child who has not been properly and verifiably immunized.

Medication requests. Most programs will administer medication to a child

Figure 9.7

**SANTA MONICA CHILD CARE CENTERS
Developmental Information**

Date_____

Child's name_____ Birth date _____ Birth place _____

What immediate circumstances make child care services necessary at this time?

_____

Age of child when mother first went to work____ What have been previous plans for care of child? _____

PRESENT FAMILY SITUATION

Parents: living together____separated____divorced____parent ill____ deceased____

Age of child at time of above change in family situation_____

If parents are divorced or separated, does child see absent parent?

Never____rarely____periodically (how often?)____regularly (how often?) _____

What helpful information can you offer about how the absence of a parent has been worked out with the child, and what has been noted about his reaction to these circumstances? (Use reverse side if more space is needed.) _____

_____

List the names, ages, and any special relationships of other children in the family:

Name _____ age _____   _____

Name _____ age _____   _____

Name _____ age _____   _____

Name _____ age _____   _____

What other persons are living in the household? (Indicate relationship to the child.)

_____

Who cares for the child at home during the mother's absence? _____

In how many different places has child lived?____How long in present home?____

Is present home: apartment_____ house_____ other _____

What play space is available? Indoors_____outdoors_____

---

only if they receive a written order from the child's physician and/or written permission from the parent. The medicine must be sent in the original container and have the child's name on it. Some centers insist that the parent hand-deliver the medicine to a staff person.

Authorized pick-up. Some programs ask that parents designate, in writing, which persons (including and/or in addition to parents) may pick the child up and take him or her from the program's official premises—either routinely or in lieu of regular transportation plans, or in specific instances of early dismissal for music lessons, Scouts, or other reasons.

Authorization for liability waiver. This is a statement of who will carry insurance for the child—the program, school, other sponsoring agent, or parent. Some programs, or the school districts in which the program is

Figure 9.8

EAKIN CARE PROGRAM

Authorization for Emergency Medical Care
Date_____
I hereby authorize emergency medical care for my child _____
during attendance at the Eakin Care Program if, in the judgement of the staff, treatment is required for an injury or illness. I hereby also authorize the administering of
anesthetics and recourse to other procedures deemed necessary by the attending
physician.

I understand that whenever possible, I will be notified prior to medical treatment of
my child. I understand that I will be notified at the earliest possible time should prior
notice prove impossible.

The physician of my choice is Dr_____;
Office phone_____; Home phone _____.
The hospital emergency room of my choice is _____

My child is allergic to the following medications and anesthetics:

_____

I understand that I am financially responsible for any expenses for medical care or
transportation incurred on my child's behalf.

_____
                                                    Parent or Guardian's Signature

A Note on Care During Program Hours:

The staff will administer prescription medicines accompanied by a signed, dated
note from a parent or guardian. The staff will not administer aspirin or other non-
prescription drugs.

Parents are requested to notify the staff when their child is ill with a communicable
disease.

---

housed, may demand that the parent sign a "liability waiver" against personal or financial claims, covering their child's participation in the program in general or on field trips only. However, it is questionable whether
courts would uphold the legality of such a statement; in some instances
programs could be sued in spite of the waiver. (See section on liability in
Chapter 12.) Here is how one Y handles the waiver:

The YWCA does *not* provide accident insurance. Please indicate your:
Type of Insurance_____
Company_____
Policy #_____

WAIVER OF CLAIMS
I hereby for myself and my child waive and release all rights and claims
for damages I may have against the YWCA Directors and Staff for any
injuries suffered by my child as a participant in the Child Care Program.

Figure 9.9

FIELD TRIP PERMISSION FORM

Field trips will be planned from time to time as part of the activity of the Adventure Club Program. This will entail walking to nearby parks, wooded areas, stores, etc. Visitations involving bussing will also be planned.

Every possible precaution will be exercised to assure the safety and welfare of your child. However, the school and its authorized agents shall not be responsible, financially or otherwise, should an accident occur.

_____ has permission to participate in the
(child's name)

Adventure Club field trip programs.

_____
                        (Signature)

Field trips. Permission must be obtained to take the child on trips, to use special transportation on these occasions, and so forth. Programs may request a blanket permission form for all trips. Some list the places to which children will be taken; for example, "swimming pool at the Y." Blanket permissions save the effort of sending out notices each time a trip is planned. The example in Figure 9.9 is from the Adventure Club in Robbinsdale, Minnesota.

Authorization for special purpose: publicity, evaluation. Some programs may be part of a project or course in child development or some other study project, or they may be visited for publicity purposes. Parents should be apprised of this before they sign up their children. For example:

In the event the children in the program are included in any newspaper, radio, or television publicity, I give my permission for my child to be included in the pictures, etc.

Programs should also obtain permission for observation on special forms, for example:

I hereby grant permission for my child to be included in evaluation (developmental, physical, and health) and in video-taping and pictures connected with the center program.

Financial information. Parents may need to fill out financial forms to be eligible for partial aid or full scholarships, or to enable the center to take part in a federal program, such as the School Lunch Program. Agencies may require that their own specific forms be completed. In the case of application for federal funds, the forms will be supplied by the appropriate federal agency.

Orientations. Certain procedures can help ease newly enrolled children and parents into the program setting. They give everybody a chance to adjust somewhat beforehand, relieving undue anxieties and putting first days on a more even keel.

Whenever possible, invite newly enrolled children and parent(s) to make their first visit to the program site together. This might be a good time for the PD to sit down with the parent(s) for a personal chat, because crowded all-parent meetings probably won't be conducive to more intimate discussion. The PD can take this one-on-one opportunity to allay any lingering doubts and to clarify last-minute contingencies.

In many programs, new enrollees will already know their SACCmates from the neighborhood or from school, but not all will. Don't just drop them in cold. Programs operating with the Tribes process have prosocial experiences prepared for new arrivals. Other programs can organize first days around empathetic ice-breakers of their own. At the very least, make sure each child gets her/his own cubby or shelf space with his/her name right on it. Having a place to belong means having a place for belongings.

Sign-ins. For accountability, each program uses some mechanism to mark children's arrivals and departures. This can range from a simple signature sheet to magnetic-stripe cards to a palmprint reader. As back-up, a program person visually confirms proper execution of the procedure.

Unexpected absences. Parents' part in accountability involves letting program people know when their child(ren) won't be coming. The concern here is threefold: child safety, the emotional and labor drain on program people, and the potential financial loss for the program. Understandably, PDs institute rather stern penalties for parents who fail to show the proper interest.

If the program has its own phone, an answering machine can take absence notifications any time, day or night. Otherwise, clearly establish who, how, and by what time parents can notify program people. Make certain parents realize the importance of keeping in touch.

When an expected child fails to show up, don't wait three days to find out why. Call the parent(s) immediately. Failing parent contact, call the emergency numbers. It's the time and trouble involved in tracking down a "missing" child that justifies the aforementioned stern penalties. Until repeated inconsideration causes a program to terminate its care contract, that time and trouble comes with the territory.

Termination/denial of program service. As with any other service agreement, either a child, a parent, or the program may choose to discontinue SACC.

Children can and often will decide for themselves simply by not showing up, and there's little this text can say about that. Some parents may argue it's the program people's responsibility to police children, and some program people may agree. That's something for them to think about.

When a considerate parent makes a conscious choice to remove a child from SACC, that parent will give the program ample notice. Programs can institute specific procedures for considerate parents to follow. With other parents, programs often set up procedures so that deposit monies are not refunded.

Every program draws a procedural line beyond which it can no longer serve in good faith. This line reflects the exhaustion of every available means at program people's disposal. Here's how a number of different people exhaust available means:

The director should have personal contact. Every two weeks you should get a sheet of unpaid bills, and phone calls should be made by the director. This is the most effective way.

First, look for the reason why parents aren't paying the bill. If we notice the bill is getting high, we write them a letter asking if they want to talk to us about it. Then we hear about all of the family circumstances.

A committee should be established to look at the exceptions. Parents should submit appeals to them.

If you have more than a handful of parents who are asking for fee reduction, your fees are too high.

A child's participation in the program will be terminated if his/her health examination form is not returned to the After School Program office within one month after the child enters the program.

Upon the discretion of the Head Teacher and after reasonable effort on the part of the program staff to integrate a child into the program, a child's participation may be terminated if that child is deemed chronically disruptive to the functioning of the program. The Head Teacher, after consulting the Program Director, will confer with the parent(s) and give notification of termination 5 school days prior to termination.

Some program administrators will go so far as to alter primary policies before they will terminate a particular child's service. But with insoluble funding cutbacks or relationships strained beyond immediate repair, termination may become inevitable. Difficult as this may be to accept, caring for the other children may finally mean ceasing to care for the one.

NOTES

1. *Child Care and Equal Opportunity for Women* (Washington, DC: U.S. Commission on Civil Rights, June 1981), p. 25.

2. State of North Dakota, Child Care Center Supplemental Parental Care, Chapter 75-03-10:23.

3. Jeanne Gibbs, *Tribes: a process for social development and cooperative learning* (Santa Rosa, CA: Center Source Publications, 1987).

4. Dale B. Fink, *School-Age Child Care Site Operations Manual* (Kansas City, MO: Camp Fire Boys and Girls, 1992), p. 83.

5. Adapted from "Roughhousing Guidelines," *School Age Notes*, March/April 1989, p. 11.

6. Gibbs, *Tribes*, p. 21.

7. *Recruiting and Enrolling Children* (Atlanta, GA: Save the Children, Child Care Support Center, 1981), p. 17.

8. Ibid, pp. 10–11.

FOR FURTHER REFERENCE

American Academy of Pediatrics. 1991. *Report of the Committee on Infectious Diseases*. Elk Grove Village, IL: American Academy of Pediatrics.

———. 1987. *Health in Day Care: A Manual for Health Professionals*. Elk Grove Village, IL: American Academy of Pediatrics.

Cherry, Clare, 1983. *Please Don't Sit on the Kids: Alternatives to Punitive Discipline*. Belmont, CA: David S. Lake Publishers. (Available from Fearon Teacher Aids, P.O. Box 280, Carthage, IL 62321.)

Child Advocacy Office of the National Council of Churches. 1984. *Helping Churches Mind the Children: A Guide for Child Day Care Programs*. New York: National Council of Churches.

Sutter, Sally A. 1988. *Safety, First Aid, and Emergency Procedures Manual*. West Decatur, PA: Pennsylvania Department of Education, Central Intermediate Unit #10, 16648.

Chapter 10

SCHEDULING

"I'm bored." What caregiver hasn't heard this familiar plaint from a child? A SACC program faces no other threat quite like monotony. The same board games, always missing the same pieces. The same apple juice and crackers. The same tables in the same places. No wonder the children either sink into dull stupor or explode into wild behavior.

To fight monotony, PDs and caregivers often strive to fill time. To achieve order, they carve out blocks of time. This much time for arriving, that much time for snack, this much time for sing-along, and mission accomplished. As the old saying among television producers goes, "They don't want it good, they want it Tuesday." Not that this fixation with time hasn't gripped most of American society in its clammy clutches. Time and motion studies, school bells, and digital technology constantly reinforce the idea of each minute as a measure of work performance.

Taken at face value, technology can easily blind anyone to their own humanity. It creates performance pressure and competition for survival that depends on nanoseconds no human can perceive. Perhaps a few not-so-foolish people still wish to entertain their human senses: to feel sand squish between their toes, to see just how long that ladybug will stay on that leaf, to listen to a train whistle until it's too far away to hear. When ticking stopwatches don't interfere, these are the ways children discover and learn to appreciate the world.

In principle, an appropriate program conducts its schedule as a way of giving children time, not stealing it from them. Perhaps Karsten Tuft can provide a more appropriate introduction to the philosophy of SACC program schedule planning.

"All genuine development takes place slowly and wastes a lot of time."[1]

Short-sighted investors intent only on quarterly interest payments will howl at this. So will anyone who regularly weaves through dense highway traffic at eighty miles an hour. So will anyone who has never planted a seed and waited for a flower to grow. Nonetheless, Tuft's words contain more than a kernel of truth.

DOES ANYBODY REALLY KNOW WHAT TIME IT IS?

Banker's hours. Swing shifts. Daylight savings. Curfews. Every little difference in life-style brings another little difference to the way people occupy their time.

In Los Angeles, the term *rush hour* once described the times during which day-shift workers traveled to and from their workplaces. It accurately described short periods of crowded highway traffic. It was a well-defined phenomenon, one that people could work into their schedules.

Not anymore. Freeway traffic in Los Angeles only eases late at night or by happenstance. *Rush hour* no longer describes life as it *really* happens.

How different people relate to different segments of time, how each of them carries out their own schedules, has a big impact on SACC scheduling. In any given program's area of service, dozens of overlapping personal schedules can affect the schedule. Arbitrary hours, days, weeks, or months of programming might look great on paper, but do they consider the partners? In practice, such a self-serving plan creates many more problems than it can ever solve.

It's true that many people let time use them rather than making time work for them. A SACC program can't afford to make this mistake. As a family support service business, a SACC program's schedule must reflect life as it really happens.

The program schedule consists of four major areas: (1) *operating hours,* or the hours and days of the week a program's doors are open; (2) *operating months,* the calendar or seasonal benchmarks providers choose to offer SACC; (3) when caregivers and PDs perform their various responsibilities, sometimes called the *caregiving schedule;* and, of greatest significance, (4) children's experiences within the program, or the *daily schedule.*

OPERATING HOURS

Daily Classroom Schedules

- Kindergarten split-days (9:00–11:30; 12:00–2:30)
- Primary grade classes' regular hours

- Early release days
- Holidays and winter/spring breaks
- Unusual or emergency school closure (heat, snow)

As long as children are subject to mandates of school attendance, a SACC program's hours must complement the pertinent schools' schedules. More than convenience or cooperation, this recognition has to do with tenets of liability. Depending on time of day and physical location, responsibility for the care and well-being of the children passes back and forth between various legal entities: parent or legal guardian, school board, city or county government, and the SACC program. When a child passes between the portals of home, school, and SACC program, the law generally assumes liability to have passed along as well.

(In order to circumvent controversy over the invocation of *in loco parentis* by child care programmers, authors of the 1990 CCDBG Act included a requirement that recipient programs permit unrestricted access to parents throughout the program day. Notably, this requirement does not generally apply to schools. See Chapter 12 for discussion of the in loco parentis issue.)

For school-sited or school-run programs, questions about mandates invariably arise. To what extent ought a SACC program to duplicate or extend regular schoolday activities? If it wishes to secure CCDBG funds, the federal government says it must not. On the other hand, parents and outside funders are indeed calling for more academics outside the classroom. And a YSA PD may not even see possibilities beyond simple group recreation. The funding web for such programs may be so highly intricate that a program may find itself in the unenviable position of having to satisfy two or three conflicting agendas with its schedule.

Having long maintained that their job descriptions don't include informal child care, elementary school teachers have the "luxury" of being able to dash from their jobs as soon as the final bell rings. Of course, a spirit of caring and volunteerism motivates some to linger afterwards, but with peer and union pressure involved, such lingering remains the exception. For this reason, it becomes even more important that when a caring vacuum occurs, a SACC program respond. This is a SACC program's raison d'être, its very reason for existence.

Parents' Employment

- Day shift and variances
- Swing shift
- Night shift

• Self-employed professionals
• Seeking work

There's a growing demand for SACC during hours other than tradition might dictate. A burgeoning 24-hour global marketplace puts increasing demands on American employers to expand their hours of operation beyond the old agrarian sunrise-sunset model. Yet the vast majority of programs in 1991 schedules their care only to accomodate typical Monday-through-Friday nine-to-fivers. Few programs addressed anyone else. Care that runs from 2 P.M. to 6 P.M. serves few of the millions who work, say, from 4 A.M. to noon or from noon to 8 P.M.

Probably the least-served children are those who are experiencing the rigors of parental unemployment, homelessness, or both. As discussed in Chapter 5, a discretionary funding policy can help alleviate short-term breaks in family life continuity. But caring and sharing encompasses more.

Precedents for continuity of care already exist. COBRA legislation requires employers to provide continuous group health insurance for up to six months after an employee's discharge. In the case of upper-management layoffs, many firms provide a safety net of outplacement assistance, which gives professionals the time and facility necessary to conduct an effective job search. Even if SACC were nothing more than an employee support mechanism, it would make sense to organize schedules in synch with prevailing conditions.

Other Partnership Members

• Caregiver pool—part-time, students, second job
• Transport—hours and days of operation
• Maintenance engineering
• Lessor (if any)
• Space sharers

Once again, the name of the game here is inclusion. Each of these groups comes to the table with preconceived ideas about their own agendas, their own time frames. Some may be willing to negotiate—but, unfortunately, confrontations are common. Like chickens in a barnyard, potential partners grapple with hierarchical pecking orders: who's bigger, who's stronger, who's older, who's richer. Since children are generally smallest, weakest, youngest, and poorest, guess who usually falls to the bottom of the list?

Like successful caregiving, successful negotiation calls for a deeper understanding of human nature. Those least willing to negotiate the schedule tend to be those who are most afraid of losing something that they highly value: money, power, prestige, or physical ease. In order to protect what they see as their own personal interests, some people absolutely refuse to step out from behind their defensive postures.

Of course, money always talks. In New York City, when the maintenance workers' union stonewalled attempts to implement SACC programs in the public schools, the School Board found that the only way to appease the union was with a big chunk of money. With no other apparent way to engender the union's cooperation, the Board bought it outright.

What's wrong with this? Here, the authority to schedule SACC in New York City schools lies completely outside the circles of the people who are most affected. Recall the PAVEWAY from Chapter 2. The union's executive authority, bolstered by its wage authority, holds sway over the proceedings. By making SACC beholden to a single industrial entity, planners open themselves up for all kinds of political fallout—not to mention discontinuation of programs—if that single "partner" balks later on.

A joint effort based solely on monetary outcomes has no rightful claim to call itself a partnership, in which each member group recognizes the others' non-economic value and integrity. Lacking this, *the SACC program eventually will fail to provide timely care*. Neither political pressure nor financial incentives can compel a potential partner to care. Instead, seek out partners whose active concern for the public weal outweighs their own selfish motivations.

OPERATING MONTHS

School Year Operation

- Traditional (August–May or September–June)
- Year-round (continuous)

When traditional schools let out for the summer, SACC takes on an entirely different role. Working parents, the mainstays of many programs, continue to face the same employment/parental care conflicts—intensified by the school shutting down for three months. That's as many as thirty empty hours a week for twelve weeks, a grand total of 360 hours. Caught between confining their children home alone or leaving them to the mercies of the "boyz in the 'hood," not only working parents want some satisfying alternative.

A successful SACC program can provide that alternative. However, because of the radical difference between supplementary schedules during school months and full-day operation in the summer, a lot of unprepared SACC programs can miss the mark entirely. One Pennsylvania PD tells what can happen:

"The kids are bored. They won't do what I say. They just won't cooperate. I don't know how I'm going to make it through the rest of the summer," said Mary. Natalie, her co-teacher, nodded her head in agreement.

"When did your summer program start?" I asked.

"Monday," replied Mary.

It was only Wednesday. Mary and Natalie were in BIG trouble. A very LONG summer loomed ahead for them and the children.

What was wrong after only two days of programming? Based on observation and discussion with staff and children, [it was clear that] program activities had changed little from the school year. With most of the children falling in age at two distinct ends of the school-age spectrum, staff found it difficult to program so all children were satisfied. What they were able to make work during the two-and-a-half hours after school, *didn't work* in a ten-hour day.[2]

Any substantial change in season or schedule calls for a substantial re-thinking of program planning priorities. As the same P.D. goes on to suggest:

Take a look at the program. Is it working? Are the children happy and involved? Are they exploring new things? Are they having fun? That's what summer programming is all about![3]

As Figure 10.1 illustrates, a year-round school with three separate tracks will have broken out about a third of its students into a non-attending or *intersession* period. Programs that complement year-round schools probably do best when they implement full-day programming throughout the year. In these communities, programs can actually benefit from increased demand for full-day care. Full-time caregivers, compensated accordingly, tend to stay longer. Also, any additional costs can be dispersed across a wider stretch of time and more parents.

Population Density

- Seasonal fluctuation (agribusiness areas or resorts)
- Steady population growth
- Steady population decline

Despite an increase of over 225 million residents since 1789, the U.S. administration still adheres to a centuries-old constitutional directive to conduct a census count only once every ten years. Aside from the phenomenal sums of federal monies that are dependent on these inaccurate population statistics, congressional districting lines disenfranchise millions of people. What's worse? As far as the statisticians are concerned, the children of those uncounted millions don't even exist.

Unlike federal census officials, a SACC program can't sit back and ignore actual neighborhood density. Factories close, putting thousands of people out of work. Seasonal industries gear up, bringing thousands of seasonal workers into a community . . . or taking them out. Under such conditions, SACC planners must attune their monthly schedules to these foreseeable fluctuations of population.

Business journals, city development agencies, and even daily newspapers often provide relatively useful data on population movement into or out of a given area. If a given number of people are expected to relocate within two to five years, the annual operation schedule may as well reflect these projected changes. For more about utilization rates, see Fees: How Parents Contribute Funding in Chapter 5, p. 107.

For the unprepared, national holidays can cause minor havoc. During its first year of operation, the Eugene Latch Key Program (ELK) in Oregon offered a year-end care option. Here's an excerpt from a subsequent ELK parent newsletter:

Christmas care was used by only half of the parents who made reservations. We arranged for staffing for all of the children. The board will consider a policy of charging for space reserved for spring vacation.

Clearly, scheduling interacts with financial management and parent relations. For this reason, set workable policies and procedures—including the establishment of special fees, if any—through which parents may formally register for these *backup care* services. Figure 10.2 illustrates ELK's solution to the problem.

Other Partnership Members

See the earlier discussion of this topic in the Operating Hours section. Whether one is planning the hours or months of operation, the same considerations apply.

THE CAREGIVING SCHEDULE

Caregiver Status

- Paid, full-time
- Paid, part-time
- Non-parent volunteer
- Unpaid student trainee
- Parent volunteer

Figure 10.1

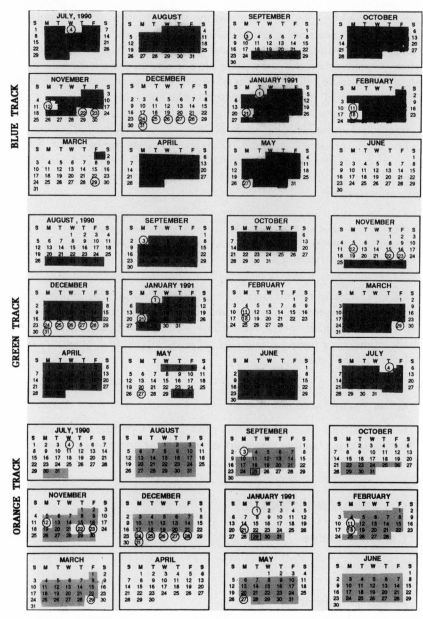

Revised 3/90

228

```
┌─────────────────────────────────────────────┐
│      VISTA UNIFIED SCHOOL DISTRICT           │
│   ELEMENTARY AND MIDDLE SCHOOLS              │
│   YEAR-ROUND EDUCATION CALENDAR              │
│             1990-91                          │
└─────────────────────────────────────────────┘
```

1990-91 YRE CALENDAR DATES

July 2 -	**FIRST DAY OF SCHOOL - BLUE TRACK**
July 4 -	**INDEPENDENCE DAY (Legal) - NO SCHOOL**
July 30 -	**FIRST DAY OF SCHOOL** - ORANGE TRACK
Aug. 24 -	**LAST DAY** - BLUE TRACK
Aug. 27 -	**FIRST DAY OF SCHOOL** - GREEN TRACK
Sept. 3 -	**LABOR DAY (Legal) - NO SCHOOL**
Sept. 25 -	**TRANSITION DAY FOR RETURN TO SCHOOL - BLUE TRACK**
	LAST DAY - ORANGE TRACK
Oct. 19 -	**LAST DAY** - GREEN TRACK
Oct. 22 -	**RETURN TO SCHOOL** - ORANGE TRACK
Nov. 12 -	**VETERANS' DAY (Legal) NO SCHOOL**
Nov. 21 -	**LAST DAY** - BLUE TRACK
Nov. 22-23 -	**THANKSGIVING HOLIDAYS - NO SCHOOL**
Nov. 26 -	**RETURN TO SCHOOL** - GREEN TRACK
Dec. 21 -	**LAST DAY** - ORANGE TRACK
Dec 22 - Jan 1	**CHRISTMAS VACATION - SCHOOLS CLOSED**
Dec. 25 -	**CHRISTMAS DAY - (Legal)**
Jan. 1 -	**NEW YEARS DAY (Legal)**
Jan. 2 -	**RETURN TO SCHOOL - BLUE AND GREEN TRACKS**
Jan. 21 -	**MARTIN LUTHER KING DAY (Legal) NO SCHOOL**
Jan. 29 -	**TRANSITION DAY FOR RETURNING ORANGE TRACK**
	LAST DAY - GREEN TRACK
Feb. 11 -	**LINCOLN'S BIRTHDAY (Legal) - NO SCHOOL**
Feb. 18 -	**PRESIDENT'S DAY (Legal) - NO SCHOOL**
Mar. 1 -	**LAST DAY** - BLUE TRACK
Mar. 4 -	**RETURN TO SCHOOL** - GREEN TRACK
Mar. 28 -	**LAST DAY** - ORANGE TRACK
Mar. 29 -	**GOOD FRIDAY - HOLIDAY - NO SCHOOL**
Apr. 1 -	**RETURN TO SCHOOL** - BLUE TRACK
May 3 -	**LAST DAY** - GREEN TRACK
May 6 -	**RETURN TO SCHOOL** - ORANGE TRACK
May 27 -	**MEMORIAL DAY (Legal) - NO SCHOOL**
May 30 -	**TRANSITION DAY FOR RETURN TO SCHOOL - GREEN TRACK**
	LAST DAY OF SCHOOL YEAR - BLUE TRACK
June 28 -	**LAST DAY OF SCHOOL YEAR** - ORANGE TRACK
July 1, 1991-	**START OF 1991-92 YRE SCHOOL YEAR**
	RETURN TO SCHOOL - BLUE TRACK
July 4 -	**INDEPENDENCE DAY (Legal) - NO SCHOOL**
July 26 -	**LAST DAY OF SCHOOL** - GREEN TRACK
July 29 -	**FIRST DAY OF SCHOOL** - ORANGE TRACK (1991-92)

Figure 10.2

CHILD CARE

Spring Vacation

PLEASE RETURN THIS FORM *NO LATER* THAN MARCH 10 *WITH PAY-MENT* IF YOU WANT CHILD CARE DURING VACATION TO:
  Eugene Latch Key
  P.O. Box 5556
  Eugene, OR 97405
  345-6358

Remember:

A. Care will be provided at:
  Patterson
  Lincoln
B. Bring a sack lunch on vacation days (no pop or sugar snacks—please).
C. Dress children warmly—the school may be cooler than usual.
D. Bring a swim suit and towel.
E. Vacation hours 7:30 A.M. to 6:00 P.M.
F. Full day rates are $3, $4, $5, $6 extra charge. Payment must be enclosed with reservation.

. . . .

I want child care during Spring Vacation for the following dates:

___ March 17 (Mon)   From ___ AM to ___ PM
___ March 18 (Tues)   From ___ AM to ___ PM
___ March 19 (Weds)   From ___ AM to ___ PM
___ March 20 (Thurs)   From ___ AM to ___ PM
___ March 21 (Fri)   From ___ AM to ___ PM

My site choice is ___ Patterson ___ Lincoln

Caregivers face the status dilemma every day. Their society places little value on their efforts, so caregivers are ill-paid. Their society views children sometimes as a nuisance, sometimes as a basis for economic transaction, rarely as critical participants, so caregivers are looked down on by members of the very professions they support. Their society revolves around the acquisition of power, and because they pursue a gentler goal, caregivers kowtow to the will of others.

If caregivers' time carries so little value, why should a program's time seem any more valuable to caregivers? How can planners afford to sweep aside caregivers' concerns as if they were totally incidental? Caregivers *are* SACC. Who they are—or who they are not—makes SACC what it is, moment to moment, day to day. A program scheduler who can accomodate school boards, parents, community agencies, and bureaucratic diktat had better also consider exactly whose time most profoundly affects the children.

Status has a great deal to do with the caregiver schedule. When scheduling volunteers and paid caregivers at the same time, does a PD intend them to divide responsibilities equally? With three full-time caregivers, will each be given a different title, different tasks, a different pay status, but the exact same number of hours? Do student volunteers want a participatory voice, or do they just want to show up and hand out the apple juice at 2:45?

PDs can make any decisions they like about the caregiving schedule, but caregivers will decide how and when they show up. When caregivers repeatedly show up late or not at all, they are either consciously or unconsciously protesting their working conditions. To resolve this, schedulers must bring their caregivers into the scheduling process. Paid or not, caregivers who *choose* to be present make a more healthful program than those who feel undervalued.

Caregiver Development

- Internal meetings
- Activity planning sessions
- In-service training
- State and national workshops
- Parent conferences
- Case consultation

If something takes caregivers away from direct caregiving, of what possible value can it be? Well, it can further their competence, improve their ability to take responsibility, and deepen their commitment to the program.

Want more? By improving their understanding of SACC, development time can strengthen caregivers' communication skills. It builds self-esteem. It engenders personal growth, self-awareness, and interconnectedness. All told, caregiver development translates into program improvement.

Rather than viewing professional development as some kind of luxury, successful PDs recognize it as an integral aspect of the schedule. They consciously encourage development by designating specific hours and days precisely for the purpose. *They build this time right into the schedule.*

THE DAILY SCHEDULE

What Every Body Desires (in no particular order)

- Relaxation
- Exercise
- Dynamic social interaction
- Solitude
- Musical interludes
- Personal expression
- Intellectual challenge
- Routine duties
- Stable structure
- Random access
- Personal attention
- Sensory stimulation
- Role model emulation
- Affection

On the face of it, scheduling dynamic daily experiences for a hundred children might seem pretty overwhelming. With a caregiver-child ratio 1:30 or higher, it might seem nearly impossible. Some schools that operate with similar teacher-child ratios, riven by administrative and academic strife, have turned to martial law techniques. They wish to cut down on dynamics. But are sheer numbers the only impediment?

Each girl and boy in a SACC program possesses a very personal mix of human desires. Each also possesses a developing awareness of how desire affects and is affected by the social universe. Some conservative pedagogues blame the world of social ills on human desire, and they aim to do away with it. Of course, that is *their* desire.

The new program director of a small, suburban SACC program inherited a program handbook that contained this schedule:

2:00–2:15	Snack
2:15–3:15	Free Time
	(games, coloring, blocks, homework, outside)
3:15–4:15	Projects
4:15–4:30	Snack
4:30–5:00	Structured Gym Game
5:00–5:30	Free Time in Gym

5:30–6:00   Back to Extended Day Room; Wind Down; Get Ready to Go Home

She considered it utterly inappropriate. Why? It locked the staff into time limits that didn't account for reality. It failed to take into account the children's human traits. Under these constraints, how could children ever begin to feel their personal desires were important to anyone? She decided to generate a new schedule, one that would meet human standards instead of ignoring them.

Here's what her new schedule looks like and what she says about it:

2:00–3:15   Arrival and Free Time
               (homework, games, outside, open snack table)

3:15–3:30   Meeting
               (chance to go over any questions, problems)

3:30–5:00   Activity Choices
               (art projects, outdoor sports, drama/music, snack with group at activity choice)

5:00–5:45   Cool Down
               (quiet activities such as homework, reading, drawing, clean-up)

This schedule allows for much more individual choices by the children. They can choose when they have their snack, whether it's right when they arrive or after they have run around outside for half an hour. By putting the second snack with the group activity, the children do not have to stop what they are doing to have snack, yet they still are eating it as part of a group. Each teacher will have a pitcher of juice and enough snacks for their group.[4]

One can imagine that the principle of choice extends beyond when and where children drink their juice. Accustomed to their own memories of childhood obedience and compliance, some adults find it difficult to think in any other terms. It's probably even more difficult for them to think of an open framework within which children might learn to organize their own lives.

Still, this PD feels herself to be on the right track. More important, she believes that to be responsive her schedule will not be carved in stone but will be a stepping stone to the next, even more appropriate schedule.

What would that more appropriate schedule look like? How would it work? What would it say about the people living their lives as part of a SACC program? Could it become even more attentive to the particulars of each boy's and each girl's personal development? Could it do this without becoming exceedingly overbearing or intrusive? In other words, can a move be made further away from *domination of* children and toward *partnership with* children?

What Every Child Deserves

- Inclusion
- Consideration
- Recognition
- Autonomy
- A chance to imagine
- A safe place to fail

At its best, SACC gives children a better handle on their futures than they might get either in an isolated security condo or on a decaying street corner. From either vantage point, childhood hinges on crucial moments. At these moments, perceptions of the self and the surrounding society transform into learned responses, or behavior. This behavior, they learn, society regards as either productive or destructive, legal or illegal, and deserving of praise, punishment or, "safest" of all, no notice whatsoever.

The issue of safety ranks high on mission statement lists. However, consider the following notion: Culturally and socially, the highest degree of safety obtains from being invisible. To be hidden from view represents the greatest safety of all. This is the view of safety many parents and SACC programs normally take with their children.

With or without SACC, children learn this lesson quite easily. They also learn the corollary: that to be visible or exposed means to be punished. In many city neighborhoods, it may even mean being shot to death. Just to survive, children quickly internalize these life lessons. They learn to hide their fears, stifle their abilities, repress their feelings, stillbear their wishes, hopes, and dreams. In fact, they learn to hide so well, they may never find themselves.

The alternative to impressing lessons in fear upon children requires some vision, some imagination, and even a little courage. (And if these qualities aren't self-evident in a program's caregivers, where else will children have a chance to observe them? On television?) Opportunity lies in easing into a new framework that facilitates the magic of growing up.

The Tribes process for social development and cooperative learning offers one powerful method for achieving this status. As the Tribes process progenitor Jeanne Gibbs puts it:

It is essential that you facilitate a series of activities that will help people present who they are, what they do well, and what they want their group to be like. They are not ready to work on curricula together unless inclusion and trust have intentionally been developed.[5]

BUILDING A SCHEDULE THAT REALLY WORKS

With each day come new dynamics, little changes to the big picture. Rather than rubber-stamping a fixed daily sequence of events onto each calendar-day box, PDs and caregivers can consciously build time around the naturally evolving dynamics of their groups. And they can do this without losing sight of real priorities. How? By borrowing a page from a most unlikely source: the motion picture industry.

A Slot Machine That Always Hits the Jackpot

A century ago, Hollywood Boulevard was a short stretch of shoe stores, and anyone with a bootleg camera and a few feet of film could be a movie producer. Production schedules were scattershot, catch-as-catch-can affairs. Whoever happened to be standing around with nothing to do might have found themselves running off to buy a hat for an actress, scissors to snip the film, or paint to cover up a hole in a wall. Nobody knew for sure what might happen from minute to minute, since nobody knew for sure when something else was going to come up.

Eventually, Thomas Ince decided to try and get *his* productions organized. On the one hand, he had some definite ideas about the kinds of things he wanted to do. On the other, he knew that a slight change in one person's plans can sometimes throw off an entire schedule. To bring flexible firmness to an otherwise unpredictable situation, he helped develop an item known as the *production board*. It was so successful an invention that even today, production managers still favor their handy, easy-to-use folding production boards.

As Figure 10.3 illustrates, a production board consists of fairly low-tech elements: a firm backing, a cardboard topic insert, several thin cardboard strips, and two retaining bands across the top and bottom. On the cardboard topic insert are listed the names and responsibilities of each person involved with the production.

Each narrow strip represents a scene from the movie's story. A scene number at the top of each strip tells the manager exactly where in the movie—beginning, middle, or end—that scene takes place. Each strip may be a different color—blue, red, green, yellow—to represent a different type of scene—night, twilight, sunrise, or daytime. The small boxes on each strip line up with the names on the topic insert, so the manager can easily check to see who goes where at what time each day.

The strip closest to the left represents the scene planned for the first day of filming. The order of strips from left to right shows the scheduled plan for everything the director wishes to do, with the last strip on the right slotted for the last day. But why are the scene numbers all out of order?

Figure 10.3

A production board shows when who goes where, what's to do, and how to get from here to there. (Photo: Jack Cash, Los Angeles, California)

Most astute readers realize that few movies are shot in the same sequence that an audience sees them. There are several reasons for this, but they all have to do with working with time.

Making Time for SACC

On a movie set or in a SACC program, no one can predict the future. The weather may turn bad, or someone may get sick. A plan requiring good weather or a healthy staffer may have to wait for another day. On the plus side, perhaps a once-in-a-lifetime opportunity presents itself, or someone suddenly comes up with a brilliant and unexpected idea. Whatever was regularly planned might better be put off for another day.

And not everyone wants or needs to be in the exact same place at the exact same time. Often, there are several different groups of people, each engaged in different types of activities at different locations, bound together by a common purpose or desire. Then, at some later point, these groups join back up to share the fruits of their experience, to form a whole greater than the sum of the separate parts.

To keep on top of the schedule, a production manager wisely uses the production board. When events call for a change in plans, the manager slips the affected scene strip out of its slot, moves it farther to the right—into the future—and replaces it with a different strip, one that allows the crew to take advantage of serendipity or to keep filming despite bad weather. Everything can still happen, just in a slightly different order. Because each event strip can be so easily moved around, the board facilitates responsive planning. No one need get bogged down by the thought of having to redo the entire schedule as if it were etched in stone.

With just a few slight modifications, the film crew's production board can easily be transformed into a SACC PD's good friend, the *Action Tracker*. On the topic insert, in place of cast and crew, fill in the names of each caregiver and child. Select different-colored strips to represent different types of daily experience: standard adult-directed, standard child-directed, off-site, special event, and so on. (A starter kit, complete with detailed instructions and basic materials, is available from SACCProject, Center for Research on Women, Wellesley College, Wellesley, Massachusetts 02181; 617-283-2547.)

Begin by slotting the strips in whatever order seems right (it won't be yet, but don't worry about that). Try to get a *feel* for how each day relates to the others. Are there too many site-based days bunched together? Are the special-event strips confined to predictable holidays? The Action Tracker visually demonstrates potential flaws or monotony in longer-range scheduling.

Try out the same exercise with program caregivers. Remember, this isn't a test, and there is no one right way to schedule the program experiences. The schedule blossoms from the imaginations and desires of people in the program.

Once the PD and caregivers have familiarized themselves with how the Action Tracker works, it's time to bring the children into the process. With a highly imaginative group, the permutations may be as numerous as the children. Also, in terms of child development, the strips serve as tangible manipulatives, physically putting time into the children's hands for them to organize.

The Action Tracker gives everyone an opportunity for inclusion, consideration, recognition, and autonomy within the schedule. Want to move something up or back? The Action Tracker gives everyone a chance to imagine the possibilities, to give vent to frustration without "ruining" the whole week. Changes in weather conditions, people, transportation, or cash flow? Slip out a strip and slot in a new one. The Action Tracker turns potential failure into a crack at creative and critical thought about how to use time.

CAREGIVERS ON THE CLOCK

Economic realities can take their toll on a labor-intensive business. Too few programs have resources enough for full-day, full-time caregivers. However, three fundamental approaches to caregiver scheduling suggest themselves. Consider these approaches as general guides. Select the aspects that seem to parallel economic reality, then customize a schedule that maximizes the potential for caring labor.

During the process, it may help to think of the caregiver schedule as a wraparound, something that embraces and enfolds the personal time and effort of caregivers. Create a schedule to which caregivers can make an honest, personal commitment. Make the schedule responsive, and caregivers can more easily respond to it.

Split Shifts

In this approach, the caring day is broken up into several discrete periods of time, each of which functions as an independent unit. In an A.M./P.M. program, two part-time caregivers might come in for the 7:30 to 9:30 A.M. unit, leave for a while, then return for the 2:30 to 6:00 P.M. unit. This approach works better in a strictly school-age program than in a multi-component program such as a full-day combination Head Start/preschool/school-age care program.

A variation on this approach involves different caregivers for each shift. Perhaps elder caregivers prefer the morning times, and student volunteers can accomodate afternoons. At least one person, usually a full-time PD, coordinates the various units throughout the day. Some overlap may occur, as when one caregiver regularly appears for both shifts, while others remain associated with just mornings or just afternoons.

Parents, college students, and those others who bear complementary responsibilities will find the split day affords them a chance to pursue the rewards of caregiving in a manageable way. For the children, it may broaden their experience of people who care. However, a typical child's daily experience of the adult clock already contains a great deal of compartmentalization: wake-up routine, A.M. program, school starts, recess, school continues, lunch, school continues, P.M. program, and so forth. By asking children to adjust to yet another adult and another, this system further compartmentalizes their experience.

Staggered Shifts

By bringing in many caregivers throughout the course of the day, programs can lower their caregiver-child ratios. The staggered approach more favorably addresses the practical reality that different school-agers have different schedules. In full-day and combination programs, it accounts for what could become, at least in split-shift programs, troublesome transitional periods. Since no one person could hope to continue unrelieved for twelve hours, this plan works very effectively for continuous-operation programs.

Figure 10.4 illustrates a sample staggered staffing plan. Note the seven-hour shifts for full-time caregivers. Jennifer, the "A.M. Kindergarten" caregiver, covers the entire morning period. Cyndi cares for the "P.M. Kindergarten" period. If perhaps only twelve to fifteen children are present between 2 P.M. and 3 P.M., at least two caregivers are always scheduled for their care. For the heavier activity of the 3 P.M. transition, Toni and William come in.

Also note Purcell's important role. During the post-lunch nap-time, he cares for kindergartners, who are just in from the classroom and probably ready for an hour or so of rest. Purcell makes time available to Jennifer, Kendall, Cyndi, and Helen for planning sessions and topical discussions while all four are there together. As mentioned earlier, this is a critical component of caregiver scheduling.

Multiple Role Responsibility

For anyone who, unaided, has funded, organized, enrolled, directed, prepared snacks for, and given care to thirty children, this approach has spoken for itself.

In badly underfunded or minimally attended programs, too few people often take on too many tasks. Commensurate with this approach comes a line of thought that runs something like, "Since no one else is going to do it, I guess I'll have to." When one person tries to step in and do it all, the results can be devastating.

Up to this point in SACC history, the most moderate vision of job combination has taken the form of the director-caregiver. One full-time position carries certain apparent advantages over two part-time ones. In fact,

Figure 10.4

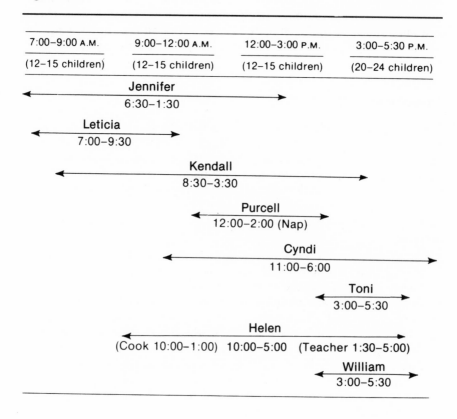

7:00–9:00 A.M.	9:00–12:00 A.M.	12:00–3:00 P.M.	3:00–5:30 P.M.
(12–15 children)	(12–15 children)	(12–15 children)	(20–24 children)

Jennifer
6:30–1:30

Leticia
7:00–9:30

Kendall
8:30–3:30

Purcell
12:00–2:00 (Nap)

Cyndi
11:00–6:00

Toni
3:00–5:30

Helen
(Cook 10:00–1:00) 10:00–5:00 (Teacher 1:30–5:00)

William
3:00–5:30

to function in a cost-controlled environment, most small programs hire one person to fill both roles. From that person's point of view, having a single full-time source of income eliminates having to make ends meet by seeking a second job.

Despite the obvious financial advantages, multiple role responsibility often leads to job overload and quick burnout. The hyphenated staffer juggles two roles in an almost schizophrenic way: The caregiver will always have arguments with the director. Besides, when is there time to go to the bathroom? Even in the short run, money saved off the backs of caregivers costs in terms of attention to children.

Multiple role-playing works best in a partnership between *at least two* caregivers. If it is carried out free of egotism and exploitation, this pairing actually provides a sturdier platform for experimentation with various roles.

Figure 10.5

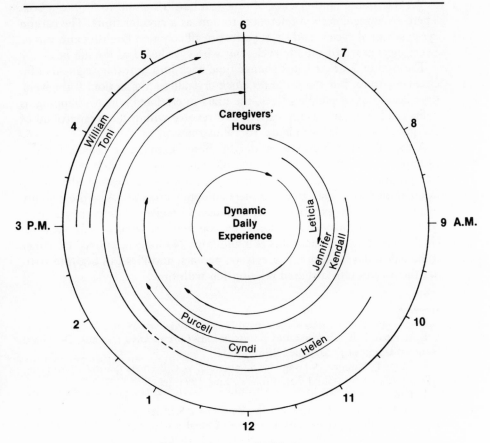

The program clock: another way to look at SACC time.

WHO PUT TIME IN A BOX, ANYWAY?

From where they sit with this book in their hands, many readers can probably glance up at a wall calendar. What will they see? The familiar design of thirty-five little boxes printed on a rectangular sheet, each little box fixed and immovable, most containing a number that locks it into place. Like square blocks, each day sits permanently imprisoned in its tiny cell, awaiting inventory, demanding a linear response.

Yet the motion and essence of time can hardly be said to fit into a box. There are quite common references to time as a circular thing. The carbon cycle, seasonal cycles, and sleep cycles are all common English expressions. Everyone's heard of the life cycle, but who ever heard of the life *box?*

The Action Tracker helps change time back into movable segments of a circular nature, but the *program clock* crystallizes the notion. Caregivers' time flows out of people's lives, the units interrelated and overlapping as befits the conditions. Daily experiences revolve within the wraparound of caregivers' schedules, as Figure 10.5 illustrates.

A calendar day begins at midnight, but a caring day begins, for this example, at 6 A.M. It stands to reason that a circular clock representing this program's schedule also begins there, continuing through the twelve hours until 6 P.M. This gives planners an opportunity to assess the viability of proposed daily experiences at a glance. Caregivers' hours may remain constant, or they may change during the course of the week, and the schedule clock effectively embraces this ebb and flow. No longer confined on paper to boxed-in days, children, caregivers, parents, and PDs can begin to partner themselves into a shared relationship with time.

NOTES

1. Karsten Tuft, *Children and Adults in Day-Care Centers* (Aarhus, Denmark: National Union of Pedagogues, 1989), p. 18.

2. Diane P. Barber, "A Long Hot Summer," *SACC Partners* (Southeastern Pennsylvania School Age Child Care Project), June 1991, p. 1.

3. Ibid.

4. Jill Leibowitz, "Revising and Implementing a Schedule for a School-Age Child Care Program" (Paper presented at Third Annual School-Age Child Care Leadership Institute, Berea College, Kentucky, July 15, 1990).

5. Jeanne Gibbs, *Tribes: a process for social development and cooperative learning* (Santa Rosa, CA: Center Source Publications, 1987), p. 53.

FOR FURTHER REFERENCE

Jorde, Paula. 1982. *Avoiding Burnout: Strategies for Managing Time, Space, and People in Early Childhood Education.* Washington, DC: Acropolis Books Ltd.

Chapter 11

TRANSPORTATION

In the days of the Roman Empire, it was common for people to observe, "All roads lead to Rome." Ever since before those ancient times, transportation has been the make-or-break planning factor for any organized human activity. Even when the enterprise is a simple afterschool program, the ability to get safely from one place to another has a lot to do with that program's success or failure.

Transportation to and from school and child care locations has quickly become one of the most telling issues for program directors, parents and children. An effective transportation policy gives everyone concerned the ability to make appropriate choices. Without an effective policy, rhetoric about selection and choice becomes meaningless. Who can come and go inevitably depends on how.

School-age care transportation planning falls into four general categories:

1. School district vehicles and personnel;
2. Program-purchased or contract vehicles;
3. Walking policies; and
4. No transportation planning.

Each category has its own philosophical motivations, its own economic impact, and its own practical effect on families. This makes it incumbent upon administrators and directors to get directly involved, to help facilitate the most appropriate transportation policy and procedures for their programs.

SCHOOL DISTRICT VEHICLES AND PERSONNEL

As in the rest of the nation, transportation to and from school-age programs stands at issue throughout New York State.[1] In 1987, New York enacted a law that allows each school district to be reimbursed for transporting children to child care facilities within district lines. The law provides for reimbursement under the same guidelines as those for transportation between home and school.

Westchester County's forty diverse school districts include dense urban centers and semi-rural areas, both containing prosperous as well as relatively poor neighborhoods, all subject to a variety of authorities. With its blend of open enrollment plans, magnet systems, and neighborhood schools, Westchester County provides fertile ground for understanding how school-age transportation law and policy affect different school systems. It also suggests a microcosm through which to understand law and policy impact on SACC transportation planning.

Whether or not a program operates in a school, the local school's or district's transportation policy tends to merge into center-based school-age care planning. That policy also affects a host of other available child care options. To make a plan that works for all takes open minds and a willingness to understand a myriad of viewpoints.

As a first step, go right to the top of command chains—or to the middle or the bottom, to the person most likely to help achieve dependable school/ SACC transport. If the school superintendent has a strong reputation for friendliness toward child care, go there. Maybe the superintendent will say, "New route? New stops? You got it!" If deed follows word, that's the end of the transportation problem.

In some areas, the bus driver has the final word on where and when the bus picks up and drops off. Maybe a direct one-on-one with the driver can easily resolve the question. The school transportation department head represents another source of speedy administrative authority and deserves a call.

However, if the quick and easy method fails, the situation may call for more elaborate effort . . . as it does in Westchester.

GOAL HELPER #1: Ascertain the existing transportation policies of enrollable children's school districts.

Based on telephone interviews its staff conducted with SACC programs, the forty district offices, and transportation departments, the Child Care Council of Westchester discerned five general transportation policy types.

Wherever they live, readers of this manual will probably find their school district's policy among the following five.[2]

- **Comprehensive**
  46 percent of all districts, 47.5 percent of elementary school population. Nineteen districts have a comprehensive child care transportation policy. They have elected to transport for all child care (regulated and exempt) throughout the whole district.

- **Participating**
  12.5 percent of all districts, 12.9 percent of elementary school population. Five districts follow the legal participation requirements and transport children to regulated family day care and exempt care within school attendance zone and to licensed centers and programs throughout the district.

- **Developing**
  7.5 percent of all districts, 10.9 percent of elementary school population. Three districts are still developing their policies and are currently transporting children to all child care within the school's attendance zone. These districts are not meeting legal requirements.

- **Non-Participating**
  20 percent of all districts, 24 percent of elementary school population. Eight school districts have elementary school transportation in place from home to school but have elected not to transport for child care.

- **Walking**
  12.5 percent of all districts, 6.3 percent of elementary school population. Five districts are walking districts, i.e., there is no transportation at the elementary level.

In the happy event that a program draws children from schools with a comprehensive or participating type of policy, finding this out may be the only planning step; some administrative follow-up by a program director or by parents can then usually fill the bill. Walking districts make school transport a moot consideration. For providers and directors in districts with developing or non-participating types of policies, there's more planning ground to cover.

> *GOAL HELPER #2: Establish a clear understanding of school transportation policies.*

Some district administrators still haven't caught up with the idea of mothers who work or the notion of one-parent families. They stonewall SACC transportation planning with intractable, outdated suppositions about family life from the "I Like Ike" years.

Other administrators, bogged down with hundreds of workaday administrative details, simply haven't the human resources to keep up with a changing world. They might not be particularly antagonistic to SACC transportation. They just might require a little nudge into the present. Even with a state law at their disposal, directors who run programs in these administrators' districts have a wide variety of concerns to address. The Child Care Council of Westchester describes its members' experiences of the major issues:

- **Cost of Transporting to Child Care**
  The new law was implemented to increase access to child care and reduce the potential cost to the school districts that could result from providing transportation for child care. Because transportation from school to child care is in lieu of transportation from school to home, the cost differential should be minimal. A full cost analysis by districts was beyond the scope of this report.

- **Optional versus Mandated Participating Requirements**
  Some anecdotal responses that we heard from transportation departments were "transporting to child care is too much trouble" and "if there is room on the bus, we will do it." In some districts, decisions regarding transportation were discretionary, left for a principal or a bus driver to decide from case to case. Inconsistencies or lack of official policy may reward the verbal, well-organized parent but offer no help for more vulnerable parents. It also leaves parents fearful of "rocking the boat" and losing what little they already have.

- **Size and Density of District**
  Large, low density districts did have a more comprehensive transportation policy. In the ten largest districts, 90 percent had at least a comprehensive or participating transportation policy. Smaller, denser districts had no pattern as to type of transportation policy. Out of the ten highest density districts, 40 percent are walking, 20 percent are non-participating, 40 percent are comprehensive.

- **District-Wide Transportation versus Neighborhood Districts**
  School districts operating with a magnet system, Princeton plan, or an open enrollment plan will draw their enrollment for each school from throughout the whole district. Our research found that every school district that was operating with a district-wide transportation system for home to school transportation also had a comprehensive child care transportation policy. Thus, a district that already transports children throughout the district is more inclined to do so for child care as well.

- **Number of Elementary Schools**
  Small districts with only one elementary school draw enrollment from the whole district and transport throughout the district. These districts are more apt to implement a comprehensive child care transportation policy. Out of the thirteen districts in Westchester County with only one elementary school, eight or 62 percent are comprehensive. Three are walking districts. One is non-participating, and one has a discretionary policy. Out of the ten districts that bus at all, 80 percent have implemented a comprehensive child care transportation policy.

- **On-Site Child Care**
  Districts with on-site child care generally tend to have a comprehensive or participating child care transportation policy. Out of the nineteen districts that have on-site child care, fourteen districts or 73.7 percent have either comprehensive

or participating policies. Two are non-participating, two are developing, and one is a walking district. Having on-site care may at times hinder development of alternative programs as districts believe they have "dealt" with the need and do not need to look beyond the one program offered.

- **Availability of Program**
  Less than 10 percent of the children enrolled in elementary school in Westchester County attend legal school-age child care programs. Several school districts were found to have no regulated program slots at all and very few regulated family day care slots. Lack of regulated programs may lead some districts to perceive that there is no need for a child care transportation policy, as the district has no program to bus to.

- **Current Busing Mileage Limit**
  A few districts had mileage limits of one and a half to two miles for elementary children, as required by law; this limits the number of children eligible for transportation. In one district there is no transport for kindergarteners, although there is transportation for grade 1 and up. In another even the kindergartener is expected to walk two miles to school. Some parents in these districts are making private arrangements with local bus or cab companies for transportation of their children. This raises the issue of how far young elementary children can safely manage to walk on their own, and where the responsibility for a safe passage to school should lie.

Any one of these issues can cause resistance to merging school transport with SACC service. In the interest of families who depend on SACC, program providers and directors often transform themselves into transportation policy consultants. Some of these issues they can think about, work on, and straighten out. Other issues, such as district cost, may prove unassailable, but only the most hardheaded school administrators will be unwilling to consider a well-thought-out alternative.

No matter how much personal planning goes into a proposed modification of school transportation policy, some district or transportation department authorities still tend to ignore a voice in the wilderness. They need to be more convincing before they become willing to cooperate fully. Far be it from this to suggest "ganging up" on a school administrator. However, several voices sometimes carry more weight than a lonely one. If school and transportation authorities seem unduly bound and determined to cling to existing policy, it may be wise to add voices to the chorus before entering the lion's den.

GOAL HELPER #3: Partner with parents and other providers.

Before setting off to re-route school transport, get some idea about who else is out there wanting to do the same thing. Although care providers may be either cooperating or competing to care for children, they all have a vested interest in setting up appropriate transportation service. Changing a district's transportation procedures affects not only children enrolled in school-age programs and their families but everyone who participates in the many child care options.

In areas where they operate, local R & Rs usually make the best source for local information about other care providers who have a stake in transportation logistics. State coalitions and school-age project directors can also help with local contact ideas. Associating and exploring mutual goals with other care providers may prove mighty helpful if it later becomes necessary to try something besides school vehicles.

Naturally enough, parents can make themselves another excellent source of support on the transportation front. They can often speak effectively to public servants at intermediate levels, and few can match a mother's interest in a policy that directly affects her and her child. Many parents have discovered the rewards to be reaped from the D.I.Y. (Do It Yourself) method.

CLOSE-UP: Parents United for Child Care (PUCC), Boston, Massachusetts

The Boston Public School system (BPS) had a developing transportation policy in place. They called it an "alternative" option for children in care programs. With bus routes centrally planned by the school transportation department, parents had the option to request that their children be picked up or dropped off somewhere other than their home—but only if that "somewhere" happened to be where the bus was already going. The deadline for requests was set for February, far too early to be helpful to most parents. BPS implemented the policy as if such requests would be unusual or exceptional.

Instead of the expected sprinkling, BPS received hundreds of requests for alternative service. Unable to cope with the demand, a BPS administrator simply sat on the applications, unable to respond one way or the other to interested parents. And when the school year began, BPS had a mess on its hands.

That was when Parents United for Child Care, a grass roots Boston advocacy group, got into the picture. PUCC took a step-by-step approach to the problem: Define the issue, survey affected parents and SACC programs, formulate a policy alternative, and make the presentation to the BPS transportation director. Professionals and volunteers combined strengths to complete these steps.

The result: Today, BPS regular enrollment forms include an inquiry about school-age care transport requirements. The deadline for new requests was moved back to June. And, to accommodate real-world demand, BPS consults students' parents about specific pick-up and drop-off locations *as an integral part* of each year's bus route planning.

As must be clear, tying school district transport to SACC encompasses a galaxy of considerations. Planners may not have, even in principle, the immediate advantage of the New York State law. Does that mean getting a bus to stop at the community college six blocks from the school takes a professional state-level lobbyist?

Don't be surprised. A lot of water goes under the bridge between the first phone call to an elected representative's office and the governor's signing of a new law. The time and trouble involved in changing state regulations can take three to five years.

Is getting this law passed worth the effort? In practice, economic downswings can transform such legislation into unfulfilled promises. When the time comes to recoup out-of-pocket expenses, districts may find state coffers in the same condition as Old Mother Hubbard's cupboard. So, even with a wildly enthusiastic district transportation department, financial resources ultimately call the tune.

So, despite the fruits of enlightened self-interest, district transport and personnel may not offer desirable, viable, or reasonable means of transportation to school age programs. Moreover, they may not offer an *immediate* solution, especially in districts or communities where programs are just starting up, beginning to gain acceptance, operating to the seeming benefit of only a few families. In these cases, another route must be taken.

PROGRAM-PURCHASED OR CONTRACTED VEHICLES

School buses can ferry children between their schools and the program site, but what about an afternoon jaunt to the high school swimming pool or a special matinee concert in the park? Even with direct cooperation from school transport authorities, PDs may still wish to pursue some form of in-house transit system. A readily available vehicle gives children a chance for experiences outside of the same old monotonous routines. For some children, it could be the only such chance they ever get.

Whatever its current financial conditions, any program may be in a position to invest in a privately owned vehicle. If not, some other pre-existing semi-private transportation service may seem economical, efficient, and worth investigating. The marketplace offers a variety of potential arrangements. As always, the cost of risk management (read "liability insurance") presents the biggest obstacle, but sometimes this can be overcome with a little inventiveness.

The Program Purchases a Vehicle

• *Single-program purchase.* Single-site directors, especially those of for-profit programs, often can make unilateral decisions about program materials and equipment, including vehicles. The Clubhouse in Tulsa,

Oklahoma, owns and maintains two passenger vans specifically for the purpose of transporting children. The overall insurance bill includes appropriate vehicular coverage.

With these vans in use, neither parents nor The Clubhouse staff have to worry about whether five- and six-year-olds will show up at the program site. Eliminated is the possibility of "wanderers" arriving at haphazard times. When one child came up with the idea for a field trip to a popular local radio station, the private transport made travel arrangements a snap.

But there is a price for all this. In fiscal 1990, for example, The Clubhouse paid an insurance bill that amounted to nearly 10 percent of annual operating costs. The majority of enrolled children's parents are upwardly mobile professionals, so, in this case, it's possible to distribute the cost of private program transport through parent charges. Programs with a similarly heeled client base might also make it work this way.

• *Multiple-program purchase.* Most nonprofit programs can't afford the luxury of bolstering their enrollment and improving activity options with 10 percent or more of their operating budgets. Directors might laugh just at the idea of coming up with a down payment for a car. But when the advantage of an interreliant partnership comes into play, all may have something where none had any.

CLOSE-UP: KARE-4, Sioux Falls, South Dakota

Four recreational organizations—YMCA, YWCA, Boys Clubs, and Girls Clubs—had been operating SACC programs at various locations in Sioux Falls. A United Way study discovered that many working parents and their school-agers were very interested in making regular use of SACC. Yet all four programs were suffering from seriously low utilization rates. The explanation? A lack of reasonable transportation.

Impressed by the United Way study results and profiles of the four programs, the Gannett Foundation channeled a $40,000 grant to pilot KARE-4, an interreliant partnership. With the KARE-4 concept, children could regularly attend any one of the four sites, or they could put together their own weekly schedule of different programs on different days. The Gannett grant facilitated bus purchases and a transportation coordinator's salary.

By linking themselves in KARE-4, all four programs witnessed an increase of utilization. While other children still dropped in occasionally, KARE-4 school-agers now had the more safe, more secure, more stimulating environment for their afternoon hours. And KARE-4 parents had the programs' assurance that transportation safety responsibilities were looked after.

State care licensing regulations include minimum standards for transportation and related liability coverage. To cover such costs, organizations, agencies, and even schools can enter into an inclusive insurance pool, defraying premiums across a multiple budget base. This way, regulations are met, and premiums become more manageable.

Major foundations and philanthropies, such as Gannett, constitute only one class of angels. Figuratively speaking, planners and administrators may find potential transportation partners right in their own backyards. Tight budgets tend to weaken the resolve of status quo supporters, and any other care provider feeling the same pinches will be looking for workable solutions. Of course, collaborations based on immediate need don't necessarily become model partnerships, but a common threat—in this case, program extinction—can rally some unexpected partners. For more ideas, see Chapter 7.

The Program Contracts for Vehicles

• *School-owned vehicles.* Even if they won't negotiate on any other basis, school transportation chiefs are almost always open to purely economic transactions. However, if checkbook diplomacy turns out to be the only way to attract school transport cooperation, chances are good that *someone* has a very sharp political axe to grind. Antagonistic contractors make pretty poor partners.

Some school superintendents just won't go for a transportation deal with an outside provider. Even if the dollars make sense, and even if the liability barrier is broken, the superintendent may still fear reprisals from the private sector. If they believe their market enterprise to be suffering from tax-supported public sector competition, for-profit providers may cry foul, as they did in Hawaii in 1990 when the governor announced plans for state-wide school-based SACC.

As part of the overall plan, PDs can make special cash-transaction arrangements for occasional or emergency school transport services. Probably most school transportation departments can function on these terms with any group or organization. If the situation warrants, PDs may find this strictly business approach useful.

• *Private bus companies.* In contrast with school districts that own their bus fleets, many districts pay private companies to drive their students to and from school. Just because the bus is yellow doesn't mean the district owns it. In fact, some districts contract out their transport service to more than one company.

A SACC program can contract with the private bus company in the same way a district can. The private carrier (1) purchases, stores, and maintains vehicles; (2) hires, certifies, and salaries drivers; (3) takes care of door-to-door insurance; and (4) can easily respond to the contingencies of transporting children. If vehicle capacities for wheelchairs or other special conditions are required, the private carrier already may be prepared and ready to serve. Smaller programs may benefit handsomely.

But what about the infamous bottom line? When he investigated the option in 1991, one PD in Louisiana faced the terrifying figures that follow:

$$10 \text{ drivers @ } \$10/\text{day} \times 140 \text{ days} = \$14,000$$
$$10 \text{ buses @ } .60/\text{mile} \times 10 \text{ miles/day} = 8,400$$
$$\text{Extra Liability---}\$1,800/\text{bus} = \underline{18,000}$$
$$\text{TOTAL} \quad \$40,400$$

Clearly, the larger program with the smaller budget had better look elsewhere for its transportation service.

• *Taxi services*. In districts that provide no transportation, or solely by dint of preference, working parents often must scramble for whatever private arrangements they can. Sometimes, that scramble leads to formal taxis or contract mini-cabs. Either can chalk up to big tabs for a single passenger, somewhat less for multiple passenger service.

Program directors may find some of their parents already spend heavily on these types of service. In the interest of cost efficiency and transportation continuity, the program might help coordinate and combine taxi service for several children. Alternatively, with enough parental interest, the PD might initiate a taxi contract as part of the program's total transportation picture.

WALKING POLICIES

As described in the Child Care Council of Westchester report, districts—and apparently taxpayers—expect five-year-olds with no recourse to make their own way to and from school, every day, perhaps alone, as far as four miles round trip. The policy reflects a belief that parents' private arrangements, costs, and concerns come with the territory. That these children are developmentally unready for dealing with most emergencies and that they lack the experience to make sound judgments seem to carry little weight in shaping policy.

Understanding what is and what isn't developmentally appropriate, top-flight PDs take the high road when they plan for children's well-being on the way to and from the site. This holds especially true for areas subject to toxic contamination, social disorder, rural isolation, and urban conflict. Factors like these can and do impact not just one afflicted child but perhaps every child in a given program.

GOAL HELPER #1: Walk with the children.

It's the most obvious and the most effective means of ensuring children's safe passage. Schools that can afford it sometimes spring for a crossing guard's wage, posting the protector within a block or so of the school-grounds. But after they leave the crossing guard behind, children's only protection from road hazards is their own judgment.

Many programs located off schoolgrounds draw the majority of their children from one school. Often, a caregiver meets these children at a des-ignated spot—if not at their classrooms—and personally escorts them be-tween school and program site. At one elementary school in Arlington, Virginia, caregivers always do this. It may be only two or three hundred yards, but the route leads through parking lots, across a street, through another parking lot and into a job training center that houses the program. That's a sixth of a mile of continuous car-filled concrete, so it makes good sense to walk with the children.

In Chicago, the Beltway Park provides one YMCA-based program with its only available outdoor play environment. Unfortunately, the program's home base sits seven long and dangerous city blocks from the park. Does that stop the director from walking the children to the park? Only when it snows or freezes.

GOAL HELPER #2: Keep apprised of current outdoor conditions.

For someone who regularly drives a car, it's easy to forget what it's like to walk down the street. In many cases, only the odd flat tire or snapped generator belt can bring someone out from behind the steering wheel and onto an unpaved easement. Anyone who's ever muddied their shoes trying to get to an emergency call box while tractor trailers and speeding com-muters whooshed dangerously close knows the feelings of helplessness and insecurity that can come from traveling on foot.

For too long, too many zone planners and land developers presumed car ownership. City managers are finally waking up to the fact that some peo-ple, including young children, have no choice but to use the sidewalk. Even so, pedestrian conditions in many areas remain perilous. PDs and care-givers can help improve children's judgment by keeping them abreast of adverse road and route conditions, construction zones, traffic density pat-terns, long signal delays—anything which might constitute a hazard.

In harsher neighborhoods where gangs ride roughshod, relative hazards can be weighed only by those on the scene. One director in Chicago keeps children indoors all day on Thursdays, because Thursdays are traditionally observed by the local gangs with intensified shootings. Any program might have its own version of Thursdays. It's advisable to take a personal interest in developments that might affect the areas through which children must walk and to advise them about what to watch for. It's also not a bad idea to keep an ear open to the children's observations: what they saw, what happened on the way home yesterday, what their friends told them to go see or watch for. In discussions about which streets to walk and when to walk them, caregivers can reinforce children's critical thinking skills and get a line on street action, all in one fell swoop.

NO TRANSPORTATION PLANNING

When school-age care planning dismisses or ignores the logistics of transportation, it's generally on the assumption that liability begins and ends with children's arrival and departure. This assumption would never be made by a prudent program director. Besides, nature abhors a vacuum, so unless PDs and administrators take some position on transportation policy, others will fill the void with an unstated de facto policy of their own.

Consider a typical district transportation policy. It normally allows children to be picked up and dropped off by school bus *only in close proximity to the child's registered home address.* To be fair, the policy may have seemed reasonable in past years, since it sought to limit liability and prevent overcrowding or abuse of bus services. In a socioeconomic climate of two-parent, single-earner, well-off nuclear families, it might still be a wonderful policy.

However, if strictly observed, such a policy handcuffs parents with children in SACC, in family and group day care, and in all the other mitigating circumstances of modern American life. Caught between this rock and a hard place, parents often choose the simplest solution: They lie. They tell the district that their children live at the care site. In this way, the district carries out its "policy," and parents and children can still obtain desired transportation service.

Are such practices illegal? Yes. Can any policy completely prevent abuses and deceptive practices? Of course not. But must widespread illegality be encouraged by policies that satisfy insurance company actuaries and nobody else? Must policymakers wholly surrender children's fates to the vagaries of self-interest and deceptive calculations? If so, only the cunning, the devious, and the brutish can thrive. Everyone else can either hitchhike or run for it.

NOTES

1. Portions of this section have been adapted and reprinted from the report *Transportation for School-Age Child Care* (White Plains, NY: Child Care Council of Westchester, 1990).

2. Listed percentages apply only to Westchester County; figures in other areas will vary.

FOR FURTHER REFERENCE

Lawren Productions. 1988. *Discipline and the School Bus Passenger* [videotape]. Evanston, IL: Lawren Productions, 930 Pitner Avenue, 60202.

Metropolitan Council on Child Care. 1991. *Transportation Issues and School Age Child Care*. Kansas City, MO: Mid-America Regional Council, 600 Broadway, 300 Rivergate Center, 64105; 816-474-4240.

Perennial Education. 1989. *How Streetproof Are You?* [videotape]. Evanston, IL: Perennial Education Film and Video; 800-323-9084. (Presents walking policy and practices.)

Chapter 12

LEGAL AFFAIRS

Many readers will recall the infamous events revolving around California's McMartin Preschool. Accusations of child abuse and maltreatment led to the longest criminal trial in that state's history. There may never be another case wherein the legal responsibility of caregivers receives such massive national attention.

More than ever before, parents, community leaders, empowering boards, partnering agencies, and children themselves require assurances that a child care program can truly "take care." Accountability for the safeguarding of children in a SACC program comes about as a result of clearly established legal frameworks, as well as an unwavering adherence to the spirit of law.[1]

AUTHORIZATIONS

It takes legal authorization to operate a legal business. Thanks to a separation of church and state, religious organizations take their legal authorizations from the U.S. Constitution. Any other administrative group that wants to operate a legitimate school-age care program has to establish its legal basis to do so.

A fundamental doctrine governing the activities of school boards is that they are created by state law and have only those powers specifically granted and enumerated by statute. So, even though they already exist as legal entities, if public school boards wish to operate, lease space to, or partner into school-age care, they still must be granted that power through enabling legislation and board resolution.

Enabling legislation is the law or group of laws that enable a school board to engage in certain activities. These usually appear in the state's education or school code. Some states only have laws that give a general description of what school boards may do. Some have more specific legislation that addresses particular uses of school property: who may lease school space, for what purposes it may be leased, what shall become of funds raised through use of school space, and so on. In the absence of state law that specifically refers to school-age care, general-powers laws and general-use laws often suffice as a school board's legal authority. However, these laws' vagueness and ambiguity leaves them open to all sorts of interpretations, and a court challenge could put the right to operate a program in the hands of a lone judge.

Several states—Tennessee, Oregon, Washington, Hawaii, Michigan, Maryland, and Massachusetts among them—have passed legislation that expressly authorizes schools to operate and/or lease out space to organizations which provide child care. The passage of specific enabling legislation may reduce judicial interference by laying the foundation for more confident local action.

Enabled by state legislation, school board members can then agree among themselves that they wish to promote school-age care. They do this by drafting and voting on a *school board resolution* (see Figure 12.1). The resolution communicates the school board's support and encouragement for SACC program operation. Also, in particular neighborhoods, it can make the proposition of school-age care more independent of personal whims or uninformed antagonism.

Churches, schools, YSAs, and municipal or state agencies can "foster in" a SACC program under the umbrella of their pre-existing legal status. Other groups who seek to collaborate with one or more of these larger entities—but *who wish to maintain administrative authority*—will want to establish their own legal identity.

INCORPORATION AND TAX EXEMPTION

If an organization can fill out the right forms, pay the fees, and wait—often as long as six months or more—for the wheels of bureaucracy to grind around, a viable legal identity can be had.

Some "organizations" consist of only one person who wishes to run a business venture for personal profit. They can file with the state and federal governments paperwork that establishes them as a *sole proprietorship*. When more than one person want to run the same business together, they can form either a *general or limited partnership,* either of which gives the small group its own legal identity. To find out about the advantages and disadvantages of these entities as they relate to SACC operations, consult a tax attorney, a business accountant, and the plethora of books and pe-

Figure 12.1
Model School Board Resolution To Authorize School-Age Child Care
Programs in Public School Facilities

WHEREAS: There is a documented unmet need in this community for supervised programs for school-age children when school is not in session, and

WHEREAS: The public schools are a logical site for the provision of care because of:

(1) their underutilized space and facilities which are already school-age appropriate;

(2) their ease of accessibility to children throughout the community;

(3) their ability to provide continuity to children who may already be involved in extracurricular activities at the school;

(4) the ability of such programs to enhance school achievement and reduce school vandalism, and;

(5) the unique configuration of their resources for, expertise in, and familiarity with children; and

WHEREAS: The provision of such care in public schools, whether by the schools themselves or other eligible entities, serves a public purpose,

THEREFORE BE IT RESOLVED:

That the Board of Education hereby encourages the use of public school facilities for school-age child care programs. Such programs may be established and operated by schools within this district or they may be

Figure 12.1 (continued)

established and operated in cooperation with eligible users.[2] Such programs may operate before, during, and after school hours, as well as during vacation session, subject to the requirement that they do not interfere with regular school instruction or ongoing school activities. Enrollment shall be open to all school-age children in the district and every effort shall be made to ensure that no child shall be denied participation in these programs because of inability to pay. There shall be no discrimination either in enrollment or hiring. Programs shall operate in conformity with all pertinent school regulations and local and state laws, including any zoning and licensing requirements; and be it further

RESOLVED:

That if such programs are undertaken by entities other than the schools themselves, that they are to be given priority in any leasing policy, second only to educational programs which are an integral part of the school's instructional function; that leases or contracts may be negotiated with such programs which do not recover all costs; and that any such leases or contracts incorporate a provision which will protect the school system and school board from any and all forms of liability that may arise out of the use of such space, as well as require providers to purchase adequate insurance naming the school board and district as the insured; and be it further

RESOLVED:

That this resolution be implemented through the guidelines and procedures established by the superintendent of schools which are incorporated by reference herein; and be it further

RESOLVED:

That the superintendent submit quarterly reports on the use of surplus space; and be it further

RESOLVED:

That this board shall annually review the guidelines and procedures established by the superintendent with respect to SACC programs to ensure their continued effectiveness.

riodicals published for the benefit of profit-seeking entrepreneurs and investors.

For larger groups, another option is incorporation. A *for-profit corporation* is a specific type of legal entity. It aims to accumulate capital profit and to distribute that profit among its directors and shareholders. The law recognizes corporations as being separate and independent from the people who operate inside them. That is, it effectively shields people from personal responsibility or liability for most of their corporate actions. Exxon is an example of a for-profit corporation.

A *nonprofit corporation* defines itself in legal documents as the provider of a charitable or educational service. A nonprofit may not accumulate profits for distribution to directors or shareholders. However, this by no means prohibits a nonprofit from making money—as long as that money goes back into providing its service. (Some states' laws make a legal distinction between corporations designated as nonprofit and those designated as "not-for-profit." Providers in these states will want to clarify their understanding of the differences. In this discussion, the term *nonprofit* refers to both not-for-profit and nonprofit.)

Once an organization has incorporated as a nonprofit, both federal and state governments may grant *tax-exempt status* to the corporation. With this status, nonprofit groups may be exempted from federal income tax, state/city income tax, and state/city sales tax. Application for tax exemption is made through a separate filing with the IRS, which reviews a nonprofit's stated definition of purpose and then determines whether or not this purpose merits the status.

Coupled with tax exemption, nonprofit incorporation probably offers SACC Providers more protection and financial benefit than any other type of legal identity. Here's why:

1. Partner institutions likely will insist that program operators or officers assume clearly defined legal accountability before consenting to a partnership. Partners naturally will want a formal dispersal of potential risks. As a legal entity, it is the corporation—not any one of its members—that bears the burden of liability.

2. Resource development often relies on external or government sources. Tax-exempt nonprofits more easily qualify for funding from these sources. In fact, many states require proof of incorporation for funding eligibility.

3. Unlike sole proprietorships and limited partnerships, the nonprofit corporation establishes a built-in group administrative structure. While particular individuals may come and go, the corporation can maintain legal program status, organization and continuity.

Sample forms and data necessary for both nonprofit incorporation and for IRS 501(c)(3) tax-exempt status appear in School Age NOTES' *Before and After School Programs*. Each state office charged with incorporation duties—frequently, the office of the secretary of state—can provide other particulars on filing requirements and fees.

Don't put away the checkbook yet. Obtaining tax-exempt status depends directly on statements made when applying for nonprofit status, so it also may be wise to consult with a legal advisor who understands the rules of the game. From time to time, legal advisors perform work on a *pro bono* basis—that is, as a community service at no charge. Legal advisors who do *pro bono* work can be found through neighborhood legal aid referral services, local bar associations, and bar-affiliated groups, all of which may be listed in the local telephone directory.

REGULATION AND LICENSING

Prior to offering SACC in a public location, providers will want to investigate potentially applicable regulations. These include not only licensing but also building code, fire code, zoning, and a range of other compliances. Generally, whether or not a given program is subject to licensure—and what administrative agency has jurisdiction—can be determined by the type of program and the type of entity that operates it.

Before granting liability coverage, insurance companies always require demonstrable compliance with civil, building, health, and other general codes. Again, the mix depends on the program location, the nature of the provider, and the demands of the insurer. But in any bottom-line consideration, licensing status and liability coverage affect a SACC program's eligibility for federal and state monies.

Licensure jurisdiction. In general, non-school-run SACC operated on schoolgrounds or in other public locations will come under the jurisdiction of the same state agency that regulates other child care programs. In California, this would be the Department of Social Services; in Tennessee, the Department of Human Services; in Illinois, the Department of Children and Family Services. Most of these agencies have a specific unit that regulates child care.

School-run programs may also be subject to agency regulations, but some states allow the state board of education or other school governance entity to set the terms. To hedge against conflicts later on, public school administrators would do well to keep in contact with the child care agency and the education department in their respective states.

• *Determinant #1: Type of care.* Many states exempt drop-in programs, special programs offered from time to time, child care offered as part of a child development laboratory, and/or programs that operate less than a minimum number of hours per week. Summer camps may also be exempted or subject to separate regulation. For the most part, though, SACC programs operate under one or more sets of administrative authorities, and that can lead to problems.

In 1980, one West Coast city's YMCA chose to pursue SACC program partnership with local public schools. The Y director discovered that the state's licensing guidelines, geared to preschool care, didn't fit SACC. Just to obtain a provisional license, the director had to negotiate with the state government for appropriate school-age standards. Those negotiations lasted three months.

State licensing regulations often have to do with ratios. They variously address ratios of children to square footage, staff to children, equipment to children, and so on. Since they were originally designed to regulate preschool operation, they also discuss such things as diaper changing and feeding practices. According to a 1988 SACCProject study, only five U.S. states reported separate regulations for preschool and SACC, and licensing officials in twenty-two states still reported confusion about whether or not some programs were subject to licensing.

Each state encourages or discourages particular types of legal accountability. While they no longer view SACC as a brand-new approach, many state and local officials continue to struggle with its bureaucratic handles. As policy evolves, and as regulations transform and develop, the licensing picture may clear up. Those who seek a SACC license in states with underdeveloped policies may find themselves catalysts to policymaking.

• *Determinant #2: Type of provider.* Some states exempt or modify requirements for programs operated by religious groups—even when these programs are open to children from the general public. Some states exempt these types altogether. The matter of religious groups operating programs in public schools continues as part of the national discussion regarding separation of church and state. It's advisable to review the most recent decisions before developing agreements in this arena.

• *Determinant #3: Personal imperatives.* When confronted by what they see as undesirable regulation, some planners choose not to seek a license. By formally designating their operation a "recreation program" or "private foundation," they sometimes avoid having to comply with certain legal requirements specific to SACC programs. However, such programs usually will not qualify for tax-exempt status or public funding.

• *Determinant #4: Credibility.* Even when it isn't required, a formal license frequently gives parents and others a higher degree of confidence in the program. In an enrollment struggle between two competing programs, the licensed program may appear more credible and, in turn, may attract more parents.

Consultation. Prior to start-up and periodically thereafter, a legal advisor—either regularly retained or on staff—reviews and analyzes regulation of SACC programs administered by schools, community agencies, religious groups, private companies, and for-profit providers. When more than one group participates in a single program's operation, each group's legal advisor is likely to have a hand in regulation compliance and paths of liability. However, child care law is as much a specialty as any other, so the advisor ought to be well-versed in this area.

ZONING

The West Coast PD who negotiated state-level licensing standards ran up against another challenge at the city level when there arose the matter of *zoning,* or civic approval to conduct business at a particular location. At the time, zoning regulations made no allowance for SACC programs, but they did describe "day care" as legitimate. In order to put SACC in elementary schools, zoning variances had to be applied for and received— one school at a time. This process consumed another three months.

Nearly every city has some kind of zoning requirements, but not all. For many years, Houston stood as the largest incorporated U.S. city without zoning regulations. This meant that, if so desired, a SACC program could be operated in almost any building with four walls and a roof, be it a warehouse, a shopping mall, or an abandoned beauty parlor!

Most cities won't be quite so casual about property usages. After a review by a city planning commission, lots are zoned for either commercial, residential, or preferential use, the latter including demonstrably religious and educational organizations. Generally speaking, a SACC program can take up residence more easily when classified for *community service,* so that it may receive the same zoning board consideration as do schools. A program so classified need not necessarily operate in a school, but it may exercise equal freedom in choice of appropriate locations.

If planning property development or new construction to house the SACC program, the site ought to be zoned appropriately before start-up. Otherwise, certain zoning restrictions and conditions may interrupt or interfere with program operation.

LIABILITY

In a SACC program, just as in any aspect of human existence, things can go wrong. No matter how well-designed or safety-minded the program's physical environment, an energetic child can still find a way to get hurt. When that happens, that child's family may sue any person or entity they hold responsible. Providers, general administrators, PDs, and even caregivers all make potential targets of liability suits.

Thanks to the absence of common law and to an antiquated tort law, U.S. courts witness a veritable avalanche of civil litigation. In 1991, American International Group, the largest U.S. underwriter of commercial and industrial insurance, related that liability costs accounted for as much as 50 percent of a product's price. Not even a small SACC program can hope for immunity from the potential ravage of liability costs.

Understandably, fears about liability impede SACC partnerships, especially those involving school boards and non-school entities. Potential partners worry about both financial loss and damage to credibility. To mitigate such fears, the agency or group that intends to administer a SACC program must be able to point to a history of responsible appearance and action. This includes the ability to secure adequate liability insurance.

Providers can usually refer liability questions and research to their regular legal advisors. PDs may be asked to supplement with specifics, and independent child care specialists may be retained as consultants. Personal injury coverage costs may be (1) absorbed by the administrator, (2) built into the fee structure, or (3) offered to parents at additional cost as a separate insurance product.

Newly formed parent groups may not have the luxury of retaining or consulting with experienced legal counsel. In these special cases, parents may have to familiarize themselves with the specifics of appropriate liability options, then negotiate terms of agreement with their partners. Such negotiations must be adversarial by definition, so it makes good sense to recruit or assign one well-informed person to play the part of adversary. If that one person knows the law, so much the better.

Negligence

When there has been a breach of duty of care that is the actual and proximate cause of the victim's injuries, negligence has occurred. In SACC, the most common breaches involve supervision; instruction in or choice of activities; failure to warn of certain dangers; maintenance, placement or location of facilities; and transportation.

Negligence itself is comprised of five basic elements: (1) duty/standard of care, (2) failure to meet the standard of care, (3) foreseeability, (4) a connection between the breach and the injury—"proximate cause," and (5) damage. While proximate cause and damage are generally self-explanatory concepts, perhaps the other elements require some additional clarification.

Standard of care. Theoretically, there is only one standard: Each person owes a duty to act as a reasonably prudent person would have acted under the same or similar circumstances. In practice, the standard depends on who is injured and who owes the duty.

Depending on whether a child is five or twelve, what constitutes adequate supervision and safety will vary tremendously. Because of relative immaturity and inexperience, a higher standard of care is owed to younger children than to older children. For example, a posted warning suffices only if a child can read, and—whether they can read or not—older children are supposed to be capable of reading. Theoretically, a higher standard of care is also owed to children with special needs, although in practice, where special needs programs have become dumping grounds for non-English-speaking or angry or abused children, standards of care have been turned upside-down.

Some providers attempt to meet the standard with differentiated treatment for younger and special children. Often, they do this by segregating children into groups by age or some other visible condition. They then apply separate sets of standards to each group.

However, if providers and caregivers are aware of a particular child's *invisible* sensitivities or propensities, they can be held to another standard of care, one that is reasonable with respect to that child. This means that a failure to treat a child in a developmentally appropriate way can conceivably constitute the basis for a claim of negligence. Herein lies the legal imperative for applying the tenets of child development to each and every child in a SACC program.

Duty to care. The standard owed will also be reflective of who owes the duty. For example, in Illinois, teachers are viewed as *in loco parentis*— literally, in place of the parent. This subjects them to the exact same standard of care as the children's parents. An Illinois' teacher's conduct must therefore be proved "willful and wanton" before being found negligent.

The question then arises as to whether or not SACC people are subject to the same standards of duty as schoolteachers and parents. As with the issue of licensing, cloudiness here stems from an absence of specific state-level attention to SACC people and programs. Sustained efforts to focus legislators' attention on school-age care may help over time to clear up the confusion.

In another important instance of differing standards of duty, a person with specialized knowledge or skills *can* be held to a higher standard. If a caregiver happens to be, say, a medical professional, that caregiver will be held to a higher standard of care in rendering emergency medical assistance than will someone with no medical training. Relatedly, caregivers who happen to be accredited SACC professionals will be held to a higher standard of care than someone with no training.

Foreseeability of harm. Liability will only occur if, in addition to a breach of duty owed, the injury that resulted was foreseeable. While some cases may seem to stretch the meaning of what is "foreseeable," the meaning reflects application of a reasonable person's so-called common sense. That is, the more easily or frequently observed the condition or behavior that results in injury, the more foreseeable the harm.

Combating Claims of Negligence

The liability picture may be painted with a broad brushstroke, or it may come together like a jigsaw puzzle. Program children may physically pass through a classroom, a playground, a city park, a bus, a crosswalk, a job training center, and a private passenger vehicle—all in the same day. Where one liability ends, perhaps another begins. What determines the lines of division and how to draw those lines constitutes the basis for liability negotiations.

• *School-run programs only.* Schools may have recourses not available to other entities. In some states, school systems (personnel, board of education, school district) may seem shielded from lawsuits by *governmental immunity* statutes. These may be seem absolute, but evolving court interpretations may render them otherwise. As one commentator has put it: "A prudent school must never presume that its students automatically shed the protective mantle of the school's duty of care when they leave the schoolhouse gate."[2]

Where governmental immunity isn't a factor, states may have statutes requiring that, prior to filing a lawsuit, persons seeking compensation for injuries file a *notice of claim* with the school district. Failing to file such a notice within a prescribed amount of time may absolutely bar the filing of a lawsuit and, as such, preclude any recovery.

• *All programs.* In the past, state courts often took the view that plaintiffs who contributed in any way to their own injury were absolutely precluded from recovering any damages. In recent years, this doctrine of *contributory negligence* has given way in most states to perceptions of relative fault, or *comparative negligence.* Some states have even adopted pure comparative negligence, which assigns liability in direct proportion to the fault of the persons who caused the injury or damage. Whether a state has a contributory or comparative negligence scheme, there remains the task of determining how much school-agers can contribute to their own injury.

Some states still retain the traditional view: Children younger than age seven are conclusively incapable of contributory negligence (they can never be proven to blame), while children from ages seven to fourteen are presumptively incapable of contributory negligence (only in light of solid evidence may they be proven partly to blame). Other states, such as Utah, have proceeded along lines that allow children of any age to be held contributorily negligent (youth is no excuse).

In making their determinations, courts have generally applied a standard that the law calls *objective.* This standard holds that when children participate in an activity characteristically engaged in by children, they are held to that degree of care ordinarily exercised by children of like age, knowledge, judgment, and experience under similar circumstances. In other words, courts generally judge a child's actions in comparison with the way other children act.

Another doctrine, known as *assumption of the risk,* occurs when the plaintiffs voluntarily and unnecessarily expose themselves to a known, specific risk of which they appreciated the magnitude. This is a recognizably *subjective* standard, requiring that the particular child knows, sees, hears, comprehends, and appreciates the particular risks involved. In this view, any child is far too unique to be compared with other children, and each child deserves to be treated as unique.

In a few states, a *charitable immunity* doctrine protects nonprofit corporations and can limit the extent of a program's liability. Statutes so based confer immunity against any civil damages for acts or omissions by persons rendering emergency care. Where applicable, the state office responsible for incorporation can provide details.

Distributing Liability

To head off adversarial claims, providers seek to establish assumption of the risk by parents. The most common method to achieve this is through the use of *waivers,* or what most people call permission slips. These authorizations and/or releases that parents sign can cover a wide range of possibilities, from field trips to discussions of human reproduction. Technically, a waiver can also be oral or evidenced in conduct, but obviously, if conflicts arise, a written waiver makes the most convincing argument.

When a provider operates in conjunction with or leases space from another entity, it is imperative to write up a formal agreement that allocates responsibilities and liabilities for various aspects of the program. Such agreements normally include a *save or hold harmless provision.* This contractual clause formally separates the indicated entity from responses to suits brought against the program. For example, the SACC lease insurance policy for Montgomery County, Maryland Public Schools, reads in part:

The lease for each user group shall include appropriate language to save the Board of Education and the school system harmless against any and all claims, demands, suits, or other forms of liability that may arise out of this use of school space.

No matter how many waivers, clauses, and policies a program employs, some liability always remains. Legal proceedings may determine personal negligence or fraudulence on the part of a group member, thereby excepting that member from corporate protection. In programs administered by a board of directors, board members can be held personally liable for the failure of the corporation to pay taxes or for gross negligence that results in financial loss to the organization. So, as long as liability sticks around, insurance companies will be happy to sell liability insurance.

Liability Coverage

Insurance policies contain highly specific terminology that affects the inclusion or exclusion of any given event's coverage. For some institutions, riders to existing policies may suffice. In other cases, new policies must be obtained.

General liability. This coverage guards against excessive claims due to physical injuries resulting from perceived negligence. A high limit of coverage, say $100,000 to $300,000, costs little more than that of $5,000 to $10,000, and it's probably worth it. In the event of a major claim, those few extra pennies will look like a very smart investment.

Vehicle. States have made this type of coverage de rigeur. An appropriate policy specifies coverage not only for regular program hours but for overlap periods such as early school dismissal. The state and insurers may require vehicles and drivers to meet special licensing requirements in order to qualify for coverage.

If vehicles used to transport children are personally owned or operated by program people, make certain these people secure high levels of coverage; liability from vehicular accidents can potentially snuff out a program. To make up the difference in cost, a good solution is to reimburse a driver directly for premiums incurred by increased coverage.

Fire. One type covers losses resulting directly from fire or lightning. Another type known as *extended coverage* guards against loss from collateral damage causes, such as smoke, and against unforeseeable acts, such as a helicopter crashing through the roof. Get both.

Theft. Programs based in metropolitan areas with unusually high crime rates will find standard theft insurance either unobtainable or prohibitively expensive. If a program falls within certain government guidelines, private insurance agents *must* make low-cost federal crime insurance available.

Fidelity bonds. These indemnify the program against employee theft or embezzlement. Many employers insist on bondability as a prerequisite for employment.

Qualified insurance agents can provide actuarial statistics and professional assessments of value on which to base decisions about necessary coverage amounts. Providers can then weigh the cost of coverage against the cost of potential loss. To re-emphasize: A program's fiscal health and longevity heavily relies on appropriate risk distribution.

SPECIAL CHILDREN, SPECIAL SITUATIONS

In light of their particular physical, emotional, or health conditions, some children seem to require unusual degrees of care. These conditions include, but are not limited to, communication disorders, developmental disabilities, emotional disturbances, health impairments ranging from allergies to cancer, learning disabilities, physical disabilities and visual impairments. Of course, these special children's well-being calls for special logistical and legal considerations.

Dale Fink's excellent volume, *School-Age Children with Special Needs:*

What Do They Do When School's Out? (Boston, MA: Exceptional Parent Press, 1988), covers various pertinent topics, including legal issues, with depth and sensitivity.

UNFAIR COMPETITION

More than once, private-sector child care business owners have leveled attacks against nonprofit SACC providers who locate in public schools. Those who declaim the schools and nonprofits for unfair competition have an argument for every occasion. First, they say that subsidies—in the form of free or reduced rent, utilities, custodial services, and the like—enable school-run programs to charge less, which gives school-based programs an unfair competitive edge. But when schools charge higher fees that more than cover their programs' operating costs, the naysayers contend that fee-based programs transform public schools into illegal commercial enterprises. It's a case of "darned if you do, darned if you don't."

Courts have uniformly rejected the notion that public school activities that simply replicate those performed by private groups constitute unfair competition. The same courts have held that statutory authorizations protect schools from such claims. The definition of what constitutes unfair competition varies widely from state to state, so, as always, it's a good idea to carefully review statutes and recent decisions.

To ensure protection against claims of unfair competition, it's also advisable to secure documented evidence of what some might call "an unmet community demand" for SACC. Herein lies the legal imperative for a CANARI (see Chapter 2). In the event of private businesses' outcries, CANARI results can substantiate the operation of nonprofit providers' programs.

CONTRACTS

Appropriate to any discussion of contracts is the famous quote attributed to movie mogul Samuel Goldwyn, who proclaimed, "A verbal contract isn't worth the paper it's printed on!"

Technically speaking, an agreement doesn't have to be in writing to be considered legally binding. However, as Goldwyn implied, proving breach of oral contract tends to be an exercise in futility. Written agreements between SACC program partners carry far more demonstrable legal weight; but be careful, because this knife cuts both ways. Formal contracts and leases aren't the only legal evidence of agreement. Signed and dated memoranda, letters, or even purchase orders can be used to prove a point.

Nor must money change hands for a contract to exist. The promise of one service in exchange for another can be just as binding as a cash transaction. For example, a parent who accepts a program's offer of SACC services in exchange for installing drywall and insulation has a legal contract with the program.

Although informal arrangements may seem less confrontational, many people's time and experience have borne out the opposite conclusion. By anticipating changes of heart and by recognizing the power of written agreements, program people stand a much better chance of avoiding unnecessary financial and emotional drain.

Effective contracts contain or make reference to concrete information regarding:

Program Purpose: The mission statement. Description of program content. Children's and parents' eligibility factors. Hours and months of operation.

Resource Availability: Program base designation. Calendar term of access to space. Parameters of shared or in-common space usage. General reference to equipment and materials deemed appropriate for program usage.

Management and Administration: Legal expectations and obligations of contractees. Lines of liability. Licensing, bonding, and/or rental fee requirements. Save or hold harmless provision. Nondiscrimination clause.

Time, Space, and Equipment (TSE) Contract

In any state, certain statutes govern the legal limits of responsibility between lessor and lessee. Wide latitude may exist within those limits, and it's up to the lessee to make satisfactory terms of agreement with the lessor. In this respect, an independent provider negotiating terms with a principal, a school board, a government agency, or a private company goes through much the same process as any renter does with any landlord. This generally indicates the execution of a legal lease or rental agreement.

When a provider seeks usage of another organization's facilities, a TSE contract goes a long way toward mitigating misunderstandings before they can happen. Such a contract formally specifies opportunities and limitations of each party. It reflects the coordination of mutual obligation.

Whether they rent or occupy donated space, providers may face another organization's standard lease as the primary written form of TSE contract. For their part, lessors frequently point a firm finger at standard lease terms and may not wish to entertain any changes. As a potential lessee and tenant, it's a provider's duty to negotiate on every standard lease term that might result in a substandard SACC program.

How could a standard contract hurt anything? It might reserve to the lessor an administrative authority to keep lessees out of a playground, a kitchen, or another shared facility without having to explain why. Going along with such prohibitive terms may seem like a gesture of goodwill, to be honored fairly by both parties, but who can say? At a later date, with another principal or another lessee involved, the program might suffer, and program people would have nothing to say about it, because "it's in the contract."

Terms of a lease must address the SACC program's actual TSE usage. In one case, a program lease was written to cover a 365-day period from September 1 to September 1 the following year. Fortunately, a lawyer who reviewed the lease prior to signing noticed that it didn't allow for the program's summer suspension. Even if the program didn't operate over the summer, it still might have been obligated contractually to pay those three months' rent! Attention to this type of detail prevents later regrets.

For programs with potential for multi-site operation, the cost and time of negotiations can sometimes give rise to a *boilerplate contract,* which providers can utilize upon entry into each new site. While this utilitarian approach may help standardize relationships between large institutions, it may also interfere with the natural growth and evolution of each site's program. In other words, a boilerplate contract may sacrifice appropriate child development concerns in the name of expediency.

Note the specificity of TSE terms in the following excerpts. From a letter of agreement addressed to a SACC program by a church board:

You will be issued two sets of keys. Children are to enter by the Merrit Avenue door and go directly to their rooms; children will not be permitted in other areas of the building.

From a school board memo:

The cafeteria can be made available five afternoons a week as the basic homeroom for the program. To clear this room will require the relocation of Girl Scout activities to another area of the school.

From a multi-site program lease:

It is understood that if a food facility is available at the designated school, then a separate agreement shall be made between the parties as to costs and services.

School Age NOTES' *Before and After School Programs* contains a sample TSE contract between a parent group and a school.

On-Site Parties Contract

Despite the way it sounds, this isn't an agreement about birthday cake and ice cream. Here, the legal term *parties* jointly refers to the people most directly responsible for day-to-day program operations. Usually, these people turn out to be (1) the on-site PD and (2) the principal, minister, community school director, or other site administrator. Even in a long-standing collaboration through which these two people have developed a solid informal arrangement, SACC program implementation sounds a call to formalize the relationship. New endeavors can sometimes strain old friendships, so a separate contract between the two can smooth around the edges before they get frayed.

An on-site parties contract clearly and appropriately (1) names the parties, (2) divides the areas and functions for which each bears direct responsibility, and (3) sets out any explicit rules about equipment, maintenance, and usage of space not expressed in the TSE contract.

As an added benefit, an on-site parties contract can help clarify relationships alluded to, but not detailed, in a TSE contract. For example, a bi-institutional TSE might invoke "a close working relationship" between the program and partner institution, then leave it to the on-site parties to figure out what constitutes such a relationship. The contract helps support whatever avenues of communication program planners and providers have in mind.

Independent Contractors

In one West Coast city, the YMCA partnered with and offered programs in the community schools. At one of these sites, during regular program hours, a child climbed on top of a community school shed, subsequently fell, and received an injury. A civil suit filed on the child's behalf named the program director personally liable and sought damages in the amount of $75,000. Question: Why wasn't the city's Community Schools Department sued?

For one thing, no school department or community education staffer had a job description that included child care.

For another, a usage standard was in effect. That is, there was no expressed or implied admission by the community schools that the shed was climbable—or even that it should be climbed—for the purpose of school-age child care. The school could be held liable only if the leased space and equipment, used as intended, proved unsafe.

Finally, the formal relationship of the PD to the YMCA and the community schools was that of *independent contractor*. The local Y bore responsibility for accidents resulting from program staff negligence.

In most states, the division of contractual liability rests on statutes that address the issue of employment. Who's at fault depends on who works for whom. Whether or not the legal entity that offers a SACC program incurs a given liability depends on the contractual relationship between that legal entity and any person who is ultimately found to be negligent.

PDs and caregivers aren't the only people whose actions may be ultimately deemed negligent. The independent contractor may be a maintenance worker hired by a site administrator for a specific purpose, services paid for on a one-time fee basis. In this event, if the worker improperly installs a light fixture that subsequently falls and injures a child, neither the program nor the director incurs liability.

In discussions of broader contracts and inherent liability, the role of the independent contractor figures prominently. Transferring liability *away* from the program through the use of independent contractors for—among other things—maintenance, transportation, and food services substantially reduces program liability expense, even if only in the reduction of premiums.

What about the $75,000 lawsuit against the YMCA program director? The local Y settled out of court, because no one wants to go into court with a losing case. The circumstances clearly pointed to the liability of an independent contractor with whom rested responsibility for a child's safety.

BEYOND LEGALESE

Whether formal or informal, verbal or written, specific or general, legal commitments inevitably depend on something more than mere words. They depend on a willingness to work together, on a desire to build reliable relationships between agencies, boards, funders, and program people. Without that willingness and desire, only hardened impersonal enforcement and spurious litigation will characterize interaction between SACC program partners—and nobody but a lawyer looks forward to that.

NOTES

1. Many of the legal considerations discussed in this chapter are condensed and adapted from Abby J. Cohen, *School-Age Child Care: A Legal Manual for Public School Administrators* (Wellesley, MA: SACCProject, 1984). This volume, prepared in cooperation with Child Care Law Center in California, may be out of print. However, Child Care Law Center offers for sale a significant number of other related publications. The Center also maintains a Law and Policy Resources Bank, which is a clearinghouse for legislation, cases, briefs, and legal memoranda on critical legal issues in child care. For more information, contact Child Care Law Center, 22 Second Street, 5th Floor, San Francisco, CA 94105; 415-495-5498.

2. W. Paul Hagenau, "Penumbras of Care beyond the Schoolhouse Gate," *Journal of Law and Education,* No. 9 (1980), p. 201.

FOR FURTHER REFERENCE

Chapman, Terry, et al. 1992. "Am I Covered for . . . ?" *A Guide to Insurance for Nonprofits.* Madison, WI: Society of Nonprofit Organizations, 6314 Odana Road, 53719.

Child Care Law Center. 1992. *Liability Insurance: Insuring Your Program.* San Francisco: Child Care Law Center, 22 Second Street, 5th Floor, 94105.

————. 1991. *501 (c)(3) Status and How to Get It*. San Francisco: Child Care Law Center.

Kotkin, Lawrence, Robert Crabtree, and William Aikman. 1981. *Legal Handbook for Day Care Centers*. Boston, MA: Kotkin and Crabtree, 61 Chatham Street, 02109.

Mancuso, Anthony. 1990. *How to Form a Nonprofit Corporation*. Berkeley, CA: Nolo Press, 950 Parker Street, 94710. (Includes all necessary forms and data for forty-nine states.)

Chapter 13

ASSESSMENTS

The laws have been examined and obeyed. The fees have been paid. There's a climbing structure outside. Caregivers have been trained. There are plenty of toys. The food's up to par. There's a rug on the floor.

But something's not quite right. Enrollment's down too low. The kids are too wild. Everybody's bumping into each other. Parents are balking at paying the full cost of care. What's a PD to do?

Or maybe everything looks just fine. Maybe there's nothing obviously wrong. But compared to what? Is the program really as good as it could be?

A *program assessment* is an examination for the sake of learning and improving. It's a process by which to step back from the program and get some objectivity. Each program has a life of its own, influenced by each of its separate planning factors. Over the life of the program, its feel can sharpen, flatten, sparkle, or fizzle. An assessment seeks to discover something about how a program's feel has developed, where it might be going, and how its people can help it feel better.

A formal assessment invites everyone who cares about the program to offer their observations. It can be as simple as a one-evening one-site workshop or as complex as a six-month district-wide survey. In either case, there's no point going in with a clipboard full of preconceived notions. Everyone who participates will have something to say, and that's the notion.

Taking stock of all the little things that make a program what it is takes some openness, some sensitivity. It takes some understanding about how different things are important to different people.

AGREEING TO MAKE THINGS BETTER

In the course of the caring day, it's easy to get preoccupied with moment-to-moment goings-on. There's usually lots of detail work, events that seem to demand immediate attention, and sometimes even a little breathlessness. But even in the midst of all this controlled chaos, it's important to make time to reflect on how a program is doing overall.

PDs generally begin the self-observation process by hearkening back to their own memories of out-of-school time. They then gather with everyone who cares about the program—caregivers, parents, Friends of the Program, site staff, and so on—to encourage them to do the same. It's a time to talk about what kind of memories the program experience creates for children. It's a time to talk about how to make the experience—and the memories—better than ever.

Formal program assessments may include questionnaires, video tapes, sensory exercises, or other ways to record and examine thoughts and feelings. Those who conduct the formal assessment are collectively known as the *assessment team*. Teams formed solely of caregivers or solely of administrators don't have as much chance for discovery as do teams that include every type of involved partner. To conduct successful assessments, directors use systems that easily permit anyone who wishes to participate as a team member, and they make a commitment to excellence the primary qualification for team membership.

One comprehensive system for this purpose was developed in the 90s by SACCProject. *ASQ: Assessing School-Age Child Care Quality* sets forth a step-by-step approach for assessment teams to take. ASQ encourages teams to explore a program's qualities in regard to four main areas:

Personal Relationships

Surroundings

Safety, Health, and Nutrition

Time and Experience

PERSONAL RELATIONSHIPS

When people interact, they communicate something about their own personal values. Some of these values they express explicity, in face-value terms. With children, they might advocate the joys of sharing, cleanliness, and conformity.

People express other values in more subtle ways. Choosing a favorite from the group tells the other children that they are less worthy. Freezing out a child's impulses tells the child that feelings aren't acceptable. With body language, turns of phrase, and little looks, caregivers unconsciously give many messages to children.

Whatever values caregivers may espouse, their actions tell the story. Their relationships with children and each other can benefit from some sensitive observation. Their pet peeves and frustrations can lead either to unspoken resentment or to considered resolution through assessment.

When it comes to the children, the same things apply. The problem with most program improvement plans is that they leave out the children's voices. Parents often base their informal assessments on what their children tell them. Why shouldn't PDs find out what's on children's minds, too?

Some Questions about Personal Relationships:

- Do children seem to have more fun when caregivers leave them alone?
- When they look at the children, do caregivers' eyes sparkle or glaze over?
- What tone of voice do caregivers take? Flat? Upbeat? And does anyone listen?
- Do caregivers have anything to say about the world children live in?
- Can children find their interests reflected in caregivers?
- Do caregivers interact with each other familially, or do children see them as actors on a stage?

SURROUNDINGS

As Lovelace wrote, "Stone walls do not a prison make, nor iron bars a cage." He might also have noted that dedicated space does not a SACC program make. Whether it is located in a church, a school, a YSA, or a single-family residence, a program can feel cozy, comfortable, and inviting. A number of ways to accomplish this are described in Chapter 4. But the space is only one factor of the place.

People take their behavioral cues from a variety of sensory stimuli. For example, some researchers believe that rooms with pink walls exert a soothing influence over people. Some have discovered that the aroma of peppermint can ease inner tension. Colors, textures, aromas, and temperature all go into the feel of a program.

Few partners will expect a PD to hire a Manhattan interior designer, and not many will consider wall color or floor surfacing particularly crucial. Opening their eyes to these issues, they fear, could mean opening their pocketbooks, but taking action on surroundings assessments doesn't have to lead to cost overruns. It might just mean opening the window.

Some Questions about Surroundings:

- Is the room lit warmly, or is everybody in silhouette?
- Children like to play on the floor, so why can't they?
- Are people afraid to use the bathrooms?

- What is that terrible smell, anyway?
- Does the echo factor lead to shouting?
- Do caregivers "go ballistic" over a little juice spill?
- Can physically challenged children move around freely? How?
- Would anyone in their right mind *choose* to be here?

SAFETY, HEALTH, AND NUTRITION

In an appropriate program, school-agers do a lot of running, jumping, falling, and bumping. Growing up has a lot to do with testing the limits of the physical universe. Imposing too many adult limits on that testing inevitably stunts children's growth.

The word *health* encompasses enough different states of being to fill an encyclopedia. Health regulations usually go toward the obvious: communicable diseases, lice, drug abuse, and the like. Regulations also speak to less obvious health risks, such as sexual or physical abuse. Evaluating compliance with these regulations presents no formidable challenge. Chapter 9 delves into these.

It's in the areas of mental and emotional health that assessments begin to help. Formal observations can paint a picture of trust or unease, of confidence or insecurity. And there *is* such a thing as group mental health, the condition of people confined with each other for long periods of time. Even after all measurable precautions have been taken, the group's relations can become twisted by a single mistaken impression.

Contrary to USDA regulations, nutrition isn't just about packing in a few grams of carbohydrates and vitamins. Everyone knows what happens to their cars if they use watered-down fuel. What happens to children running on lard crackers and artificially flavored drinks is even more damaging. On top of this, there's a veritable chemistry set lurking in much of the low-cost "nutritious" food that programs serve. How safe or healthy is a mouthful of sulfites, sodium nitrites, and MSG? The Food and Nutrition Standards section in Chapter 9 goes into a little more detail about this, and Chapter 10 contains a discussion about scheduling snacks.

How children behave when they eat gives observers another kind of understanding about how children feel. If they're always throwing it more than eating it, maybe they just don't like it. Or maybe it's an indication that something *else* is wrong. A formal assessment looks at this.

Some Questions about Safety, Health, and Nutrition:

- Is someone spreading rumors or innuendos?
- When children want to hide, can they do it safely without having to ask permission? How?
- Does one child always seem to get ganged up on?

- Is there some kind of law against fruits and vegetables?
- Who keeps leaving the street door open?
- Are children afraid to ask for more food?

TIME AND EXPERIENCE

Chapters 4 and 10 deal extensively with this assessment area. Formal observations can reveal the different ways in which time influences the depth of experience. They give substance to developmental theory about experiences and children's ages. They also provide an overall view of the program's success at accomodating children's interests and abilities.

Some Questions about Time and Experience:

- Do older children ever get to handle some real equipment, or are they stuck with the preschool toy hammer?
- Are adults always toting clipboards and checking their watches?
- What's all this military lining-up stuff?
- Why does it feel like everyone's just waiting around for something to happen?
- Why don't parents like to come in?

ON THE ROAD TO ASSESSMENT

Sometimes, providers, administrators, PDs, and parents have a tough time agreeing to the terms and methods of assessment. Each of them comes to the table with a different personal and political agenda, so it may be difficult for one to identify with another's point of view. What one thinks of as perfectly acceptable might give another nightmares. While their discussions drag on, self-assessment and its objective—program improvement—remain unaccomplished.

In order to break the gridlock, any one of the players might retain or lobby for an *independent program evaluator*. Ideally a knowledgeable outsider who can apply cool-headed expertise, an independent program evaluator, will have an established reputation in the school-age care field. She or he will have previously conducted research, published findings, successfully directed or administered school-age programs, and consulted to civic or state policymakers.

Depending on the size of the program, the number of sites, and the depth of the investigation, an independent evaluator's work can take from two weeks to six months. The evaluator may work alone or may employ a team of observers who visit program sites and collect preliminary data. A professional evaluation will shed light on a wide range of assessment issues, clearing the way for more informed cooperation between program people and partners.

The cost of independent evaluation varies with the scope of the work, but in no case does it come cheap. A statewide evaluation of program service can run thousands of dollars. However, if the evaluation spurs the cause of program improvement, the cost-to-benefit ratio might look surprisingly reasonable.

Although it can offer additional incentives to improve service, an independent evaluation cannot substitute for an agreement to make things better. Responsibility for that agreement always rests with program people and partners. It rests with their ability to see and understand their own contributions, to confront facts, to welcome growth and change.

SOME PARTING WORDS ABOUT QUALITY

If a program mission statement fails to reflect at least some notion of moral obligation, it fails as a mission statement. And herein lies the strange contradiction of the well-intentioned SACC program: It is an island of moral imperatives in an ocean of commercial values. Yet even this contradiction pales beside the more immediate debate over the issue of "quality."

In his classic *Zen and the Art of Motorcycle Maintenance*, Robert Pirsig describes his own philosophical search for the elusive meaning of Quality, with a capital *Q*. Perhaps SACC practitioners would do well to recall the complete nervous breakdown Pirsig experienced as a result of that search. Might one not wonder whether *Quality* has fast become an overused child care buzzword, already devoid of value?

The "Q" word crops up in just about every discussion about a SACC program's worthiness. For years, child care professionals have uttered the words "quality child care," usually in seeking to promote curriculum, caregiver training, policy statements, and regulated environments. The concept of child care has been imbued with industrial language. Caregivers are "workers" hired to use developmentally appropriate "tools," serving "consumers" or "clients," all in order to "yield measurable results" as quantified by "experts." Is this Quality?

Instead, perhaps they would do well to explore how people *feel* about *qualities*, with a small *q*. The quality of a unique emotional bond. The quality of a smelly gymnasium or a windowless basement room. And especially the quality of a child's smile, which can never be assessed.

FOR FURTHER REFERENCE

American Academy of Pediatrics and American Public Health Association. 1992. *Caring for Our Children: National Health and Safety Performance Standards (Guidelines for Out-of-Home Child Care Programs)*. Washington, DC: AAP/APHA, Dept. 5037, 20061-5037; 202-789-5667.

Bredekamp, Sue, ed. 1991. *Accreditation Criteria and Procedures of the National Academy of Early Childhood Programs*. Washington, DC: NAEYC.

———. 1987. *Developmentally Appropriate Practice in Early Childhood Programs Serving Children from Birth Through Age 8*. Washington, DC: NAEYC.

Child Welfare League of America. 1993. *Standards of Excellence for Child Day Care Service*. New York: Child Welfare League.

Appendix 1

STATE CHILD CARE LICENSING AGENCIES

ALABAMA
Office of Day Care and Child
   Development
Department of Human Resources
64 North Union Street
Montgomery, AL 36130
(205) 242-1425

ALASKA
Division of Family and Youth Services
Department of Health and Social
   Services
P.O. Box 110630
Juneau, AK 99811-0630
(907) 465-2145

ARIZONA
Office of Child Day Care Facilities
Department of Health Services
100 West Clarendon, Suite 520
Phoenix, AZ 85013
(602) 255-1272

ARKANSAS
Division of Children and Family
   Services

Department of Human Services
Slot 720
Little Rock, AR 72203
(501) 682-8590

CALIFORNIA
Community Care Licensing Division
Department of Social Services
744 P Street, Mail Station 17-17
Sacramento, CA 95814
(916) 973-3846

COLORADO
Department of Social Services
1575 Sherman Street, First Floor
Denver, CO 80203-1714
(303) 866-5961

CONNECTICUT
Community Nursing, Home, and
   Health Division
Department of Health Services
150 Washington Street
Hartford, CT 06106
(203) 566-2575

DELAWARE
Division of Program Support
Department of Services to Children,
  Youth, and Families
1825 Faukland Road
Wilmington, DE 19805
(302) 633-2700

DISTRICT OF COLUMBIA
Department of Consumer and
  Regulatory Affairs
614 H Street NW, Room 1031
Washington, DC 20002
(202) 727-7226

FLORIDA
Day Care Licensing
Department of Social and
  Rehabilitative Services
1317 Winewood Boulevard
Building 7, Room 203
Tallahassee, FL 32399-0700
(904) 488-4900

GEORGIA
Day Care Licensing Section
Office of Regulatory Services
Department of Human Resources
878 Peachtree Street NE, Room 607
Atlanta, GA 30309
(404) 894-5688

GUAM
Department of Public Health and
  Social Services
P.O. Box 2816
Agana, GU 96910
(671) 477-8907 x28

HAWAII
Public Welfare Division
Department of Human Services
P.O. Box 339
Honolulu, HI 96809
(808) 586-8107

IDAHO
Family and Children's Services
Department of Health and Welfare
450 West State Street, 3rd Floor
Boise, ID 83720-5450
(208) 334-5702

ILLINOIS
Department of Children and Family
  Services
406 East Monroe Street
Springfield, IL 62701
(217) 785-2688

INDIANA
Licensing Unit
Department of Public Welfare
402 W. Washington St., Room W-364
Indianapolis, IN 46204
(317) 232-4442

IOWA
Day Care Services and Licensing
  Bureau of Adult, Children, and
  Family Services
Department of Human Services
Hoover State Office Building, 5th Floor
Des Moines, IA 50319
(515) 281-6074

KANSAS
Child Care Facilities Licensure
Bureau of Adult and Child Care
  Facilities
Department of Health and
  Environment
900 SW Jackson Street
Topeka, KS 66612-1290
(913) 296-1272

KENTUCKY
Division for Licensure and Regulation
Department of Social Services
275 East Main Street, CHR Building,
  Fourth Floor East
Frankfort, KY 40621
(502) 564-2800

LOUISIANA
Health Standards
P.O. Box 3078
Baton Rouge, LA 70821
(504) 342-4131

MAINE
Child Care Licensing Unit
Bureau of Social Services
221 State Street, Station 11
Augusta, ME 04333
(207) 289-5060

MARYLAND
Office of Child Care Licensing and
    Regulation
2701 North Charles Street
Baltimore, MD 21201
(410) 333-0193

MASSACHUSETTS
Day Care Licensing
Office for Children
1 Ashburton Place, Room 1111
Boston, MA 02108
(617) 727-8900

MICHIGAN
Day Care Licensing
Department of Social Services
Grand Tower, Suite 1212
P.O. Box 30037
Lansing, MI 48909
(517) 373-8300

MINNESOTA
Department of Human Services
444 Lafayette Road
St. Paul, MN 55155-3842
(612) 296-3768

MISSISSIPPI
Bureau of Health Resources
Department of Health
P.O. Box 1700
Jackson, MS 39215-1700
(601) 960-7504

MISSOURI
Division of Family Services
Broadway State Office Building
P.O. Box 88
Jefferson City, MO 65103
(314) 751-2450

MONTANA
Audit and Evaluation Division
Department of Family Services
P.O. Box 8005
Helena, MT 59604
(406) 444-5910

NEBRASKA
Licensing Unit
Department of Social Services
P.O. Box 95026
Lincoln, NE 68509
(402) 471-3121

NEVADA
Bureau of Child Care Services
Department of Human Resources
Kinkead Building
711 East 5th Street, Capital Complex
Carson City, NV 89710
(702) 687-5982

NEW HAMPSHIRE
Bureau of Child Care Standards and
    Licensing
6 Hazen Drive
Concord, NH 03301
(603) 271-4624

NEW JERSEY
Bureau of Licensing
Division of Youth and Family Services
Department of Human Services
CN 717
Trenton, NJ 08625
(609) 292-4834

NEW MEXICO
Licensing and Certification Bureau
Public Health Division

Department of Health
Harold Runnels Building, 1st Floor
  South
1190 St. Francis Drive
P.O. Box 26110
Santa Fe, NM 87502
(505) 827-2389

NEW YORK CITY
Bureau of Day Care
Department of Health
65 Worth Street, 4th Floor, Room 452
New York, NY 10013
(212) 334-7803

NEW YORK STATE
Office of Family and Children's
  Services
Department of Social Services
40 North Pearl Street, Floor 11-B
Albany, NY 12243
(518) 474-9454

NORTH CAROLINA
Division of Facility Services
701 Barbaur Drive
Raleigh, NC 27603-2008
(919) 733-4801

NORTH DAKOTA
Department of Human Services
600 East Boulevard Avenue
Bismark, ND 58505
(701) 224-4809

OHIO
Office of Child Care Services
65 East State Street, 5th Floor
Columbus, OH 43215
(614) 466-3822

OKLAHOMA
Office of Child Care
Department of Human Services
4545 North Lincoln, Suite 100
Oklahoma City, OK 73105
(405) 521-3561

OREGON
Children's Service Division
198 Commercial Street SE
Salem, OR 97310
(503) 378-3178

PENNSYLVANIA
Bureau of Child Day Care Services
Office of Children, Youth, and
  Families
Department of Public Welfare
Bertolino Building, 4th Floor
P.O. Box 2675
Harrisburg, PA 17105-2675
(717) 787-8691

PUERTO RICO
Department of Social Services
P.O. Box 11398
Fernandez Juncos Station
Santuce, PR 00910
(809) 723-2127

RHODE ISLAND
Department for Children and Their
  Families
610 Mt. Pleasant Avenue, Building 2
Providence, RI 02908
(401) 457-4540

SOUTH CAROLINA
Office of Children, Family and Adult
  Services
Department of Social Services
P.O. Box 1520
Columbia, SC 29202-1520
(803) 734-5740

SOUTH DAKOTA
Child Protection Services
Department of Social Services
Kneip Building
700 Governor's Drive
Pierre, SD 57501-2291
(605) 773-3227

TENNESSEE
Licensing Unit
Social Services Division
Department of Human Services
400 Deaderick Street
Nashville, TN 37248-9800
(615) 741-7129

TEXAS
Licensing Branch 550-W
Department of Human Services
P.O. Box 149030
Austin, TX 78714-9030
(512) 450-3265

UTAH
Office of Licensing
Department of Social Services
120 North 200 West, Room 317 3rd
    Floor
Salt Lake City, UT 84103
(801) 538-4242

VERMONT
Division of Licensing
The Children's Day Care Unit
Department of Social and
    Rehabilitation Services
103 South Main Street
Waterbury, VT 05676
(802) 241-2158

VIRGIN ISLANDS
Office of Preschool Services
Department of Human Services
Barbee Plaza South
St. Thomas, VI 00802
(809) 774-0930

VIRGINIA
Division of Licensing
Department of Social Services
8007 Discovery Drive
Richmond, VA 23239
(804) 662-9025

WASHINGTON
Division of Children and Family
    Services
Department of Social and Health
    Services
P.O. Box 45710
Olympia, WA 98504
(206) 753-0204

WEST VIRGINIA
Division of Social Services
Department of Human Services
Capital Complex, Building 6, Room
    850
Charleston, WV 25305
(304) 558-7980

WISCONSIN
Office for Children, Youth, and
    Families
Division of Community Services
Department of Health and Social
    Services
1 West Wilson Street
P.O. Box 7851
Madison, WI 53707
(608) 266-8200

WYOMING
Division of Public Assistance and
    Social Services
Department of Health and Social
    Services
Hathaway Building, 3rd Floor
Cheyenne, WY 82002
(307) 777-6595

Appendix 2

REGIONAL AND STATE COALITIONS

ALASKA
Alaska School-Age Child Care Alliance
Barbara Dubovich
Camp Fire, Inc.
3745 Community Park Loop
Anchorage, AK 99508
(907) 279-3551

Beth Edmunds
YMCA
5353 Lake Otis Parkway
Anchorage, AK 99507
(907) 563-3211

ARIZONA
School Age Child Care Coalition
Governor's Office for Children
Marti I. Lavis, Director
Dolores Casillas, Early Childhood
  Specialist
1700 W. Washington, Suite 404
Phoenix, AZ 85007
(602) 542-3191

CALIFORNIA
*California School-Age Consortium
  (CSAC)*

Julie Sinai, Executive Director
CSAC
111 New Montgomery Street, #302A
San Francisco, CA 94105
(415) 957-9775

COLORADO
*Colorado Alliance for Quality School-
  Age Programs (CAQSAP)*
Sandy Whittall, President
CAQSAP
Tower Rd. Learning Center
18707 E. Hampden Ave., Ste. 140
Aurora, CO 80013
(303) 680-6111

CONNECTICUT
*Connecticut School-Age Child Care
  Association (CSACCA)*
Joan Benson
CSACCA
P.O. Box 224
Marlborough, CT 06447
(203) 295-9400

DELAWARE
Work/Family Coalition
Patricia Tanner Nelson
Cooperative Extension
125 Townsend Hall
University of Delaware
Newark, DE 19717-1303
(302) 831-2509

FLORIDA
Florida SACC Coalition
Tom Mueller
Latchkey Services
4910-D Creekside Drive
Clearwater, FL 34620
(813) 573-1060

GEORGIA
*Georgia School-Age Childcare Council
  (GSACC)*
Anne Bramlette, Executive Director
GSACC
119 East Court Square, Ste. 205
Decatur, GA 30030
(404) 373-7414

ILLINOIS
Illinois SACC Network
Christine Todd
113 Child Development Lab
1105 West Nevada
Urbana, IL 61801
(217) 244-1290

INDIANA
*Indiana Association for School-Age
  Child Care, Inc. (IASACC)*
Ellen Clippinger, President
IASACC
4701 N. Central
Indianapolis, IN 46205
(317) 283-3817

IOWA
Iowa School-Age Child Care Alliance
Lynn Graham
Child Development Building
Iowa State University

Ames, IA 50011
(515) 294-1648

KANSAS
*School-Age Child Care Committee,
Kansas Association for the Education
  of Young Children*
Diane Purcell
911 Clay
Topeka, KS 66606
(913) 232-1603

KENTUCKY
*Kentucky Coalition for School-
Age Child Care*
Norma Meek
2785 Terrace Boulevard
Ashland, KY 41102
(606) 325-4896

MAINE
*Maine School-Age Child Care
  Coalition*
Karen Upton, President
Kennebec Valley YMCA
33 Winthrop St.
Augusta, ME 04330
(207) 626-3488

MARYLAND
Maryland Child Care Alliance
Dale Jackson, Chair
Howard County Government
3430 Courthouse Drive
Ellicott City, MD 21043

Louise Corwin, Administrator
Governor's Office for Children, Youth,
  and Families
301 W. Preston St., Ste. 1502
Baltimore, MD 21201
(301) 225-4160

MASSACHUSETTS
*Massachusetts School-Age Child Care
  Consortium*
Irene Denty
2618 Massachusetts Ave.

Lexington, MA 02173
(617) 862-8318

MICHIGAN
Oakland Professionals for SACC
Deborah Shepard
Troy Adult and Community Education
201 W. Square Lake Rd.
Troy, MI 48098
(313) 879-7557

MINNESOTA
*Minnesota School-Age Child Care
Alliance (MSACCA)*
Shari Rachac, President
357 9th Ave., North
South St. Paul, MN 55075
(612) 457-9493

Linda Sisson
5701 Normandale Road
Edina, MN 55424
(612) 928-1420

MISSOURI
School-Age Child Care Committee
Harry Kujath
State Department of Elementary and
    Secondary Education
P.O. Box 480
Jefferson City, MO 65102
(314) 751-0857

NEBRASKA
*Before and After School Child Care
    Project*
Phyllis Chandler
2240 London Court
Omaha, NE 68102
(402) 345-9118

NEW HAMPSHIRE
School Age Child Care Council
Cynthia Billings
Child and Family Services of New
    Hampshire
13 Green Street
Concord, NH 03301
(603) 224-7479

NEW JERSEY
*New Jersey School-Age Child Care
    Coalition*
Diane M. Genco, Chairperson
225 Edgewood Avenue
Westfield, NJ 07090
(908) 789-0259

NEW YORK
SACC Network of Albany
Sharon Montaginino
P.O. Box 357
Guilderlind, NY 12084
(518) 456-3634

*School-Age Director's Network—
    Westchester County*
Jill Stewart, Director
Chappaqua Children's Workshop
P.O. Box 254
Chappaqua, NY 10514
(914) 328-3295

NORTH CAROLINA
*North Carolina School-Age Childcare
    Coalition (NCSACC)*
Kim Cline
111 W. 8th Street
Newton, NC 28658
(704) 464-9355

*Metrolina Alliance of School-Age
    Professionals (Charlotte area)*
Karen Callahan
Child Care Resources, Inc.
700 Kenilworth Avenue
Charlotte, NC 28204
(704) 376-6697

OHIO
*Ohio Professionals for School-Age
    Child Care*
Tracey Ballas
1742 Norwood Blvd.
Zanesville, OH 43701
(614) 453-7743

OKLAHOMA
*Oklahoma School-Age Child Care
Coalition*
Lu Ann Faulker
Office of Child Care
4545 North Lincoln, Suite 100
Oklahoma City, OK 73105
(405) 521-3561

OREGON
*Oregon School-Age Child Care
Alliance*
Colleen Dyrud
SACC Project, Department of
Education
700 Pringle Parkway SE
Salem, OR 97310
(503) 373-5585

PENNSYLVANIA
Community Services for Children, Inc.
Joyce Lang
431 E. Locust St.
Bethlehem, PA 18018
(215) 691-1819

Western Pennsylvania SACC Alliance
Sharon Schweninger
Mt. Lebanon Extended Day
P.O. Box 10434
Pittsburgh, PA 15234
(412) 323-1922

*Western Region School Age Child Care
Project*
Karen Schwarzbach
Child Care Office
YMCA of Pittsburgh
600 West North Avenue
Pittsburgh, PA 15212
(412) 323-1922

*Central Region School Age Child Care
Project*
Ann Rodomski
116 S. Allegheny St., Ste. 314
Bellefonte, PA 16823-1962
(814) 353-6110

*Southeast Pennsylvania School-Age
Child Care Project*
Diane P. Barber
Day Care Association of Montgomery
County
601 Knight Rd.
Ambler, PA 19002
(215) 643-0569

*Philadelphia School-Age Child Care
Coalition*
Christine Davis
Parents Union
311 S. Juniper St., Rm. 602
Philadelphia, PA 19107
(215) 546-1166

RHODE ISLAND
*Rhode Island School-Age Child Care
Project*
Joanne Howard, Coordinator
Rhode Island College
600 Mt. Pleasant Avenue, HM103
Providence, RI 02908-1991
(401) 456-8594

TENNESSEE
SACC Network
Robert Ecklund/Lisa Beck
Metropolitan YMCA
900 Church Street
Nashville, TN 37203
(615) 259-9622

TEXAS
*Texas Association for School-Age
Child Care*
Nancy Baker
Texas Department of Human Services
P.O. Box 149030, Mail Code E-311
Austin, TX 78751
(512) 450-4011

VIRGINIA
*Virginia School-Age Child Care
Network*
Karen Starner

St. John's Early Childhood Center
271 Winchester Street
Warrenton, VA 22186
(703) 374-5341

WASHINGTON
*Washington School-Age Child Care
Alliance*
Mari Offenbecker
YWCA of Seattle-King County
1118 Fifth Ave.
Seattle, WA 98101
(206) 481-9082

WISCONSIN
*Wisconsin School-Age Child Care
Coordinating Council*

Jeanette Paulson
Wisconsin Child Care Improvement
Project
1245 E. Washington Ave., Ste. 210
Madison, WI 53703
(608) 257-0909

WYOMING
*Wyoming School-Age Child Care
Project*
Bernita Quoss and Peggy Cooney
Child and Family Studies Program
Department of Home Economics
P.O. Box 3354, University of Wyoming
Laramie, WY 82071
(307) 766-4011; (307) 766-4145

Appendix 3

SCHOOL-AGE CARE RESOURCES

NATIONAL ORGANIZATIONS

American Academy of Pediatrics, Division of Child and Adolescent Health, 141 Northwest Point Boulevard, Elk Grove Village, IL 60007 (708) 228-5005

American Library Association, 50 E. Huron St., Chicago, IL 60611 (312) 944-6780

American Public Health Association, 1015 15th Street NW, Washington, DC 20005 (202) 789-5627

ASPIRA Association, Inc., 1112 16th Street NW, Suite 340, Washington, DC 20036 (202) 835-3600

Association of Junior Leagues International, 660 First Ave., New York, NY 10016 (212) 683-1515

Boys and Girls Clubs of America, 771 First Ave., New York, NY 10017 (212) 351-5900

Camp Fire Boys and Girls, 4601 Madison Ave., Kansas City, MO 64112 (816) 756-1950

Center for Early Adolescence, University of North Carolina at Chapel Hill, Carr Mill Mall, Ste. 211, Carrboro, NC 27510 (919) 966-1148

Child and Family Justice Office of the National Council of Churches, 475 Riverside Dr., Rm. 572, New York, NY 10115 (212) 870-3342

Child Care Action Campaign, 330 Seventh Ave., 17th Floor, New York, NY 10001 (212) 239-0138

Child Care Law Center, 22 Second St., 5th Floor, San Francisco, CA 94105 (415) 495-5498

Child Welfare League of America, 440 First Street NW, Suite 310, Washington, DC 20001 (202) 638-2952

Children's Defense Fund, 25 E St. NW, Washington, DC 20001 (202) 628-8787

Concerned Educators Allied for a Safe Environment, 17 Gerry Street, Cambridge, MA 02138 (617) 864-0999

Congress of National Black Churches, 600 New Hampshire Ave. NW, Ste. 650 Washington, DC 20037-3914 (202) 333-3060

Early Adolescent Helper Project/National Center for Service Learning in Early Adolescence, CASE/CUNY Graduate Center, 25 West 43rd St., Suite 612, New York, NY 10036-8099 (212) 642-2946

ERIC Clearinghouse on Elementary and Early Childhood Education, University of Illinois, 805 W. Pennsylvania, Urbana, IL 61801 (217) 333-1386

4-H Clubs, National 4-H Council, 7100 Connecticut Ave., Chevy Chase, MD 20815 (301) 961-2800

Families and Work Institute, 330 Seventh Ave., New York, NY 10001 (212) 465-2044

Family Resource Coalition, 200 S. Michigan Ave., Ste. 1520, Chicago, IL 60604 (312) 341-0900

Girl Scouts USA, 420 5th Ave., New York, NY 10018 (212) 852-8000

Girls Inc., 30 East 33rd St., New York, NY 10016 (212) 689-3700

Kiwanis International, 3636 Woodview Trace, Indianapolis, IN 46268 (317) 875-8755

League of Women Voters Education Fund (LWVEF), 1730 M Street NW, Washington, DC 20036 (202) 429-1965

NACCRRA (National Association of Child Care Resource & Referral Agencies), 2116 Campus Dr. SE, Rochester, MN 55904 (507) 287-2020

NAEYC (National Association for the Education of Young Children) & NAECP (National Academy of Early Childhood Programs), 1509 16th Street NW, Washington, DC 20036-1426 (800) 424-2460

NAESP (National Association of Elementary School Principals), 1615 Duke St., Alexandria, VA 22314 (703) 684-3345

NAIS (National Association for Independent Schools), 75 Federal St., Boston, MA 02110 (617) 451-2444

National Association for Regulatory Administration, Department of Services for Children, Youth, and Their Families, 1825 Faulkland Road, Wilmington, DE 19805 (302) 633-2700

National Association of State Boards of Education, 1012 Cameron St., Alexandria, VA 22314 (703) 684-4000

National Black Child Development Institute, 1023 15th Street NW, Suite 600, Washington, DC 20005 (202) 387-1281

National Catholic Educational Association (NCEA), 1077 30th St. NW, Suite 100, Washington, DC 20007 (202) 337-6232

National Coalition for Campus Child Care, c/o Jane Ann Thomas, Child Development Program, William Rainey Harper College, 1200 W. Algonquin Rd., Palatine, IL 60067-7398 (708) 397-3000

National Coalition for Parent Involvement in Education, c/o Linda Moore, Council of Chief State School Officers, 1 Massachusetts Ave. NW, Ste. 700, Washington, DC 20001 (202) 408-5505

National Council of Jewish Women, 53 West 23rd Street, New York, NY 10010 (212) 645-4048

National Council of La Raza, 810 First Avenue NE, Suite 300, Washington, DC 20002 (202) 289-1380

National League of Cities, 1301 Pennsylvania Ave. NW, Suite 608, Washington, DC 20004 (202) 626-3000

National Park and Recreation Association, 2775 South Quincy St., Suite 300, Arlington, VA 22206 (703) 820-4940

National PTA (Parent-Teacher Association), 700 N. Rush St., Chicago, IL 60611-2571 (312) 787-0977

National School-Age Child Care Alliance, c/o California School-Age Consortium, NSACCA Membership Department, 111 New Montgomery St., San Francisco, CA 94105—FOR MEMBERSHIP INFORMATION ONLY. Address all other inquiries to: NSACCA c/o Tracey Ballas, 1742 Norwood Boulevard, Zanesville, OH 43701

National School Boards Association, 1680 Duke St., Alexandria, VA 22314 (703) 838-6722

Parent Action, B & O Bldg., 2 N. Charles St., Ste. 960, Baltimore, MD 21201 (301) 752-1790

PhoneFriend, 101 Beecher House, Penn State, University Park, PA 16802 (814) 865-1751

Project Home Safe (a program of the American Home Economics Association), 1555 King St., Alexandria, VA 22314 (800) 252-SAFE

School-Age Child Care Project, Wellesley College Center for Research on Women, Wellesley, MA 02181 (617) 283-2547

United Neighborhood Centers of America, 1319 F St. NW, Suite 603, Washington, DC 20004 (202) 393-3929

United Way, Inc., 621 S. Virgil Ave., Los Angeles, CA 90005 (213) 736-1300

YMCA of the USA, 101 N. Wacker Dr., 14th Floor, Chicago, IL 60606 (312) 977-0031

YWCA of the USA, 135 W. 50th St., New York, NY 10020 (212) 621-5115

NEWSLETTERS, MAGAZINES, AND JOURNALS

Child Care Employee News, available from Child Care Employee Project, 6536 Telegraph Ave., Suite A-201, Oakland, CA 94609 (415) 653-9889

Child Care Information Exchange, published by Exchange Press, Inc., P.O. Box 2890, Redmond, WA 98073 (206) 883-9394

Day Care USA, published by United Communications Group, 11300 Rockville Pike, Suite 1100, Rockville, MD 20852-3030 (301) 816-8950

NSACCA News, published by NSACCA, Rockwood School District, 111 E. North St., Eureka, MO 63025-1229 (314) 587-2531

Report on School-Age Child Care, published by Business Publishers, Inc., 951 Pershing Drive, Silver Spring, MD 20910-4464 (301) 587-6300

School-Age NOTES, published by Richard T. Scofield, P.O. Box 40205, Nashville, TN 37204 (615) 242-8464

Young Children, published by NAEYC, 1509 16th Street NW, Washington, DC 20036-1426 (800) 424-2460

BIBLIOGRAPHY

Barber, Diane P. "A Long Hot Summer," *SACC Partners* (newsletter of Southeastern Pennsylvania School Age Child Care Project, Ambler, PA), June 1991.

Beaver, Nancy H. *Somebody Cares: Eight Model Child Care Programs for School-Age Children in Texas*. Austin, TX: Corporate Child Development Fund for Texas, 1987.

Blank, Helen. "The Child Care and Development Block Grant and Child Care Grants to States Under Title IV-A of the Social Security Act: A Description of Major Provisions and Issues to Consider in Implementation," Washington, DC: Children's Defense Fund, 1991.

Child Care Council of Westchester. *Transportation for School-Age Child Care*. White Plains, NY: Child Care Council of Westchester, 1990.

Child Care Support Center. *Recruiting and Enrolling Children: Tips on Setting Priorities and Saving Time*. Atlanta, GA: Save the Children, 1981.

Cohen, Abby J. *School-Age Child Care: A Legal Manual for Public School Administrators*. Wellesley, MA: SACCProject Publications, 1984.

Dittman, Laura, ed. *Curriculum Is What Happens: Planning Is the Key*. Washington, DC: NAEYC, 1970.

Eisler, Riane. *The Chalice and the Blade: Our History, Our Future*. San Francisco: HarperCollins, 1988.

Fink, Dale B. *School-Age Child Care Site Operations Manual*. Kansas City, MO: Camp Fire Boys and Girls, 1992 draft edition.

Gannett, Ellen. *City Initiatives in School-Age Child Care*. Wellesley, MA: SACCProject Publications, 1989.

Gannett, Ellen, and Lynn Hatch. *State Initiatives on School-Age Child Care*. Wellesley, MA: SACCProject Publications, 1989.

Genser, Andrea, and Clifford Baden, eds. *School-Age Child Care, Programs and*

Issues. Urbana, IL: ERIC Clearinghouse on Elementary and Early Childhood Education, College of Education, University of Illinois, 1980.

Gibbs, Jeanne. *Tribes: a process for social development and cooperative learning.* Santa Rosa, CA: Center Source Publications, 1987.

Greenman, Jim. *Caring Spaces, Learning Places: Children's Environments That Work.* Redmond, WA: Exchange Press, 1988.

Gross, Malvern J., Jr., and W. Warshauer, Jr. *Financial and Accounting Guide for Nonprofit Organizations.* New York: John Wiley and Sons, 1979.

Halpern, Robert. "The Role of After School Programs in the Lives of Inner-City Children." Chapin Hall Center for Children, University of Chicago, unpublished paper.

Hendon, Kay, John Grace, Diane Adams, and Aurelia Strupp. *The After School Day Care Handbook: How to Start an After School Program for School-Age Children.* Madison, WI: Community Coordinated Child Care/4-C in Dane County, Inc., 1977.

Jones, K. Craig, and E. Ray Dockery, eds. *Influences on Development.* Littleton, MA: Copley Publishing Group, 1988.

Katz, Lillian. *Talks with Teachers.* Washington, DC: NAEYC, 1977.

Lawyer-Tarr, Sue. *How to Work with School-Age Children and Love Them.* Tulsa, OK: Clubhouse After School Caring and Sharing, 1980.

Leibowitz, Jill. "Revising and Implementing a Schedule for a School-Age Child Care Program." Paper presented at Third Annual School-Age Child Care Leadership Institute, Berea College, Kentucky, July 15, 1990.

Levine, James A. *Day Care and the Public Schools: Profiles of Five Communities.* Newton, MA: Education Development Center, 1978.

Loney, Gerry. *Thunderburg: An After-School Program.* Addison County, VT: Addison County Vocational Center, 1979.

Lombardi, Joan. "New Federal Dollars: How Are They Being Used?" *Child Care Information Exchange,* December 1991; 8(6): 56–57.

Marx, Fern. "School Age Child Care in America: Final Report of a National Provider Survey." Wellesley, MA: Center for Research on Women, Wellesley College, 1990.

McAdoo, Harriet, and Vanella Crawford. "The Black Church and Family Support Programs." *Prevention and Human Services,* Spring 1991; 9(1).

Morgan, Gwen. *A Hitchhiker's Guide to the Child Care Universe.* Boston: Wheelock College, 1991.

———. *Managing the Day Care Dollars.* Boston: Wheelock College, 1982.

Nall, Susan W., and Carol S. Klass. *School-Age Child Care in Illinois.* Edwardsville: Southern Illinois University, 1991.

Neugebauer, Roger. "Building a Center—Habitat-Style." *Child Care Information Exchange,* August 1990; 7(4): 14–17.

———. "Fifth Annual Child Care Center Management Software Buying Guide." *Child Care Information Exchange,* December 1990; 7(6): 53–58.

———. "Money Management Tools—Sliding Fee Scales," *Child Care Information Exchange,* June 1979; (8): 27–33.

O'Connor, Susan. *ASQ: Assessing School-Age Child Care Quality.* Wellesley, MA: SACCProject Publications, 1991.

Pirsig, Robert. *Zen and the Art of Motorcycle Maintenance.* New York: Bantam Books, 1975.

Prescott, Elizabeth. "Dimensions of Day Care Environments." Keynote address, Day Care Environments Conference, Iowa State University, June 15, 1979.

Prescott, Elizabeth, and Cynthia Milich. *School's Out! Group Day Care for the School-Age Child.* Pasadena, CA: Pacific Oaks College, 1974.

Richards, Mary McDonald. *Before and After School Programs: A Start-Up and Administration Manual.* Nashville: School Age NOTES, 1991.

Riley, David. "Grass Roots Research on Latchkey Children Leads to Local Action." Paper presented at Extension National Invitational Conference on School-Age Child Care, St. Louis, May 1990.

Scott, Andrew. "What Is an Adventure Playground?" *CSAC Review* (newsletter of California School-Age Consortium, San Francisco), Fall 1988.

Seligson, Michelle, and Dale B. Fink. *No Time to Waste: An Action Agenda for School Age Child Care.* Wellesley, MA: SACCProject, 1989.

Steinberg, Jill Ellen. *The After School Day Care Association Activity Book.* Madison, WI: ASDCA, 1978.

"Toward Seamless Service: Some Key Issues in the Relationship between CCDBG and AFDC-Related Child Care." Washington, DC: Center for Law and Social Policy, 1991.

Travis, Nancy, and Joe Perreault. *The Effective Day Care Director: A Discussion of the Role and Its Responsibilities.* Atlanta: Save the Children, 1981.

Tuft, Karsten. *Children and Adults in Day-Care Centers.* Arhus, Denmark: National Union of Pedagogues, 1989.

U.S. Commission on Civil Rights. *Child Care and Equal Opportunity for Women.* Washington, DC: U.S. Government Printing Office, June 1981.

Williamson, Jack. *The Humanoids.* New York: Avon Books, 1980.

Wolfe, Alan. *Whose Keeper?: Social Science and Moral Obligation.* Los Angeles: University of California Press, 1989.

INDEX

(Entries for school-age child care programs are listed in **bold**.)

About the Authors

MICHELLE SELIGSON is Director of the School Age Child Care Project at Wellesley College's Center for Research on Women. She is a nationally recognized authority on child care.

MICHAEL ALLENSON is an independent writer and educator.